Compulsory Compassion

Law and Society Series
W. Wesley Pue, General Editor

Gender in the Legal Profession: Fitting or Breaking the Mould
Joan Brockman

Regulating Lives: Historical Essays on the State, Society, the Individual, and the Law
Edited by John McLaren, Robert Menzies, and Dorothy E. Chunn

Taxing Choices: The Intersection of Class, Gender, Parenthood, and the Law
Rebecca Johnson

Collective Insecurity: The Liberian Crisis, Unilateralism, and Global Order
Ikechi Mgbeoji

Unnatural Law: Rethinking Canadian Environmental Law and Policy
David R. Boyd

Murdering Holiness: The Trials of Franz Creffield and George Mitchell
Jim Phillips and Rosemary Gartner

People and Place: Historical Influences on Legal Culture
Jonathan Swainger and Constance Backhouse

Feminist Activism in the Supreme Court: Legal Mobilization and the Women's Legal Education and Action Fund
Christopher P. Manfredi

The Heiress vs the Establishment: Mrs. Campbell's Campaign for Legal Justice
Constance Backhouse and Nancy L. Backhouse

Tournament of Appeals: Granting Judicial Review in Canada
Roy B. Flemming

LAW AND
SOCIETY

Annalise Acorn

Compulsory Compassion:
A Critique of Restorative Justice

UBCPress · Vancouver · Toronto

09   08   07   06   05   04   5   4   3   2   1

Printed in Canada on acid-free paper

National Library of Canada Cataloguing in Publication Data

Acorn, Annalise E.
  Compulsory compassion : a critique of restorative justice / Annalise E. Acorn.

  (Law and society 1496-4953)
  Includes bibliographical references and index.
  ISBN 0-7748-0942-6 (bound); ISBN 0-7748-0943-4 (pbk.)

  1. Restorative justice. I. Title.
HV8688.A26 2004   364.6'8   C2003-907008-5

Canadä

UBC Press gratefully acknowledges the financial support for our publishing program of the Government of Canada through the Book Publishing Industry Development Program (BPIDP), and of the Canada Council for the Arts, and the British Columbia Arts Council.

This book has been published with the help of a grant from the Canadian Federation for the Humanities and Social Sciences, through the Aid to Scholarly Publications Programme, using funds provided by the Social Sciences and Humanities Research Council of Canada.

UBC Press
The University of British Columbia
2029 West Mall
Vancouver, BC V6T 1Z2
604-822-5959 / Fax: 604-822-6083
www.ubcpress.ca

For my glorious kinswoman, Mary C. Moore,
a passionate and inspiring lover of books

Had Cain been allowed to pay off his score, he might possibly have killed Adam and Eve for the mere sake of a second luxurious reconciliation with God afterwards.

– George Bernard Shaw, *Major Barbara*

Contents

Acknowledgments

In the initial stages of my project, I received tremendous assistance from Robert Howse. He was amazingly kind and generous with his time, insight, and encouragement. His unshakable faith that I would actually write a book about this topic never failed to astonish and energize me.

Bill Miller overcame his abhorrence of the general subject matter sufficiently to read the manuscript with patience and care. He gave me the benefit of his substantial knowledge of revenge cultures. I wish I could have remained truer to his intolerance for platitudes and pious academic canting. But the book is significantly less tedious than it would have been without his critical influence.

The support of a McCalla Fellowship from the University of Alberta was of great assistance to me in the completion of the manuscript. A seminar on "Passion and Politics" with Shane Phelan and Cheryl Hall at the University of Hawaii helped to form my early thinking on the relation between love and justice. The Law Commission of Canada Roundtable on Restorative Justice, convened by Rod MacDonald, was an excellent event from which I benefited enormously. A colloquium on "Justice and Repair" at the Congress of the Social Sciences and Humanities in Edmonton was also very helpful. Discussions at the Legal Theory Workshops at McGill and Michigan Law Schools assisted me immeasurably. I am also grateful to Kathleen Clark, Ted Decoste, Natalka Freeland, Trevor Farrow, Judy Garber, Don Herzog, Richard Janda, David Kahane, Jennifer Llewellyn, Charles May, Jenny Nedelsky, Fran Olsen, Michael Pratt, Shane Phelan, Rebecca Sober, Melissa Williams, and Bruce Ziff, who all offered useful comments, insights, and bibliographical suggestions. I am especially grateful to Dan Markel and Bob Zuber, who read the manuscript from beginning to end and gave me a number of very helpful suggestions. I am much indebted to David Cayley for saving me from a particularly embarrassing error. In addition, I owe a great deal to the anonymous readers at UBC Press. I would also like to thank Greg Fingas for bringing his lively intellect and scrupulous eye for detail to the creation of the index.

Hearty thanks also go to my meticulous dad, Glen Acorn, for his expert help with proofreading.

Extracts from the *Handbook of Victim Offender Mediation* by Mark S. Umbreit (Jossey-Bass, 2001) © John Wiley and Sons are reproduced with the permission of John Wiley and Sons; extracts from *Restoring Justice*, 2nd edition, by Daniel W. Van Ness and Karen Heetderks Strong (Anderson Publishing, 2002) © Anderson Publishing Company are reproduced with permission of Anderson Publishing Company; and extracts from the radio program *Ideas*, "Justice as Sanctuary," with Herman Bianchi, Part 1, 27 October 1997, © Canadian Broadcasting Corporation, are reproduced with the permission of the Canadian Broadcasting Corporation.

Annalise Acorn

Compulsory Compassion

1

The Seductive Vision of Restorative Justice: Right-Relation, Reciprocity, Healing, and Repair

When I first encountered "restorative justice," I was filled with enthusiasm. Restorative justice took a positive, forward-looking approach to crime. It focused on repair instead of punishment, on healing the wounds of injustice instead of inflicting further retributive suffering.[1] It conceptualized crime as the wrongful violation, not of an impersonal set of rules, or an abstract notion of "the state," but of individual victims.[2] It was concerned with the humanity of both victim and offender, and sought to restore the dignity of each by reintegrating both into respectful and healthy communities. It saw the community as the source of resolution of conflict.[3] Restorative justice seemed to hold a credible promise of something that had always appeared too illusive to hope for: a reconciliation of meaningful – even strict – accountability for wrongdoing with compassion for both victim and perpetrator.[4] I was powerfully drawn to restorative justice in many of these particulars. I was persuaded by its rejection of our cultural obsession with punishment as satisfying proxy for justice; its critique of our faith in imprisonment as necessary and sufficient assurance that justice has been done;[5] its claim that punishment as imprisonment is gratuitously cruel and counterproductive.[6] Most importantly, however, I was persuaded that our conflation of justice with punishment as imprisonment – or as any pure infliction of suffering on the wrongdoer – belied an impoverished, shallow, unsophisticated, and ultimately empty understanding of justice itself.[7] Llewellyn and Howse's claim that "there is no positive value for justice in the *very fact* of the perpetrator's suffering or sacrifice of well-being" sounded right.[8] Understanding justice as the creation of relations of reciprocal respect seemed a far fuller and more enlightened understanding than the crude and brutal equation of justice with punishment. I became convinced that our obsession with retribution had created, and was serving to perpetuate, habits of mean-spiritedness that were doing untold damage in every facet of our lives, from international conflicts to our most intimate micro-interactions.

In place of this nasty and destructive retributive obsession, restorative justice offered an array of spiritually expansive ideals. It conceived wrong-doing in terms of wrong-relation and justice in terms of "right-relation."[9] Drawing on the spiritually sumptuous ideas of Martin Buber, restorative justice envisioned an escape from our bondage in so many "I-It" relationships. It envisioned justice as the repair of the world; the struggle toward ever more sustaining "I-Thou" relationships. Justice, then, was to be found in an authentic experience of mutuality, reciprocity, and regard between and among individuals. In place of the spiteful aspiration to inflict suffering on the wrongdoer as a means of achieving justice, restorative justice offered a loving aspiration to heal the damage of the wrong and to repair the injury to the relationship between the victim and the perpetrator. Such healing was to be supported and sustained by a community committed to mutual equality and respect. In place of the bleak procedural labyrinths of traditional legal institutions, restorative justice offered immediate and dramatic encounters between victims and offenders.[10] It offered both victims and offenders an experience of justice as a personal achievement.[11] Justice would no longer be imposed from on high but would be imaginatively and actively created and enacted by individuals and communities.[12] We would no longer look for justice in the substance of judicial decisions, jury verdicts, or prison sentences. We would expect and demand to find justice in relationships.[13]

I was enticed by all these wholesome carrots held out as alternatives to the sinister stick of retribution. It seemed so right-headed to organize the energy of our sense of justice around these far more positive goals: renewal of the victim's dignity, security, and sense of belonging in community; the perpetrator's contrition, his coming to accept the validity of shared norms prohibiting harmful conduct, his active participation in helping to repair the harm to the victim; and, ultimately, through this process of accountability and repair, the social redemption of both victim and perpetrator and their return – without stigma – to a position of acceptance and participation in the community.[14]

The point of justice (along with the point of a career devoted to justice) would no longer be merely the infliction of retaliatory suffering. Nor would it even be the piecing back together of some banal *status quo ante*.[15] Instead, the goal of justice might become something far more worthy of devotion. Restorative justice could also be seen as an approach to crime that was working toward social justice and the broader goals of the creation of relations and communities of mutuality, respect, peace, harmony, and equality.[16] And, though this idealized goal of right-relation might always elude our grasp, and though we might be forever stuck in an agonistic struggle toward this idealized conception of justice, at least, with right-relation as the target of justice, we could be confident we were aiming at something genuinely desirable and worthwhile. We could be certain that justice – not only in its abstract understanding, but in its day-to-day applications in the resolution of specific wrongdoing – was at least on the trail of something indisputably good, something indisputably connected with the pursuit of peace and with the creation of sustaining communities and relationships. This promised no small gain given that the value of the pursuit of criminal justice in the form of ever-longer prison sentences seemed so utterly doubtful.

The rhetoric of restorative justice speaks very personally to the listener, and I was aware that my attraction to it had some very personal pulls. First, my own weariness of feminist rage exhaustion was significant. The feminist commitment to anger and to a retributive sense of what was needful to bring about greater equality for women in areas such as sexual assault, domestic violence, pornography, and sexual harassment was becoming a heavy emotional and energetic burden. Many of the feminist stars in the academy were skilful rhetoricians of rage.[17] Being a legal feminist seemed to require emulation of those performances and, as a result, negotiating the difficult terrain of the negative emotions of justice: anger, resentment, vengefulness, and bitterness.[18] To be publicly committed to eliminating injustice caused by sexism in the law often meant incurring the risk that others would instantly collapse one's persona into the toxic trope of the angry feminist. At the same time, within the feminist community, a pose of anger, at the very least, was necessary lest one be seen as lax in one's feminist commitments.[19]

And, in all good conscience, it was cowardly and complacent to refuse to participate in the anger to which gender injustice gave rise. The retributive sentiments of feminism were often rightly fuelled by compelling evidence that the system was set up so that men could and did "get away with it." Exercise of police and judicial discretion sympathetic to accused men and dismissive of victimized women and children made convictions hard to come by in cases of private violence. The only available antidote to this bias in favour of the accused seemed to be to advocate that more credence be given to women and child victims and harsher penalties be dealt out to male offenders.

Restorative justice seemed to offer a better alternative. It was committed not only to holding offenders accountable, but also to repairing relations and to establishing communities capable of supporting practices of equality and respect. Feminist retributivism, while it perhaps offered justice to women on some level, also seemed to entail ever more gender animosity.[20] Restorative justice, by contrast, seemed to promise something better than mere retribution.[21] It potentially offered better solutions to the intractably complex problems of intimate violence. It aimed at hard-nosed accountability for male offenders as well as at the possibility of improved, more respectful, more harmonious gender relations in the future. Perpetrators of sexual assault, child sexual abuse, and domestic violence would be forced to look their victims in the eye and acknowledge the damage they had done rather than simply hiding behind aggressive defence counsel or bitterly doing time without acknowledging responsibility. Perpetrators would suffer genuine shame about their conduct, but restorative institutions would channel the energy of that shame toward better futures for both victim and offender.[22] Thus restorative justice, accompanied by genuine community support for victims, was perhaps a better means of ensuring accountability as well as effective deterrence.

My attraction to restorative justice was also motivated by the malaise that afflicts many lawyers, law professors, judges, and other actors in the legal system: weariness of squabble in general. Not propelled by any first-order thirst for revenge, stuck in that sorry niche of the world set up to manage the energy of other people's resentment, and, worse still, knowing that the legal system, even when it does deliver on its own terms, never really delivers a particularly satisfying experience of justice, we can fall prey to a dejected disgust with our own endeavour. We are encumbered by a guilty awareness that the usual rights and remedies afforded – imprisonment, fines, probation, conditional sentences – all too often fail to fulfill the aspirations behind victims' decisions to participate in the criminal process.[23] Even when, on those rare occasions, the court's pronouncement of a guilty verdict inspires the victim to burst out with a victorious "Hooray!" the celebration seems somehow artificial and hollow – relief masquerading as satisfaction. Or perhaps the outcry is itself an attempt to grasp in the last moment some more immediate encounter, some catharsis of genuinely relational gloating, that the process of adjudication has failed to deliver. This lacklustre sense of what the present system has to offer by way of experiential justice inspires a longing for something more. To be able, then, to approach the endeavour of justice with a sense that, at least theoretically, one might be able to offer something as seductive and rich as encounter and experiential justice-in-relation seemed to lend a new-found nobility to the task.

If, as Martin Buber claims, "All actual life is encounter,"[24] then institutions of justice, set up to facilitate the possibility of actual encounter, would surely yield a more life-giving conception of justice than institutions that do all they can to prevent encounter. Or as restorative justice advocate John Braithwaite puts it: The restorative movement is attractive because it is "to justice as jazz is to music."[25] Restorative justice seemed to have a freer form and deeper soul than do our traditional institutions.

Moreover, restorative justice seemed to offer hope to those who recognized the importance of, and felt a need to participate in, the legal process but who also claimed no desire to deal in the currencies the system has to offer. For those victims who cared more about apologies than imprisonment – those who weren't interested in seeing the offender punished but who would have been gratified by the offenders' acknowledgment of responsibility, expression of remorse, and making of meaningful reparation – restorative justice offered the possibility of principled participation in institutions of justice.[26] Likewise, restorative justice seemed to offer an important alternative for victims uninterested in punishment but deeply concerned as responsible citizens to try to ensure that the offender would not go on to victimize others.

Thus the tremendous appeal of restorative justice seemed to lie primarily in its validation of my own and other peoples' dissatisfaction with a legal system that depersonalizes, desiccates, and fetishizes justice in a way that deprives people of meaningful experiences of justice *in relation*. Restorative justice was appealing because, while it offered to put the *doing* back into doing justice, it did not at the same time validate the impulse toward revenge.[27] It held out a refreshing optimism that the desire for revenge – though not the desire for a personal experience of actively participating in bringing about justice – is a product of our reluctance to use our imaginations to envision other ways of creating accountability in the victim-offender relationship.[28] Restorative justice respected the desire for a personalized experience of justice as an individual and relational achievement, and it set the imagination to the task of envisioning positive, nonviolent ways of creating that experience.[29]

Perhaps we were not hardwired for revenge after all. Perhaps, by strengthening connections between compassion, equality, mutuality, reciprocity, and respect, on the one hand, and justice, on the other, we could be true to our need for justice while ending cycles of retributive suffering. Vengeful longings would, therefore, gradually be replaced with desires for the experience of respectful relation.[30] Successful practices and supporting discourses of justice-as-repair would become mutually reinforcing in their pedagogical and practical effects.

Along with being drawn into the theory of restorative justice, I was also moved by its success stories. I was inspired by stories of the proceedings of the South African Truth and Reconciliation Commission, by moments in which victims and perpetrators of the most horrific crimes of apartheid faced one another across a table and recounted the unimaginable suffering of their victimization, recounted the details of their crimes, and struggled, however ambivalently, however painfully, to work toward an understanding of how to move forward together into a more humane society.[31] Likewise, I was amazed by compelling stories of victims of sexual abuse who have been able to encounter their abusers, speak their suffering, and educate their abusers about the harm caused by their conduct. Some victims had clearly received benefits from such encounters. They had obtained information about the details of the abuse that they had repressed and had been able to set out strict guidelines to be followed by their offenders in assuring that the offenders would not interfere in the victims' lives again.[32] Others had benefited simply from the experience of hearing their abuser accept blame. I was moved also by stories of healing restorative encounters between murderers and the surviving loved ones of their victims.[33]

One of the most powerful aspects of these stories was the degree to which their focus on "encounter" showed an astute awareness of the mysterious exclusivity in the relation between victim and perpetrator.[34] Restorative practices seemed singularly capable of accessing and redirecting the energy of that sinister intimacy – bringing it out in the open and enlisting it in the service of justice and right-relation. It brought the tie between victim and offender out of the closets of shameful and mutual stigma and into the open, where it could be seen, heard, and healed.[35]

Some Skeptical Anxieties

Eventually, however, I began to experience twinges of doubt. I had a niggling but persistent embarrassment about my willingness to be seduced by the restorative justice movement. And the embarrassment grew as my commitment to an intellectual defence of restorative justice seemed to be pushing me into more and more situations where I was answering too many difficult questions about the viability of restorative justice with rhetorical platitudes about right-relation, mutuality, equality, and respect.

Inasmuch as I was drawn to this project of trying to find a nicer way of doing justice, as much as I tried to effect the necessary conceptual uncoupling of justice and punishment and to effect the necessary new coupling of justice and right-relation, I couldn't quite do it. I remained unable to let go of my moral intuition that a just response to wrongdoing often requires "throwing the book" at wrongdoers, with equal emphasis on the "throwing" and the "book." Justice persisted in being bound up with both violence and consistency. Compensatory *schadenfreude* for victims and nasty comeuppance for wrongdoers still felt just. Moreover, "the book" (by which I mean the ideal of the rule of law) and its commitment to consistency, predictability, precision, and universal application also continued to have compelling and even essential connections to any sane and workable notion of justice.[36] Thus the restorative aspiration to divorce justice from reciprocal infliction of suffering, along with its faith in context supersensitivity, which sees the shape of relational justice as ever springing from the particulars of this victim, this wrongdoer, and this community, caused me considerable anxiety. Perhaps justice just wasn't nice. And perhaps it had to be tied to a notion of fairness which held that a just response to wrongdoing required some kind of parity in the consequences of wrongdoing among perpetrators of the same kind of wrong.[37]

Thus I became concerned that, in my enthusiasm for restorative justice, I was indulging in what Jonathan Allen so aptly calls the "wishful thinking (or at least, not very thoughtful wishing)" of restorative justice.[38] I began to feel that there was a shamefully Panglossian aspect to the whole restorative justice movement for which someone, though most likely not the advocates of restorative justice, would have to pay.[39]

I also identified an element of hypocrisy. I discovered that I felt this discomfort most intensely when I stopped thinking about the beauty of the ideas; stopped luxuriating in the voyeuristic moral gratification of looking on at the allegedly healing encounters of others; and started to think about whether in my own life and my own conflicts I was really willing to sign up for restorative encounters and restorative solutions. There was something troubling about my own hesitancy and about my lack of confidence in my own willingness and ability to apply the theory to myself. Restorative justice seemed just fine for other people, for harms I had not suffered, but when it came to *me*, restorative justice wasn't what I wanted. I did not feel competent as an advocate for restorative justice because I doubted both my ability to repair relationships marred by wrongdoing and my commitment to doing so.

Of course, I was not alone in thinking that if I wanted to promote restorative justice I would have to be able to claim a few impressive restorative successes of my own. Most advocates of restorative justice are aware of their obligation to "walk the talk." The territory of envisioning grand-scale social, communal, and relational transformations for the better generally comes with a recognition that (like analysts who must submit to analysis) advocates of restorative justice need to have a track record of successful healing and transforming in their own lives and relationships. Van Ness and Strong in their book *Restoring Justice* write:

> A hallmark of restorative justice must be ongoing transformation: transformation of perspective, transformation of structures, transformation of people. It begins with transformation of ourselves, for we too have recompense to pay, reconciliation to seek, forgiveness to ask, and healing to receive. We look not only for justice "out there," but must turn the lens on ourselves as well – on our daily patterns of life and on our treatment of and attitudes toward others. Restorative justice is an invitation to renewal in communities and individuals as well as procedures and programs. Transformation of the world begins with transformation of ourselves.[40]

Similarly, Michael Hadley concedes that restorative justice "requires all of us to come to grips with who we are, what we have done, and what we can become in the fullness of our humanity."[41]

So the primary optimism is about the possibility of recompense, reconciliation, forgiveness, and healing in the context of the criminal offender-victim relationship. The application of this optimism to oneself is an earnest and well-meaning nod to the problems of hypocrisy that the primary optimism creates.

Thus the stumbling block for me came with my recognition of my own inability to put myself forward with a straight face as a competent participant in reconciliation, healing, and forgiveness. On the one hand, it was clear to me that my zeal for restorative justice was springing, in part, from an essentially romantic desire to get in on this starry-eyed notion of right-relation that restorative justice was so sanguine about. Surely, if it could happen for murderers and the survivors of their victims, it could happen for me in my troubled relationships fraught with petty, low-stakes conflicts and trivial insults. Surely, I too could participate in and experience reciprocal, mutual, and compassionate justice-in-relation.

Of course, it wasn't as if there were no "right-relations" in my life. Taking an honest stock of things, so long as I didn't go too far in idealizing this notion of right-relation, I could reasonably say that some of my relationships were pretty much "right." But in looking at the right ones, it was also clear that they tended to have a number of other characteristics, such as: spontaneous affinity, shared purpose, shared interests, shared history, absence of a history of serious wrongdoing, mutual commitment to respectful engagement, and the investment of much (richly rewarded) time and effort, sensitivity, and hard work, with no small assistance from affection, humour, and fun. So these were the precious right ones. These were the ones that could plausibly be thought of in terms of some kind of "I-Thou" mutuality.

But there were lots of wrong ones too – lots of relationships that were marred by resentment, wrongdoing, bitterness, and small-minded pettiness on all sides. And what struck me, in reflecting on these relationships, was that I was far less cheery about the possibility for recompense, reconciliation, forgiveness, and healing in the context of these – my own comparatively trivial, low-stakes – "wrong relations" than I was in the context of relations between murderers, burglars, sexual abusers, even the most heinous of war criminals, and their victims. Something had to be seriously wrong here. Reflecting on the trivial problems in my botched relations, it was evident that, in most cases, I did not have the will or desire necessary to repair them. Moreover, reparation did not seem either likely or possible even if sought with the best of intentions. In any event, why not save my energy for those pretty-much-right relationships that were not marred by any of these difficulties but nevertheless required lots of time and devotion to maintain? Wrong-relations seemed to have a kind of incorrigibility to them that made the project of repair a waste of time. So I had to admit that I personally was not up for sinking my energy into relational transformations.

How, then, was I to avoid the pessimism prompted by my own experience? And how was I to square this pessimism with the feel-good optimism about healing that had been induced in me by reading, rather than living, tales of restorative justice in the contexts of apartheid, ethnic cleansing, assault, rape, murder, robbery, and criminal negligence causing death?

Here I permitted my thoughts to follow a troubling trail: Could it be that right-relation stood a better chance of being restored when the wrongs to be overcome were big rather than trivial? Restorative justice advocate John Braithwaite says: "The more evil the crime the greater the opportunity for grace to inspire a transformative will to resist tyranny with compassion."[42] So perhaps the wrongs that marred the rightness of *my* relations were too subtle – they just didn't constitute sufficiently jarring events – to serve as the powerful blast-off needed to propel a journey into wholeness and healing.

My thoughts strayed to a singularly wrong relation in my life. I thought to myself: "Perhaps if I were to break into her house and, well, I probably couldn't bring myself to actually assault her but let's say maybe I could just steal her TV or her stereo. Might we not then be forced into a cathartic and ultimately transformative encounter? And propelled by its momentum, might we not be flung out of this terrible lock of hostility and into healing and right-relation? Might we not then embark, with the support of a respectful community, upon a restorative journey toward equality, right-relation, and mutual respect for each other's dignity?" Heaven knows, there did not appear to be any other way forward. So, perhaps crime was the answer.

This curious logic got me more than a little worried. And what troubled me most was that I was not *exactly* misapplying the theory. The rhetoric of restorative justice *was* evoking a fantasy of idealized harmony in relationships between victims and perpetrators of crime – often purely injury-generated relationships – and not even remotely desired by either party, least of all by the victim. But the rhetoric of transfor-mation, healing, repair, love, compassion, equality, and respect in the context of victim-wrongdoer relations was shamelessly bypassing the obvious: that relationships marred by big wrongs and serious violations *have* to be more difficult to fix than relationships marred by petty wrongs and trivial insults and annoyances. Moreover, this rhetoric was bypassing the perhaps even more incontrovertible fact that harmony, mutuality, equality, reciprocity, and respect are hard won even in our most significant and well-intentioned relationships. The achievement of relations of equality and respect in the context of those core everyday relationships – the ones we put so much of our energy and intelligence into maintaining, the ones that receive the food, water, and sunshine of our spontaneous affection and desire – are themselves so painstakingly difficult and uncertain in success. So how can we – without hypocrisy – embrace a notion of justice grounded in a vision of right-relation, mutuality, reciprocity, equality, and respect between victims and perpetrators of unthinkable, unforgivable evils?

Thus confused, I turned to Derrida for help. His discussion of forgiveness offers one possible answer to this question. Justice-as-reconciliation can be seen as anticipating or requiring forgiveness,[43] and impossibility is, for Derrida, at the core of the very concept of forgiveness. If you don't have a grand-scale wrongdoing that defies the possibility of forgiveness, then it's not merely that you are in the minor leagues of forgiveness; you aren't even playing the game: "If one is only prepared to forgive what appears forgivable ... then the very idea of forgiveness would disappear ... From which comes the aporia, which can be described in its dry and implacable formality, without mercy: forgiveness forgives only the unforgivable. One cannot, or should not forgive; there is only forgiveness, if there is any, where there is the unforgivable. That is to say that forgiveness must announce itself as impossibility itself."[44] Forgiveness is a logical possibility only in respect of the inexpiable, unforgivable wrong that defies even the attempt to imagine a proportionate response. It does not require the contrition or apology of the wrongdoer or the possibility of punishment.[45] Nevertheless, Derrida commends forgiveness to us (or to those who have the opportunity to forgive: the victims of unforgivable wrong) as a worthy existential challenge. Worthy, it appears, primarily because of its richness as a paradoxical puzzle. Forgiveness is an impressive – possibility-defying – exercise of existential willpower. The audacious impossibility of forgiveness goads one to dare to try it. Forgiveness is a conceptual "attractive nuisance" (like the running bulldozer parked next to the school yard) for a paradox-crazed sensibility like Derrida's. It appeals as an exhilarating form of ethical bungee jumping.

Derrida's insights give us some sense of the potential intuitive appeal attaching to the idea that horrendous wrongs are, on some level, easier to repair and restore than trivial ones. There is no existential glory in forgiving the forgivable. Forgiveness of the unforgivable appeals because of its impossibility and its unquestionable status as a breathtaking achievement. Thus the worse the wrongdoing is, the greater is the power of the paradox of forgiveness to goad us into trying – if, like Derrida, we are inclined that way. The unavailability of a proportionate response likewise recommends forgiveness as a way out of an otherwise immobilizing conundrum.[46] Forgiveness of the unthinkably egregious has more drama and is worth the effort because, if successful, it clearly counts as seriously impressive ethical and existential muscle flexing. Forgiveness of the garden variety crimes and misdemeanours of ordinary life is too low stakes to have any existential cachet. In Derrida's formulation, such wrongs don't even give rise to the opportunity to forgive. So why bother? Thus we see how it is possible to conclude that repair and reconciliation as effected between victims and perpetrators of horrific crimes are potentially more attainable than repair and reconciliation between the victims and perpetrators of commonplace wrongs. Forgiveness of the unforgivable evokes the possibility of existential sainthood. Forgiveness of the forgivable is too mediocre to have any really compelling payoff for the victim.

Thus it might be that restorative justice – insofar as it is seen as a challenge to forgive – would have more appeal in relation to unimaginable atrocities than in relation to run-of-the-mill wrongdoing. Yet Derrida is quick to point out that "one could never, in the ordinary sense of the words, found a politics or law on forgiveness."[47] As Derrida rightly notes, for example, the South African Truth and Reconciliation Commission was founded on a legal category of amnesty completely distinct from any notion of forgiveness.[48] It was Desmond Tutu who later urged South Africans and the world to reinterpret the process in terms of the Christian vocabulary of repentance and forgiveness. But forgiveness, especially in Derrida's formulation, cannot be a matter of justice. It is a "hyperbolic ethics," an "ethics beyond ethics"; it is the unthinkably supererogatory.[49] Thus it is outside the realm of justice.

Moreover, in Derrida's formulation, forgiveness – superdemanding though it may be – is, in some senses, not as demanding as restorative justice. Forgiveness for Derrida seems to be primarily an inner state, constituted by a once-off leap of will. But restorative justice requires something more. If forgiveness is a necessary element of restorative justice, it is only instrumentally so.[50] The significance of forgiveness to restorative justice lies in its possible contribution to the ultimate restorative goal of right-relation — that is, a lived relationship of mutual equality and respect. Most restorative justice advocates see repentance and forgiveness as important parts of the process toward right-relation; but it is right-relation, not forgiveness, that is equated with justice. Thus to achieve justice-as-repair, one must actually persevere in the relationship with the offender and work toward something better. This expectation is a constitutive element of restorative justice no matter what kind of wrong we are dealing with. Thus, even if Derrida helps us to see how forgiveness as an ethical feat might have greater allure the worse the wrongdoing, once we add the requirement of working things out in the relation between victim and perpetrator, we are thrown back on our initial puzzle. Why would one do it unless committed to an ethic of self-sacrifice and saintliness? And how can a system of justice be structured around a general demand for such supererogatory patience and devotion from victims?

The question of expenditure of resources alone would seem to rule out restorative justice as a viable possibility.[51] The resources, care, and attention that serious and workable institutions of restorative justice would have to bestow on relationships either generated or marred by criminal violation would be enormous. When the right-relations that we have the good luck to create take so much of our time and energy, why would we sink a necessarily far greater amount of time and energy into the wrong ones? Why would anyone pour so many resources into these least promising of relations? Why would victims want to expend their time and energy on a bad and unwanted relationship that they would prefer to erase from their lives?[52]

Though I have difficulty coming up with positive answers to these questions, it is apparent to me that the problem with my skepticism here may be merely my own moral failing. Restorative justice may well be for people who are much more patient than I; more committed to peace, healing, and harmony; less curmudgeonly; more pious; more morally inclined toward the endeavour of working things out for the sake of building community; more willing to persist with people who have wronged them. Yet (and I hope there is no self-righteousness in this claim), if the success of restorative justice is contingent upon consistently finding participants (victims, offenders, and community members) who are significantly more morally patient than I, then it is in some considerable trouble – and not because I am morally good but because neither am I a moral monster. I am pretty much the run of the moral mill. Yet restorative justice seems to anticipate that it will be drawing its participants (including its offenders) from the ranks of the morally supererogatory. I am worried about how such a system is to protect the interests of victims and even (although to a lesser extent) the interests of perpetrators of crime. I am concerned about a system of justice that asks victims in particular to take on the onerous task of working things out in relation to their offenders. But I am also worried about a system that purports to be able to deliver caring and compassionate assistance in effectively healing the admittedly terrible wounds suffered by offenders, wounds that go some way toward explaining the participation of offenders in wrongdoing.

Consider the following example. Restorative justice proponent Herman Bianchi tells a story of two young men who had brutally assaulted a cab driver.[53] The assault left the victim permanently confined to a wheelchair. The assailants were arrested. While awaiting trial, however, they became extremely remorseful and very much wanted to make reparations to the victim. Their lawyer suggested that they write the victim a letter. They then wrote to the victim, offering to take care of him for twenty-five years as compensation for the harm they had done. The victim did not answer the first letter, so the perpetrators wrote to him again. The victim was initially very skeptical about the offer, but the victim's friends were enthusiastic and persuaded him to accept, assuring him that the offenders "will do their utmost to make your life bearable." The victim was convinced by his friends' arguments and accepted the offer.

Bianchi celebrates the agreement as a restorative move from damage to repair, from wrong-relation to right-relation, from wrongdoing to true penitence and meaningful accountability: "This is now a wonderful case as it should be. This is divine justice. Now, just do it!" However, the perpetrators, whom we are to assume are not particularly wealthy, would not be able to care for their victim were they in jail, so the agreement needed ratification from the judge. But the judge refused, finding that the victim's consent did not obviate the need for punishment; other potential assailants needed to be taught a lesson. Bianchi laments the judge's refusal to grant a stay of proceedings against the two offenders and to allow the agreement to be put into practice. He also bemoans the refusal of our system to support this restorative solution, arguing that the default solution that our system offers – the offenders go to prison, and the victim is supported by the state in an institution – exacerbates and perpetuates the damage to all concerned. Bianchi's position seems compelling enough. At a glance, the plan seems to be a perfect example of restoration of balance in the relation between victim and perpetrator.

Now, the story as told does not give us any explanation of what it would mean for the perpetrators to "take care of" the victim for twenty-five years, and it asks us to assume that the victim accepted the offer without any further clarification – apart from the interpretation offered by his friends (who had presumably never met the perpetrators) that the offenders meant to "do their utmost to make his life bearable." In all events, we can assume that the arrangement would require extensive close contact between the perpetrators and the victim. Depending on the degree of the victim's disability, he might need something close to twenty-four-hour care, which would most likely require that the perpetrators live with the victim.

As Bianchi's research demonstrates, this kind of response to crime has its historical precedents.[54] Feuding cultures provide interesting support for the basic idea that meaningful reparations can be made when a wrongdoer voluntarily agrees to care for the victim or the victim's dependents.[55] This idea also gleans some historical support from the work of William Ian Miller. Miller notes that in medieval Iceland wrongdoers would commonly agree to foster one or more of the victim's children as a means of pacification. Miller describes an incident in the sagas where "Sturla forced his young son on a man who had sold him wormy meal."[56] By fostering children belonging to a victim, the wrongdoer was relieving the victim of the financial burden of feeding the child. Significantly, he was also symbolically accepting a one-down status in relation to the victim since, in the context of medieval Icelandic culture, "he who fosters another's child is always considered the lesser man."[57] Yet even in a culture where such fosterage was an accepted means of offering reparation and effecting reconciliation, Miller notes that the practice must give us a pang of anxiety about the fate of the poor child. How could this father so cavalierly send his son into the house of the man who was his enemy? Yet Miller concludes with the assurance that nothing in the sagas suggests that such children were treated at all like hostages: "The children, it seems, were treated no differently than any other child would have been."[58] Means of caring for children were already in place in the households; thus the foster children could simply take up an equal place with the other children.

This arrangement seems all very nice. But can we apply this cheery picture to our case of the disabled man and his two assailants? Imagine living for even one week as a disabled person in the same space as the two men who have caused your misery by brutally assaulting you – with men who have no skills in the care of the disabled, whose general "life skills" are likely to be less than optimal, and for whom your presence can only be an annoying and possibly painful reminder of their guilt. I fear that the outcome of this story, even at its most optimistic, would likely resemble the predictable tale of the well-meaning person who, in a rush of compassion, decides to care for an abandoned puppy only to find weeks later that it is far too much to handle and that its presence has become a source of overwhelming frustration and hostility. Even if some extraordinary victim might wholeheartedly take on the risks of such a vulnerable life, can we, in good conscience (and could this cab driver's friends in good conscience), support a system that would encourage the subjection of victims to this kind of intense intimacy with those who have harmed them? How can we endorse a system of justice that rests on the prediction that equality, mutuality, reciprocity, and respect will be achieved in such relationships?

It is doubtful that the fosterage practised by such a profoundly communal people and culture as that of medieval Iceland can really serve as an adequate precedent or inspiration for similar practices in modern society. Nor does a relationship as hopelessly unpromising as that between the victim and the wrongdoers in Bianchi's story provide a stable foundation for the creation of a more cohesive community. There is no good reason to feel any less anxious about the fate of the disabled man's living in such prolonged intimacy with his assailants than we might about the fate of the Icelandic children going off to be cared for in the houses of their parents' enemies.

Before leaving this anecdote, let's consider it from a slightly different angle. Let's imagine that the perpetrators were very wealthy men. And let's then imagine that instead of extending this imprecise offer "to take care of him for twenty-five years," the perpetrators made a very precise, and indeed far better, offer of, let's say, three million dollars to provide the victim with professional home care for life, compensation for pain and suffering, and so forth. Now one would assume that, under our present system, if such a payment were made spontaneously by the perpetrators, this gesture would figure as a mitigating factor in a judge's determination of the appropriate criminal punishment. But to conclude that the offer of monetary compensation should completely extinguish the state's obligation to proceed with the criminal charges (which Bianchi's story seems to entail) would collapse the present system of a dual civil action and criminal prosecution into a single civil action. As long as the perpetrators were in a position to pay compensation, they would be excused, as it were, from criminal prosecution. But what if the perpetrators were not in a position to pay compensation, which would seem to be the case in the story as told? It appears that the restorative solution would then also collapse the criminal prosecution into a civil action but would allow the impecunious offender to pay by working for the victim.

This arrangement, of course, is an ancient practice tried and true. It is found, for example, in the Bible, the laws of Hammurabi, and Roman law. It is called debt-slavery.[59] Where an offender was unable to pay compensation to a victim or to pay a debt owed to a creditor, he was made to fulfill the obligation by handing over the only thing he did have: his body and its labour. In other words, he became the slave of the victim or creditor. We can easily read the story of the cab driver and his assailants in a similar light. Presumably, any agreement to be ratified by the judge would have to provide for the consequences of breach. The perpetrators could not simply decide after a year or two that they didn't much like the arrangement and preferred not to look after the victim. One would assume that if the perpetrators were to default on the agreement, the criminal jurisdiction would be resurrected, and the perpetrators would either honour the agreement or go to jail. It would appear, then, that what is being promoted in the story is an arrangement between victim and perpetrators in which either the perpetrators continue to work for the victim or suffer incarceration.

We should also note that such an arrangement, if universalized, would give rise to a significant disparity in the treatment of rich and poor offenders. The present system, of course, has wealth disparity to be sure. Things like quality of representation, prosecutorial zeal, and judicial sympathy are not distributed evenly across class lines. But, to the extent that our system prosecutes them at all, it potentially makes the rich pay twice: once by subjecting them to criminal punishment and again by requiring them to pay civil damages to compensate their victims. Under our system, the impecunious offender can pay only once through criminal punishment. The story of the cab driver and his assailants, inasmuch as it is being offered as a model for a system of justice, would risk a different and significant inequity between rich and poor. The story writ large would give rise to a system that treated poor offenders more harshly than their wealthy counterparts. The repentant rich would be able to pay up without doing time, but the penitential poor, those without the option of paying-up, most likely would have to do time either as the employee/caretaker of the victim or in prison.

Given these difficulties, why does Bianchi's story remain nevertheless so oddly persuasive and even moving? I suggest that the appeal of this story depends largely on the judge's rejection of the plan.[60] The momentum of the story takes our imaginative focus off the details of what such an arrangement would really be like for the victim and the perpetrators. It is only because we give superficial imaginative consideration to the rejected restorative fantasy that we find the overall vision of restorative justice in the story persuasive.

Admittedly, not all or even most restorative solutions anticipate this kind of ongoing intimate bond (or bondage) between victim and offender. Yet the theory, in its idealization of equality and respect in the relationship between victim and offender, and many of the testimonial success stories of restorative justice tend to envision some kind of amiable optimality in the victim-offender relation. The concepts of mutuality, reciprocity, healing, equality, and respect to be achieved between victim and offender may be staggeringly vague and open to many divergent conceptions, but all these conceptions reach toward a vision of shared satisfaction between victim and offender.[61]

The seductive vision of restorative justice seems, therefore, to lie in a skilful deployment – through theory and story – of cheerful fantasies of happy endings in the victim-offender relation, emotional healing, closure, right-relation, and respectful community. Yet, as with all seductions, the fantasies that lure us in tend to be very different from the realities that unfold.[62] And the grandness of the idealism in these restorative fantasies, in and of itself, ought to give us pause.

Moreover, the contexts in which restorative justice is most vigorously and successfully promoted are the same contexts in which other powerful emotional pulls are inducing us to, as Jonathan Allen again aptly puts it, "confuse aspiration with prediction."[63] Enthusiasm about restorative justice thrives best in contexts already conducive to optimistic fantasy. For example, South Africans of all races experienced a heady idealism at of the end of the apartheid regime. There was an exuberant sense that South Africa, newly freed of the yoke of apartheid, would surely become a country of unprecedented cultural richness, economic prosperity, and political enlightenment. This exuberance, in part, inspired the wave of willingness to go along with the vision of justice offered by the Truth and Reconciliation Commission. The shared anticipation of a glorious new era of national flourishing opened South Africans to an understanding of justice that was sunny and forward-looking. Apartheid had been a long and shameful yesterday, and to focus national energy on punishing its past might destroy the possibility of the brilliant tomorrow just beyond the horizon.

This mood factor also surfaces in our assessment of other contexts in which restorative justice might be appropriate. Consider, for example, two common settings in which restorative justice is advocated: Aboriginal and juvenile crime. Take the Aboriginal context first. The restorative justice movement in Aboriginal contexts is bound up with both the political push toward Aboriginal self-government and a more general renaissance of traditional Aboriginal culture.[64] The distant Aboriginal past evokes a spiritually enlightened culture that fosters harmonious interconnections between people and nature.[65] The recent Aboriginal past represents oppression and pollution by a spiritually inferior white culture that privileged acquisition and egoism over shared purpose and relationship. The Aboriginal future promises a proud renewal of traditional values and practices. Thus, in the Aboriginal context, as in South Africa, restorative justice is supported by an atmosphere of shared anticipation of a soon-to-be-celebrated future. Optimism that Aboriginal peoples are on their way out of a toxic condition of oppression – a condition that contributed significantly to high crime rates in Aboriginal communities – supports the idea that healing of relations between victim and offender is an appropriate and viable response to wrongdoing.

In the context of juvenile crime, youth itself supports an optimistic focus on the future. We are more willing to see the wrongdoing of the young as attributable to lack of maturity rather than to actual malevolence or viciousness. The juvenile criminal's whole life stretches out before him. We are reluctant to abandon hope either for the possibility of spontaneous change of a young offender's ways or for their improvement through better education and socialization.[66] To presume that a young offender doesn't deserve a chance to make amends seems culpably cynical – just as it seems culpably naive to give adult offenders the benefit of the same set of doubts. The fairness of this disparity in our assessment of the young and the older is beside the point. Youth puts us in the optimistic mood necessary for restorative justice.[67] It opens us up to the idea that the appropriate response to wrongdoing is to try to educate offenders about the harm they have done, attempt to engender a compassionate response both in offenders for their victims and in victims for their offenders, and give the young every reasonable chance to redeem themselves.

Again the emotional pulls that render us susceptible to optimistic fantasy and aspiration do not necessarily map onto the practical conditions that would make restorative healing and repair more likely. The probability of the success of restorative justice seems to depend primarily upon the character and resources of the offender.[68] Restorative justice is possibly the perfect solution to crime where the offenders have the capacity for serious critical self-reflection, the resources and ability to repair the damage caused, and a bona fide desire, along with sufficient self-command, to behave respectfully in their relations with their victims and their communities in the future. It is difficult to imagine how one could isolate particular contexts or types of crime in which one was likely to find a critical mass of these good bad guys capable of transformation and participation in relations of equality and respect.[69] Moreover, it would seem that in promoting restorative justice at the theoretical level and in seeking victims' consent to restorative processes at the practical level, we are asking victims to wager that their particular offenders fall into this category of redeemable rogues capable of taking responsibility for their actions and making meaningful amends.

Of course, there are many more factors beyond just the character of the offender that will influence the success or failure of restorative justice: whether the damage is reparable, whether the victim is amenable to forgiveness, whether the victim supports the goal of re-establishing the worth of the offender or continues to desire the offender's suffering. Yet, at the end of the day, the primary control over the success or failure of restorative justice seems to lie in the hands of offenders. Nevertheless, the credibility of restorative justice is absolutely contingent upon its ability to deliver some version of its promise of equality, respect, mutuality, reciprocity, and healing in the relation between victim, offender, and community.

Aims of the Book

The primary aim of this book is to examine critically the aspiration of restorative justice to effect a practical and theoretical reconciliation between the values of love and compassion, on the one hand, and justice and accountability, on the other. Restorative justice offers a vision of justice as "tough love." It also, however, places an extraordinary amount of faith in the idea that compassion itself, when extended toward and effected between victims and wrongdoers, will have an overwhelming and magically transformative power in the direction of justice. The book critically examines the emotional, spiritual, dramatic, and rhetorical pulls behind the aspiration to reconcile love and justice. It takes this aspiration to be the source of enthusiasm and excitement behind the restorative justice movement. In doing so it attempts to take seriously Jonathan Allen's charge that restorative justice confuses aspiration with prediction.[70] I take the view here that to separate aspiration from prediction, as we ought, we first need to unearth the affective foundations of these aspirations — that is, understand why the ideal of a harmonious and compassionate solution to the problem of injustice is compelling. The book, therefore, attempts to investigate and critique the multiple emotive pulls that draw us into zeal about justice-as-repair and right-relation. It critically examines the longings that inspire the wishful thinking of restorative justice. Moreover, it seeks to expose much of this rhetoric and the aspirations it inspires as culpably sentimental and dangerously naive.

The book assumes that the emotional and theoretical aspects of restorative justice are inextricably intertwined. Such is the case, in part, because so many of the philosophical roots of restorative justice are theological. Pulls toward and away from institutions of restorative justice are bound up with our feelings about a relationship to the divine. The more we are emotionally drawn to a religious ethic of love, the more we will be motivated to struggle to make restorative justice work.[71] The more we have both a longing for some conflation of love or compassion and justice (and some theoretical framework within which to situate the possibility of that conflation), the more we will be motivated to persist in the project of justice-as-repair. The more we are committed to an ethic of nonviolence, the more we suffer at the thought of inflicting suffering on others.[72] The more we are drawn to the value of harmony, the more the aspirations of restorative institutions will appear worthwhile to us.

The intertwining of the theoretical and emotional aspects of restorative justice is also explained in part by the fact that so much of the advocacy of restorative justice comes in the form of examples or success stories. Since the theory of restorative justice locates justice in the experience of relationship, restorative justice proponents often lead with accounts of people's experiences of restorative success. These accounts are meant to and often do elicit an emotionally open-hearted and optimistic response. These restorative success stories (like so much of the self-help industry) seek to induce people to buy into a theory on the basis of selective and simplified examples of cases in which adherence to the theory purportedly worked miracles.[73]

A third aspect of the enmeshment of theory and emotion in restorative justice derives from the fact that so much of restorative rhetoric explicitly requests that we access or cultivate emotional states of compassion and love when thinking about wrongdoing and justice.

The Goal of Right-Relation: The Single Unique Feature of Restorative Justice

I do not attempt to put forward a comprehensive definition of restorative justice. Yet I do attempt to engage with restorative justice as a distinctive approach to wrongdoing. With this objective, I focus particularly on its embrace of the notion of right-relation as the essence of justice and on how this understanding of justice leads to the even more idealistic attempt to harmonize the restorative understanding of justice with an understanding of love. A few words of explanation are needed here to clarify my focus on the idealized notion of right-relation as *the* distinctive element of restorative justice, and on its link to the restorative aspiration to reconcile love and justice.

Restorative justice is not the same thing as plain old alternative dispute resolution or mediation, though it shares aspects of these. Its aspirations exceed those of mere corrective justice, though clearly it aspires to correct. It is quite different from deterrence and rehabilitation theory, though it prides itself on its ability to help offenders both to internalize and to act in accordance with the view that crime doesn't pay. Like retributivism, restorative justice seeks to rectify the imbalance created by crime, yet it abhors the retributive notion that deliberate infliction of suffering on the wrongdoer helps to restore that equilibrium.[74]

In its rejection of the wilful infliction of suffering on the offender, restorative justice does resemble deterrence and rehabilitation theories about the best way to respond to crime. Yet deterrence and rehabilitation theories, unlike restorative justice, judge that we ought to bracket the question of justice per se and concentrate on the question of how to bring about change for the future. In other words, we should forget about pouring our energy into making past wrongs right. Rather, we should focus our efforts on making sure the wrongdoing doesn't happen again. As *A Clockwork Orange* – Stanley Kubrick's superdisturbing film about the ultimate mode of deterrence and rehabilitation – puts it: The point about "the Ludovico treatment" is "that it works." The offender is reoriented toward nonviolence. Justice, by contrast, is not the point.

Restorative justice, however, *is* a theory of *justice*.[75] Though it is primarily future oriented, it cares, as a matter of principle, about improving the future by addressing (if not redressing) past wrongs. Reduced recidivism and rehabilitation may be the happy, inevitable by-products of the restorative understanding of justice, but they are not its first-order ends.[76] Thus, though it rejects wilful infliction of suffering on an offender as having justice value, restorative justice also shares important ground with retributive justice. Both insist that wrongs must be *put right*. Both see an essential relation between justice and reciprocity. Yet restorative justice is committed to a radical debunking of the retributive idea that proportionate suffering deliberately inflicted on the offender has intrinsic justice value. It seeks to right the balance, to be sure, yet it holds that retributive theory mistakenly (even arbitrarily) identifies one particular practice – punishment – with the goal of rectification.[77] Restorative justice seeks creative, positive, nonviolent, and even noncoercive ways of putting things right. Moreover, it holds that the appropriate means of righting the balance are highly context-sensitive. Restorative justice is necessarily vague about what is going to count as restoration of the balance in any given situation. The theory must remain underdetermined on this point because what will bring about the restoration of social equilibrium in the context of any given wrongdoing is dependent entirely on the social, political, economic, and cultural relationships in play. As Braithwaite puts it: "One answer to the 'What is to be restored?' question is whatever dimensions of restoration matter to the victims, offenders, and communities affected by the crime. Stakeholder deliberation determines what restoration means in a specific context."[78] Yet there are also some basic procedural elements that restorative justice embraces as a matter of principle. In particular, it is committed to encounter and reciprocal truth-telling as effected between the victim, the offender, and their communities as an essential step toward the goal of justice-as-repair.

Restorative justice also shares much common ground with corrective justice in the Aristotelian sense.[79] Most importantly it wholeheartedly embraces the idea that the offender should compensate the victim for the losses suffered as a result of the wrongdoing – that the offender should disgorge and restore to the victim the advantage gained from the wrong, thus making the victim whole again. Corrective justice, like restorative justice, does not place value on the wilful infliction of suffering on the offender but focuses on repair of the victim's loss. Yet the ambitions of restorative justice are both less precise and more expansive than those of corrective justice. Restorative means of repair of relations can achieve justice despite their departure from the strict transfer of wrongful gain back to the victim. In other words, the impossibility of strict correction does not preclude restorative justice from being achieved. Where the wrongdoer cannot compensate the victim for the wrong done, either because the wrongdoer does not have (or no longer has) the means to do so or because the loss does not admit of material compensation, things can still be put right by other means – for example, by apology and forgiveness.[80] Further distinguishing restorative justice from corrective justice is its effort to widen the net of our concern in understanding who is affected by wrongdoing. Corrective justice tends to narrow the focus to the primary victim and wrongdoer. Restorative justice, by contrast, seeks to involve and restore all members of the community potentially affected by the wrongdoing.[81]

Moreover, restorative justice, though it encourages compensation, is not satisfied with mere compensation understood as a return to the *status quo ante*.[82] It requires – as a matter of justice – something more. It requires that we build better, more respectful, more mutual relationships than those that existed prior to the wrong. It reaches toward an idealized state of right-relationship as its model of the just. The justice to be restored is the experience of relationships of mutuality, equality, and respect in community.[83] And it is this extravagant ambition – this understanding of justice in terms of an idealized conception of right-relation – that is the single distinguishing element of restorative justice. All other aspects of restorative justice are drawn from elsewhere. The sense of the importance of face-to-face encounter is drawn from alternative dispute resolution and mediation theory, as is the idea that conflict belongs to the community as a whole and that the community ought to be included in its resolution. Repudiation of the wilful infliction of suffering on the offender as an intrinsic good is drawn from rehabilitation and deterrence theories of punishment and corrective justice. The idea that justice involves the restoration of a social equilibrium and a return to a situation of some form of reciprocity is drawn from retributive justice.

Thus the singularity of restorative justice lies in its ambitious and seemingly good-hearted aspiration to understand justice in terms of right-relation – in its aspiration to locate justice in the experience of relations of mutuality, equality, and respect. The degree of idealization involved in this understanding of justice as right-relation can be either intensified or downplayed. However, it is this notion of right-relation – and its potential associations with harmony, wholeness, caring, compassion, reciprocal regard, and mutual valuation of intrinsic worth – that paves the way toward a communion between the restorative understanding of justice and an (also idealized) notion of love. It is via this idea of right-relation that the aims of restorative justice often escalate into the aspiration to reconcile, and even conflate, our values, experiences, and practices of love and justice. Indeed, right-relation, explicated in terms of respect, mutuality, reciprocity, and regard, can serve equally well as a conception of love, and perhaps much better as a conception of love than of justice. In fact, restorative justice theory sees the notion of right-relation as mediating and harmonizing these two presumptively conflicting realms of love and justice. It is in this distinctive move that the case for restorative justice becomes tied to the age-old human hope for the convergence of love and justice. The purpose of this book is to explore the nuances of that hope and to attempt to expose it as not only illusory, but also dangerous.

Sources

The sources I draw from are varied. In relation to restorative justice itself, I draw from theorists such as Dutch criminologist Herman Bianchi, whose impassioned and charming style make him still one of the most compelling advocates of restorative justice. I also look to Howard Zehr, Daniel Van Ness, Karen Heetderks Strong, John Braithwaite, Charles Colson, Mark Umbreit, and Christopher Marshall, as well as to Michael L. Hadley's collection on the spiritual roots of restorative justice. I draw, to a considerable extent, on the coauthored work of Robert Howse and Jennifer Llewellyn, both of whom were involved in the South African Truth and Reconciliation Commission.[84] Their work remains, in my view, the most theoretically sophisticated and persuasive writing there is on the topic.

I also draw extensively on theoretical sources that deal not so much with restorative justice per se but nevertheless advance strong connections between love, compassion, fellow-feeling, mercy, and justice. Here, I take the work of Martha Nussbaum as a foil. To a large extent I am attempting to transplant Nussbaum's ideas into foreign soil. I am assuming that it is possible to uproot her articulation of the relations between love, eros, compassion, and fellow-feeling, on the one hand, and justice and morality, on the other, and plant them in the context of restorative justice.

The opposite theoretical pull for me is found in the writing of William Ian Miller. It is Miller's unapologetic sympathy for vengeful desire, more than any careful and measured defences of retributivism within our criminal justice system, that I find to be the most compelling lure away from the piety of restorative justice. Miller's work is not entirely hostile to restorative justice in the sense that it can be read as promoting the value of encounter between victim and offender as well as a conception of justice as grounded in reciprocity. However, his work also forces us to concede the dark side of these ideas: the inevitability that encounters between victim and offender will be fraught with feelings of mutual contempt, disgust, and desires for revenge; that reconciliation between victim and offender will take place when both are motivated by powerful external and practical reasons for saying "uncle"; and that, to a considerable degree, justice-as-reciprocity will necessarily cash out in the currency of the infliction of reciprocal suffering.

Novelists are perhaps the most important source for this work. Restorative justice promotes itself on the basis of success stories and victim satisfaction surveys. If we immerse ourselves in the world of restorative justice narratives and testimonials, we acclimatize ourselves to their sensibility and are increasingly convinced by them. My intention in turning to novels is to break out of the world of stories generated by the restorative justice movement. Authors with more sophisticated, less evangelical sensibilities generate stories that very often run counter to all the restorative justice intuitions. My purpose in turning to such stories is to ask whether these counter-stories resonate as more true to human experience than do the simplified stories that come out of the restorative justice movement.

I am convinced that we need the great novelists here because they have the ability to show us more facets of human personality and interaction than the professionalized and hence bowdlerized "I hear your anger" restorative justice culture is capable of perceiving or relating. I will try to show that stories from the pens of these writers, which so often contradict the premises of restorative justice, ring truer with our honest perception of ourselves and each other than do the stories that restorative justice asks us to buy as the foundation for a new conception of justice. Jane Austen, Saul Bellow, Charles Dickens, George Eliot, Mark Twain, and Sinclair Lewis are authors upon whose ability to perfectly capture sentiments I rely extensively.

The Road Map

A basic outline of the chapters proceeds as follows. In Chapter 2, "'Essentially and Only a Matter of Love': Justice and the Teachableness of Universal Love," I begin by setting out the multiple points of contact between the rhetoric of restorative justice and ideals of universal love and agape. From there I embark on a critique of the aspiration to reconcile love and justice, noting first its latent conservatism. Then I go on to compare the restorative justice aspiration to reconcile love and justice with the techniques of people like Mohandas K. Gandhi and Dr. Martin Luther King, Jr. I subsequently move to the problem of the cultivation of an inner state of love as a requisite of justice and question our ability to cultivate universal or brotherly love between perpetrator and victim in the context of wrongdoing.

Chapter 3, "Three Precarious Pillars of Restorative Optimism," looks at three interrelated aspects of the optimism inherent to restorative justice. First, it examines the restorative justice aspiration to change radically what we mean by justice. Restorative justice is optimistic that we can retain a notion of justice as fundamentally concerned about reciprocity, while at the same time debunking the notion that justice is achieved through punishment that imposes reciprocal harm. In the first part of this chapter, I examine and critique this element of restorative optimism. Next, I turn to the second pillar of restorative optimism: its sense that the offender's character is likely to change for the better as a result of the restorative process. Here again I attempt to question the foundations of that optimism. Finally, I turn to the third pillar of restorative optimism:

the idea that, supported by the restorative process, the victim will come into healing and meaningful recovery from the effects of the crime.

In Chapter 4, "Sentimental Justice: The Unearned Emotions of Restorative Catharsis," I begin by noting that some squeamishness about restorative justice and its aspiration to reconcile love and justice may be mere aesthetic distaste for the sentimental. Yet to object to theories or practices of justice on grounds of their sentimentality seems overly fastidious in an ethically impoverished way. It wrongly raises matters of taste to the level of matters of justice.[85] In this chapter, I ask whether sentimentality in a theory or practice of justice is necessarily a bad thing and ask whether what appears to be an essentially aesthetic distaste for the sentimental has any legitimate place in ethical or moral theory. I ultimately argue that there is indeed something wrong with a sentimental theory of justice. And I conclude by noting also that proponents often use sentimental storytelling as an (unscrupulous) means of boosting the so-called magic of restorative justice.

In Chapter 5, "'Lovemaking Is Justice-Making': The Idealization of Eros and the Eroticization of Justice," I turn to the erotic in its relation to justice. Here I take up various strands of the idea that the erotic impulse is a primal energetic and psychological force capable of propelling us toward right-relation. I begin by looking at Martha Nussbaum's defence of the erotic as an ethical energy that brings us into a more lively sense of the other. From there I turn to a different but related argument for the relevance of desire to justice. Lesbian theologian Carter Heyward makes the claim that eros and justice are related and reconciled through the value of mutuality.[86] I conclude that the motivation behind these efforts to equate justice and the erotic is primarily to improve the public respectability of sexuality and, therefore, that sex stands to gain far more than justice in the association.

In the final chapter, "Compulsory Compassion: Justice, Fellow-Feeling, and the Restorative Encounter," I take a comprehensive look at the relation between compassion and justice. I begin by taking up Martha Nussbaum's claim that Aristotle's discussion of pity in *The Rhetoric* provides the foundation for a rationalist account of compassion as a vital element of justice in adjudication.[87] Having critically examined some of the problems with positing a major role for compassion in adjudication, I go on to note that the ideally anticipated role of compassion in restorative justice is drastically different from that envisioned by advocates of compassionate judging. In the second part of this chapter, I attempt to draw a picture of the kind of compassion restorative justice anticipates. In the third part of the chapter, I note that the notion of compassion relied on by restorative justice is grounded in a practice of egalitarian humility and must be deliberately cultivated. Here I discuss the extreme emotional stamina and commitment required to cultivate the authentic capacity for such compassion as well as the emotional and physical risks entailed in extending that compassion to a potentially dangerous opponent.

In the Epilogue, "Restorative Utopias – 'The Fire with Which We Must Play'?" I conclude with grave reservations about restorative justice, which are grounded not so much in its utopianism but in its failure to provide us with a desirable vision of utopia.

That is the road map. Let's proceed now to explore these disparate domains of love and justice and to examine how restorative justice attempts to reconcile the two.

2

"Essentially and Only a Matter of Love": Justice and the Teachableness of Universal Love

"Besides, taking an unjust revenge (and no revenge can be just) is acting directly against the holy religion we profess, whereby we are commanded to do good to our enemies, and to love those that hate us; a precept which, though seemingly difficult, is really not so to any but those who have less of God than of the world, and more of the flesh than the spirit: for Jesus Christ, true God and man, who never lied, nor could nor can lie, who is our legislator, has told us, *his yoke is easy and his burden light:* and therefore he would not command us any thing impossible to be performed. So that, gentlemen, you are bound to be quiet and pacified by all laws both divine and human."

"The devil fetch me," quoth Sancho to himself, "if this master of mine be not a tologue;[1] or, if not, he is like one, as one egg is like another."

– Miguel de Cervantes, *Don Quixote de la Mancha*, Part 2, Chapter 27

Can one love every one, all men, all one's neighbours? I have often asked myself that question. Of course not. It's unnatural indeed. In abstract love of humanity one almost always loves no one but oneself.

– Fyodor Dostoyevsky, *The Idiot*

Restorative justice stands in need of some explosive force powerful enough to demolish our moral intuition that justice demands the infliction of a painful comeuppance upon the wrongdoer. It needs something big enough to snap offenders out of their propensity to offend; strong enough to quell victims' desire for revenge and to inspire genuine forgiveness; and deep enough to restore the moral bonds of community. And, since *amor vincit omnia*, how about love? Restorative justice sees universal love as the primary fuel for accomplishing all of these feats. It aspires to harmonize the virtues, values, and practices of love and justice. Restorative justice takes Augustine's conception of love – to love is to will the being of the other – and folds this understanding of love into its understanding of justice.[2] Justice is not achieved until all manifestations of the will to annihilate the other are extinguished. It is not achieved until the victim, offender, and community can authentically proclaim to one another: "I will that you be." Restorative justice simply is whatever it takes to make that happen.[3]

This restorative aspiration to transform justice by reconciling it with love is often explicitly cast in religious terms. For example, restorative justice advocate Howard Zehr speaks of the aspiration of restorative justice to emulate biblical justice, which "grows out of love. Such justice is in fact an act of love which seeks to make things right. Love and justice are not opposites, nor are they in conflict. Instead, love provides for a justice which seeks first to make right."[4] For Zehr, justice is based on love and mercy rather than opposed to it.[5]

Christian proponents of restorative justice such as Zehr, Van Ness, and Strong, and (to a lesser extent) Herman Bianchi, see restorative justice as the emulation of Jesus' love. Zehr writes: "Love must govern your relationships within your own community. The boundaries of love are expanded over the course of biblical history, until Jesus urges us to love not just our own kind but also our enemies and to practice forgiveness."[6] Van Ness and Strong also speak of their work in promoting and practising restorative justice as having been supported by the presence of: "One who speaks to our own brokenness: 'I have loved you with an everlasting love; I have drawn you with loving-kindness. I will build you up again and you will be rebuilt.' One who calls on us to 'let justice roll on like a river, righteousness like a never-failing stream.'"[7] They urge Christian churches to give financial, moral, and personal support to restorative justice initiatives by claiming that the Christian commandment to love one's enemy obliges the church to do so.[8]

Pierre Allard and Wayne Northey also see restorative justice as the emulation of Jesus' love. They write: "Jesus is the great 'restorer' ... Jesus' option for forgiveness, for merciful restoration, is sealed forever in the mystery of his death and resurrection ... Jesus' love, as the faithful insist, is boundless, amazing, extravagant. It reaches out to all without distinction, offering hope, fellowship and new beginnings ... From his time on, no enemy may ever be put outside the circle of God's love – or indeed ours."[9] Likewise, Archbishop Desmond Tutu's advocacy for restorative justice is peppered with allusions to the power and demands of Christian love.[10] Restorative justice aims at generating that superabundant (more on the superabundance problem soon), all-inclusive kind of love that extends ever outward, even to the enemy, and overcomes the overwhelming inclination to respond to brutality and wrongdoing with hatred and disgust.

Of course, extension of loving regard to the victim of crime in a restorative processes is encouraged. However, since love of victims comes

relatively naturally, the preponderance of effort is devoted to the cultivation of love of the offender. As Zehr notes, for the offender "a precondition for healing may be an awareness that they are loved and of
value rather than further confirmation of their worthlessness."[11]

Perhaps daunted by the abysmal track record of this centuries-old Christian rhetoric of love of the enemy – indeed, much of Western history can
be read as the history of its failure – some Christian proponents of restorative justice turn to the Old Testament and the Hebrew language, as well
as to the theological/philosophical writings of Martin Buber, for fresher
sounding rhetorical tropes. They speak of restorative justice in terms of
shalom, meaning peaceful and harmonious relations; *tsedeka*, a conception of justice evoking relational equality and respect; and *teshuwa*, an
understanding of turning away from wrongdoing and returning home to
loving community.[12]

Drawing on Buber's discussion of the "I-Thou" relationship, some proponents also see the tension between love and justice being resolved
once we begin to think about justice in terms of right-relation. If we
understand justice as a quality of relationship – as inhering not in the
judgment of a court or the infliction of a punishment but in the lived
experience of respectful interaction between people – and if we understand the attainment of justice as being located in the improvement of
relationships, then the conflict between love and justice disappears. Justice simply *is* lived relations of reciprocal respect and nonexploitation.
When we then view love as the desire for the well-being of the other, all
conflict between love and justice is resolved. Restorative justice aims
directly at the re-establishment of right-relation, taking right-relation as
a unifying justice-based end. As Christopher D. Marshall puts it in his
book *Beyond Retribution,* the difference between love and justice shrinks
when we conceptualize "justice in relational and liberationist terms, justice as the existence of right-relationships, where there is no exploitation,
and all parties exercise appropriate power."[13] Speaking of Jesus' commandment to love the enemy, Marshall writes: "genuine justice, the justice that makes things better, is never satisfied merely by following the
rules, however equitable they are, or by asserting one's legal rights, however fair that may be. It is satisfied only when relationships are restored
and the destructive power of evil is defeated, and this requires a freely
chosen relinquishment of the logic of – and legal right to – an eye for
an eye and a tooth for a tooth."[14]

Readings of restorative justice as the fulfilment of a spiritual yearning
for a confluence of values and practices of love and justice hail not only
from the Judeo-Christian tradition, but from a wide variety of faiths.
Pashaura Singh, looking to Sikhism, argues that the case for restorative
justice is made through the claim that "brotherly love rises above justice

in a manner that it includes justice but so transforms it that it becomes consistent with the spiritual unity of [hu]man kind."[15] Speaking of the spiritual foundations of restorative justice in Chinese philosophy, Edwin C. Hui and Kaijun Geng write: "In the [restorative] process, lawbreakers are helped to practice a universal love and mutual benefit."[16] Coming from a Buddhist perspective, David M. Loy writes: "Buddhist justice grows out of a compassion for everyone involved when someone hurts another ... If fear is indeed the opposite of love, we are faced with two contradictory paradigms about the origins and role of justice. The issue becomes which kind of society we want to live in."[17]

Some restorative justice advocates attempt a more humanist, less explicitly religious, reconciliation of love and justice. Jonathan Burnside and Nicolas Baker speak of restorative justice as aspiring to "a passionate construal of justice [that] would emphasise love, compassion and the vindication of the weak."[18] John Griffiths, whose critique of the criminal justice system was an early precursor of restorative justice, brought the value of love into conversation with the value of justice by arguing that the ideology of criminal law might presume background conditions consistent with a loving family in its approach to offenders. Griffiths argued that we should exercise our ideological freedom to break the bad habit of assuming background conditions of "disharmony, fundamentally irreconcilable interests, a state of war."[19] He thought we should replace such assumptions with those of "reconcilable – even mutual interests, a state of love."[20]

John Braithwaite is perhaps the most influential and prolific proponent of restorative justice. He is also an ostensibly purely secular thinker. Yet even he speaks of the restorative encounter as a "ritual of love"[21] and refers to restorative justice as "justice administered with love."[22] Again, focusing on the importance of extending love to the offender as part of the restorative process, Braithwaite writes: "The literature on restorative justice conferences shows that love is central to understanding what makes them succeed. The attitude item with the highest loading on the reintegration factor in a factor analysis of offender attitudes toward the conference was 'During the conference did people suggest they loved you regardless of what you did?' In court cases, this item had the lowest loading on the reintegration factor of all the reintegration items. In short, the feeling by offenders that they were in receipt of unconditional love seems a crucial ingredient for the success of circles."[23] It is clear that he sees the extension of love to the offender as a necessary element of restorative transformation.

Other advocates for love as an element of restorative justice focus on the euphoric experiential – almost revival meeting – character of the restorative encounter. The energetic, emotional, and cathartic momentum of the restorative encounter is seen as shifting parties into a loving state of mind toward one another. Van Ness and Strong enthusiastically quote Lila Rucker: "It is enlivening to observe, much less experience, the process at work: affirmation, love, openness, honesty, laughter, respect, diligence, genuineness ... Ancient doors have creaked open. Tears spill down radiant cheeks."[24]

Of course, there are many powerful writers and thinkers on whom restorative justice can draw that have explored the relation between love and justice. Though Reinhold Niebuhr was a forceful skeptic about the Christian aspiration to a conflation of love and justice, he was also tremendously articulate in evoking a sense of the reliance of justice on some conception of love and the partial and provisional contributions that love could make to justice: "Insofar as justice admits the claims of self it is something less than love. Yet it cannot exist without love and remain justice. For without the 'grace' of love, justice always degenerates into something less than justice."[25] Zora Neale Hurston also gives us lavishly seductive words relating love and justice to one another: "Power at its best is love implementing the demands of justice. Justice at its best is love correcting everything that stands against love."[26]

One can also turn to Gene Outka's excruciatingly painstaking work *Agape: An Ethical Analysis* for a drier, less evocative, yet more philosophically exacting elaboration of an understanding of justice in terms of the commandment to love. There Outka seeks to derive from love-as-agape a comprehensive ethical system along the lines of utilitarianism. He seeks to elaborate love as "a normative ethical principle or standard with perhaps unvarying meaning or content."[27] He concerns himself "with agape in its utmost generality ... [and with] the kinds of 'material' or substantive content which it has been said to possess irrespective of circumstances."[28] Despite the aridness of this endeavour, one has to give Outka credit for putting himself to the task of at least trying so meticulously to bear out the philosophical implications of the rhetoric of love and justice. But, in the end, as Paul Ricoeur points out, all Outka's careful analytical skill fails to surmount the radical disproportionality between justice and love.[29]

Of course, one of the major reasons to worry about this disproportionality and to distrust idealistic talk about love and justice as "not opposite and not in conflict" is the track record of such arguments on the justice playing field. Generally speaking, such rhetoric has been less effective as a force toward greater justice than as a support and justification for oppressive hierarchical institutions. Love-talk in the context of injustice tends toward conservatism inasmuch as it argues against angry agitation or resistance and in favour of cheerful acquiescence in the status quo. People in positions of power preach brotherly love as a means of condemning resistance. As the verse in Proverbs says: "By long forbearing is a prince persuaded, and a soft tongue breaketh the bone."[30]

Sinclair Lewis demonstrated the manipulative nature of the rhetoric of love beautifully in his novel *Babbitt*. There we see a conservative minister, the Reverend Dr. Drew, preaching a sermon condemning a strike:

> What is not generally understood is that this whole industrial matter isn't a question of economics. It's essentially and only a matter of Love, and of the practical application of the Christian religion! Imagine a factory – instead of committees of workmen alienating the boss, the boss goes among them smiling, and they smile back, the elder brother and the younger. Brothers, that's what they must be, loving brothers, and then strikes would be as inconceivable as hatred in the home![31]

The vision of harmonious, loving relations is held up as the desirable standard. It is then insinuated that harmony would be perfectly achieved if everyone would lovingly accept the value and correctness of established power elites. It is the lower-downs – the victims of injustice – who are asked to act lovingly first. Trusting acceptance on their part is a prerequisite for the higher-ups to connect with their beneficence. A beautiful paradise of loving harmony is there for the taking if only the lower-downs will stop engaging in nasty and uglifying resistance. It is their agitating about injustice that deprives all of us of the heaven on earth attainable if they would just practice (younger) brotherly love with greater sensitivity. The perpetrator of injustice chastises the victim both for the victim's failure to love and for the perpetrator's own consequent inability to be loving the way he'd ultimately like to be.

Of course, the Reverend Dr. Drew's concluding reference to the inconceivability of hatred in the home is very telling. The idea that the family is and ought to be a sphere of harmonious shared purpose and affection – that it is and ought to be much like the kingdom of heaven – has long been a conservative force silencing women's complaints about injustice in the family. The fictional ideal that, within the family, love subsumes the demands of justice while offering a superior and richer set of aspirations becomes an impossible but compulsory standard for emulation. The expectation that families meet this standard in turn makes shameful any discussion of injustice and any revelation of hatred arising out of injustice in the home. The burden of this expectation has fallen on women, whose worth is questioned when they inevitably fail to infuse the home with values of selflessness, caring and giving, and shared purpose.[32]

Similarly, in the context of race relations, Derrick Bell has criticized the rhetoric of love of the enemy as an antiprogressive force.[33] Preaching of love as the first best response for victims of injustice, when not combined with daring strategies of resistance, carries the overriding message that victims ought to endure their frustrations and just "be nice" to the perpetrators of injustice in hopes that their niceness and love will some-day heal and transform the wrongdoers. The perpetrators of race, gender, and class injustices have every motivation to counsel such strategies of love. They have every motivation to try to inspire others to strive for rela-tions of mutual, spontaneous, happy love wherein love abolishes the impulse to think about whether one is being treated justly in the rela-tion and the impulse ever to punish or chastise the other.

Of course, the presence of authentic personal love between intimates does dramatically influence their sense of what counts as justice between them. We are both more lenient and more demanding in what we expect as matters of justice from those we love. La Rochefoucauld writes: "We forgive so long as we love."[34] On the other hand, love can also heighten the desire for revenge against lovers or loved ones who betray us. But our usual sense of the effect of love, especially of desiring love, is that the wronged party will so desire the restoration of the benefits enjoyed in the relationship that he or she will become lax about enforcing the demands of justice. Love deprives the injured party of the will to insist on justice. La Rochefoucauld speaks here of romantic love that indulges the wrongdoer and quashes all concern about justice. Here, love does not subsume or transcend justice; it simply lets the offender off the hook. Nietzsche goes further than La Rochefoucauld when he says that "every-body will revenge himself unless he is without honor or full of contempt or full of love for the person who has harmed or insulted him."[35]

Yet restorative justice looks to a kind of "tough love" that does not temper the demands of justice-as-accountability but that nevertheless does transform the world into one where Nietzsche's words are anath-ema. It aspires to dislodge the conception of honour that goads victims of wrongdoing toward vengeance and to replace it with a code that hon-ours the power to forgive. In this endeavour, it can take some assistance from de Tocqueville, who points out that codes of honour can command vengeance and forgiveness with equal vigour: "In some cases feudal honor enjoined revenge and stigmatized the forgiveness of insults; in others it imperiously commanded men to conquer their own passions and required forgetfulness of self."[36] Yet de Tocqueville's proviso about forgetfulness of self is key. And, inasmuch as a code of conduct demands forgetfulness of the claims of the self, it is unable to accommodate the legitimate demands of justice. No viable conception of justice can be founded on repudiation of the rightful claims of the self. This is true even though a compelling conception of honour can be so founded. A code of honour is essentially an attempt to infuse a collective or individual commitment to any virtue or practice with heightened ethical and dramatic significance. Honour is promiscuous in relation to the virtues. It can be grafted onto any nor-mative ideal – be it fearlessness or prudence; compassion or violence; the ability to work hard or the ability to drink hard. Justice is not as flexible a concept. It is immutably, conceptually tied to protection of and concern for the claims of individuals concerning their rightful entitlements and legitimate interests.

Nevertheless, restorative justice hopes it can simultaneously validate and protect the claims of the individual and promote an ethic of forgiveness while at the same time repudiating punishment. It hopes to correct wrongdoing, insist on the making of amends, and lovingly support both the victim's and offender's return to a caring community.

Yet, inspiring though this talk of the transformative power of love can be, it often seems either so abstract as not to offer any guide toward action at all or so supererogatory that it requires unconscionably grand-scale sacrifices on the part of victims and communities in the cause of promoting the welfare of offenders. Consider, for example, John Braithwaite's endorsement of a Palestinian restorative justice institution called Sulha: "A wise old man is asked in an ancient Arab story, 'How do you make peace between people?' The old man answers, 'If a bad man and a good man quarrel, I take from the good man and give to the bad man.' Then he is asked, 'What if it is two bad men who quarrel?' 'If it is two bad men,' he replies, 'then I take from myself and give to both of them.'" Braithwaite then comments: "Accepting the anger of victims with love no matter what they do, of peacemakers sacrificing themselves to absorb that anger, may bring victims to a state of grace."[37] Again, superabundant sacrifice, either on the part of the victims themselves or on the part of the mediator or peacemaker, is anticipated to have drastically beneficial results.

There is arrogance in this element of restorative justice. Do we think we are so much more likely to succeed than every other well-meaning generation of those who have aspired to conquer their enemies through loving embrace? Moreover, might one not legitimately mistrust this rhetoric of love as a potential power grab? Reconciliation of the values of love and justice seems to be an illusion and a potentially very dangerous one at that – dangerous both because it renders us vulnerable to the threats of those who will never be constrained by anything but violent coercion and because it fosters the expectation and desire for frictionless harmonies that will never be achieved.

While all of these charges can be levelled against the project of conflating love and justice, we can't be completely dismissive about the power of love to render assistance to justice either. History provides us with some undeniable success stories where love has worked as a force toward justice. The movements led by both Mohandas K. Gandhi and Dr. Martin Luther King, Jr., provide moving and dramatic instances of universal love deployed as a political practice and strategy toward greater justice. Both

Gandhi and King employed a strategy characterized by the extension of love and nonviolence (in Gandhi's terms *ahimsa*) to the enemy.[38] King spoke in terms virtually identical to those employed by restorative justice advocates:

> When we speak of loving those who oppose us we refer to neither *eros* nor *philia*: we speak of a love which is expressed in the Greek word *agape*. *Agape* means nothing sentimental or basically affectionate; it means understanding. When we love on the *agape* level we love men not because we like them. Not because their attitudes and ways appeal to us, but because God loves them.[39]

King's strategy vividly illustrates the power of the impersonally loving stance toward one's opponent as a fungibly loveable fellow-creature-of-God. The technique is to will oneself to ignore all authentic negative emotional responses to wrongdoers so as to enable oneself to take up a stance of dignified nonviolence in relation to them. Yet it is the steadiness of the loving posture, rather than its internal authenticity, that counts when one uses love as a political strategy toward greater justice.

The method is clearly grounded in an insight found in Proverbs[40] that is later quoted by Paul in his letter to the Romans: "Dearly beloved, avenge not yourselves, but rather give place unto wrath: for it is written, Vengeance is mine; I will repay, saith the Lord. Therefore if thine enemy hunger, feed him; if he thirst, give him drink: for in so doing thou shalt heap coals of fire on his head. Be not overcome of evil, but overcome evil with good."[41] We are assured that God keeps to himself the pleasure of and the duty to exact revenge. In reliance on that guarantee, we are told to reverse all normal expectations of reciprocity in our relations with wrongdoers. Instead of responding to harm with harm we are asked to repay harm with goodness. Yet it is clear that the extension of love and kindness to the enemy – if not an out-and-out form of revenge – is a strategy that still seeks to humiliate, infuriate, and thereby disarm the enemy. The point of the beneficence is to cause pain. The strategy disrupts our expectations and understandings of reciprocity. Yet the game of reciprocal exchange of insult and injury is at once both repudiated and more skilfully played. Moreover, in Paul's estimation, though God may love our enemies, we can also count on him to punish them for wrongs they commit against us. The commandment to love is coupled with this assurance that God can be trusted to take revenge. This assurance makes the extension of love to the enemy all the more palatable; loving the enemy is essentially a matter of biding our time.

Thus, although the goal of this method is most certainly to end the game of reciprocal insult and injury, one seeks to end that game by winning it. By striking a strategic pose on the higher moral ground of loving kindness, one disappoints and frustrates the opponent's expectation of hostile exchange while at the same time delivering the (metaphorical) knockout blow. The strategy was particularly brilliant in both the colonial and the civil rights contexts faced by Gandhi and King. Since it was their full humanity and capacity for civilization that was being denied by their oppressors, the humaneness and civility of their stance was particularly disarming. By taking up the stance of paternalistic beneficence toward their more powerful opponents, both Gandhi and King were able to cultivate an image of greater refinement than the most refined of their white, self-appointed superiors. This vivid image of greater civility was a powerful weapon in the humiliation of the opponent.

These political experiments in love and justice were indisputably, breathtakingly impressive, and Gandhi and King are arguably the two unrivalled moral heroes of the twentieth century. Yet, interestingly, while restorative justice advocates appropriate the rhetoric of Gandhi and King, they do not often refer to the legacies of Gandhi and King in seeking either inspiration for restorative practices or grounding in practices of love and justice.[42] The Gandhian strategy, though it uses the same rhetorical tropes, doesn't map conveniently onto restorative justice in the criminal context. There are a number of reasons for this. First, Gandhian strategy is developed as a weapon of the weak-but-numerous against the purportedly legitimate and unquestionably powerful few. The Gandhian strategy is a kind of one-two-no-punch that ends up effectively defeating the moral power, and thereby immobilizing the physical power, of the stronger opponent.[43] The strategy cleverly (not to mention bravely) goads the enemy into openly exercising his superior physical power with unconscionable brutality. The Gandhian counters this violence with dignified, serene, and stubborn insistence on clearly defined political demands coupled with absolute defencelessness. The enemy comes off as an obscene bully and, exposed in this unfavourable light, is stripped of his pretense to moral authority.

The method plays on the incongruousness of the opponent's pretense to a status of moral authority and his public violation of all norms of honour prohibiting the use of violence against the defenceless. Yet it is the enemy's pretense to a status of moral legitimacy, reasonableness, and beneficence that sets the trap for the requisite humiliation.[44] Private wrongdoers in the restorative justice context are, therefore, significantly different from the political opponents of Gandhi and King. First, the private wrongdoer is generally not invested in his or her credibility as a moral authority.[45] Second, and more significantly, that the wrongdoer in the context of restorative justice is usually less powerful than the victim and community put together (ironically) poses a problem. The extension of loving kindness in the restorative encounter is not a strategy for a weaker victim to wrest coercive power away from the more powerful wrongdoer. On the contrary, extension of loving kindness to the offender in a restorative encounter is a relinquishment of the state's presumptive coercive power over the offender.

The Gandhian method is used by oppressed persons who have no means of effectively punishing the wrongdoing of the colonial power. It makes very good sense to talk about love of the wrongdoer when the wrongdoer has all the guns and one needs some means of helping one's followers to resist despair. In the context of criminal wrongdoing, the state presumptively holds the power of punishment.[46] This complete reversal of the power relation in the restorative justice context renders the loving stance of restorative justice far more akin to an indulgent kind of love of wrongdoers: love that lets them "get away with it."[47]

A further significant aspect of the Gandhian method that renders it inconvenient as an inspiration for restorative justice is its requirement for extreme physical courage.[48] The Gandhian method is a tactic of war with all the physical risks that war entails; it requires an army and anticipates casualties. The Gandhian extension of nonviolent regard to the opponent is impressive and effective precisely because it courts real physical danger. Its shaming strategy works only because it *does* bring out the violence and brutality of the opponent. It works because the more dignified yet physically weaker party becomes vulnerable to that brutality in public view. Gandhi, King, and their followers disrupted the usual reciprocity of justice by meeting violence with nonviolence. But both their moral heroism and their success lay not primarily in their rhetoric about love of the enemy, but in their readiness to be murdered before a horrified on-looking world.

Inasmuch as the Gandhian method repudiates the reciprocal ethic of the *lex talionis*, and rewards violence with nonviolent insistence on equality and respect, it participates in what Paul Ricoeur describes as that "logic of superabundance that ... opposes itself to the logic of equivalence that governs everyday life."[49] As Ricoeur says, "there are those unique and extreme forms of commitment taken up by St. Francis, Gandhi and Martin Luther King, Jr. Yet from what penal law and, in general, from what rule of justice can we deduce a maxim of action that would set up non-equivalence as a general rule?"[50] The courage to assume a fiction of superabundance comes from extreme religious devotion combined with absolute faith in the rectitude of one's position and with a certainty that one's aspirations for change are incontrovertibly more significant than one's life. As Don Quixote puts it in the quotation above, such courage requires only that one be more of the spirit than of the flesh, more of God than of the world. The leap to an assumption of superabundance is inspired by a religious sense that one has access to that supreme source of eternal love and life. The credibility of one's declaration of superabundant love is always testable by one's willingness to lay down one's life.

The naivety, or perhaps the hubris, of restorative justice lies in its aspiration to disrupt the reciprocity and equivalences of everyday life while remaining more concerned about the world than about God and more concerned with the flesh than with the spirit. It seeks to bring love to justice without being underwritten by that great otherworldly insurer who will indemnify worldly losses with supreme concessions in the hereafter. Restorative justice, then, is both too spiritual and not spiritual enough. In other words, it seems to aspire precisely to be a form of penal law that "sets up non-equivalence as a general rule." Yet proponents of restorative justice do not personally take on, and cannot in good conscience suggest that victims take on, the physical risk always inherent in this steadfast insistence on nonequivalence. They are not ready to die, nor do they even anticipate any physical risk, in the exercise of disrupting the expected reciprocities of justice.

The turning of the other cheek that restorative justice envisions on the part of the victim and community is meant to work its magic on the offender instantaneously. Yet, in Gandhi's and King's estimation (not to mention Jesus'), the strategy of nonequivalence – of the turning of the other cheek – was recognized as presumptively entailing, and did entail, physical martyrdom and death. While Gandhi's method required that one rein in one's authentic desire to lash out at the wrongdoer, it certainly did not question that the wrongdoer would continue to behave violently. Restorative justice, by contrast, assumes its own ability to subdue immediately the violence of the offender through the gifts of withdrawal of punishment and the extension of brotherly love. It assumes that people tend to become what you take them to be and that treating perpetrators as trustworthy will transform them into people deserving of trust. As restorative justice advocate Aleksandar Fatić puts it, "the only way to make offenders trustworthy is to trust them, and moreover, to create a culture in which trust itself will be seen as the only legitimate means for maintaining and restoring itself."[51] The Gandhian method makes no such sunny assumption.

Moreover, the purely physical nature of the Gandhian method renders the inner state of loving regard for the opponent ultimately unimportant. As long as you can stand your ground and take it, thereby provoking your opponent into ever-more-despicable acts of violence, it doesn't matter how sincere your loving regard for him is. The method provides its own external means of faking the inner state of love embraced in its rhetoric. It clearly spells out the motions one needs to go through. Of course, the courage to do so needs to be real, and, for some, talking themselves into loving people they would spontaneously hate may be good practice for talking themselves into standing still when they would spontaneously flee or fight. Thus the rhetoric is not just for the benefit of the enemy and the on-lookers. This talk of love is also a rhetoric inspiring solidarity and endurance. But the success of the method depends mostly on sheer physical courage, partly on the shaming bite of the rhetoric of brotherly love, and not very much at all on the inner state of agape achieved by the Gandhian practitioner. When Gandhi and King talked about brotherly love as action rather than affection, they knew exactly what sort of action they meant. They meant actively and openly taking up a defiant but dignified stance of equality in relation to the enemy, righteously disobeying his commands, and then taking the enemy's blows without lashing out in return. Gandhi and King were moral heroes without a doubt. But they were also resolutely practical men.

Howard Zehr is aware of the tension between love for the wrongdoer as an inner affective state and as a name for a particular strategy or action. Zehr wants to follow Gandhi and King to disclaim any need for tender feelings toward the opponent in a practice of justice that seeks to accommodate the demands of love.[52] Zehr, like Gandhi and King, seeks in particular to distance the kind of love he is advocating from romantic or personal love:

> It is worth noting here that Western concepts of romantic and emotional love complicate our understanding of love as a source for action. Biblical concepts of love do not rule out how we feel. Certainly Christ makes it clear that feelings of hate are as serious as actions. Yet love is not defined as a mushy emotion. Love is, rather, a conscious act of looking after the good of another. When the Bible talks of love, the words usually connote action and volition more than feeling.[53]

But Zehr's observation begs two questions. First, what actions or volitions on the part of the victims are called for by restorative justice? And, second, why would victims be inclined to act this way in the absence of a motivation drawn from pure religious devotion? Both Gandhi and King had very specific answers to these questions. The actions they called for comprised collective, deliberate, but defenceless noncooperation with oppressive state action. The very apparent and clear motivation for doing so was to attain the desired position of political autonomy and equality. But Zehr does not give us clear answers to these questions in the context of restorative justice. It remains completely unclear as to exactly what action the victim should take (other than turning up at the restorative encounter, telling his or her story, and forbearing from vengeance) to promote the good of the offender. More perplexing still, we are given no explanation as to why the victim should be motivated to take such action. In the tactics of Gandhi and King, the extension of love to the wrong-doers was a clearly intelligible part of a larger attempt to wrest power and control from them. If it worked, the strategy was patently in the best interests of the victims. The victims of injustice got what they wanted through the loving strategy: home rule for India or desegregation in the American South. It is not clear, however, in the context of restorative justice what, if anything, is on offer for the heroically loving victim who succeeds in caring for the well-being of the offender.[54] Thus restorative justice demands a more thoroughgoing selflessness on the part of the victim than the Gandhian method ever did. In restorative justice there is no clearly defined victory in sight that sensibly motivates the victim's forbearance.

Thus, in the absence of a clear sense of what it is that the victim is to *do* strategically in extending love to the offender and how it is that this extension of love to the offender is supposed to assist the victim in righting the balance and regaining a sense of dignity, we are thrown back onto the inner-state-oriented notion of a vague kind of feeling of universal loving compassion to be generated between the victim and the offender and the members of the community.

This conclusion, of course, brings us up against the difficulty that feelings are notoriously hard to command. We have a sense that, to be authentic, love must be spontaneous and perhaps even overwhelming – something that we would feel even if our will and better judgment were to forbid it. Does love that we deliberately, painstakingly fabricate count as love at all? But love of the wrongdoer in the criminal context – love of the burglar who breaks into your house, the stranger assailant who rapes you, the drunk driver who leaves you a paraplegic – has to be of this deliberately and painstakingly fabricated kind. It can't be spontaneous, nor can it be authentic (at least not initially). It is "put on" against all spontaneous inclination. And while devout practitioners may manage to fool themselves in the bargain, the process toward such success must involve striking the inauthentic pose of brotherly love in the hopes that this phoney posture will transmute by habit of self-discipline into genuine feeling capable of honestly motivating action.

Arguments for the viability of agape as a realistically powerful ethical force concede the indisputably self-conscious and self-generated nature of this kind of love. Arguments for the ethical viability of brotherly love tend to elaborate brotherly love in its relation to spontaneous personal love and (most often) romantic love. Some proceed by highlighting the similarities between spontaneous personal or romantic love and agape, arguing that (at the end of the day) personal and even romantic love are not actually so very spontaneous either. If love is going to succeed as a steady force in a long-term relationship, such personal love must (like agape) be a product of self-conscious effort, deliberate self-discipline, and intentional action. Thus, since our personal loves are a product of self-directed effort, such effort directed toward those who have wronged us is not so different from what we are used to already in our relationships of love. The other opposite strand of argument in favour of agape proceeds by drastically distinguishing agape from the spontaneous excitement of personal love. Let's first consider the arguments that liken agape to personal love.

Some thinkers who argue for agape – not only in political but also in personal life – see the very arbitrariness of passionate, spontaneous love as a source of optimism about our capacity to command deliberately feelings of an agape-type love in personal relations with others. Denis de Rougemont in *Love in the Western World* sees eros as being ever in need of rescue by agape. De Rougemont takes the very whimsy and caprice of spontaneous romantic love as a reason to be optimistic about our power to cultivate authentic agape for specific others by force of will. The very arbitrariness of love can inspire hope that we might discipline and domesticate it in the service of other interests. Left to its own spontaneous devices, love is but the work of so many magical but out-of-control mischief makers: Cupid or Puck or Hollywood or even that luckless Queen of Ireland whose love potion accidentally made its way down the gullet not of King Mark, for whom it was intended, but of the wanderer Tristan, thereby making a disastrous match for her daughter Iseult.[55] If love is thus so utterly arbitrary, so absolutely lacking in any grounding in intrinsic affinity, then why shouldn't it be amenable to direction toward anyone or anything?[56] For de Rougemont love would "cease to be a demon only when it ceased to be a God."[57] The quickest way of stripping love of its pretense to godlike status must be to bring it to heel in the service of rationality and domesticity. The very absurdity of love, as well as its propensity to be led by shallow fashion, inspires the belief that love – if utterly arbitrary – must also be capable of being tamed and directed in the interests of reason, prudence, and justice.[58]

If we can successfully fool ourselves in such matters – and overcome our knee-jerk likes and dislikes in relation to romantic passion – then why shouldn't it be even easier to fool ourselves when it comes to knee-jerk feelings of hatred and moral disgust in relation to relative strangers? If we can hunker down and learn to love a lover – say a partner in an arranged marriage – why shouldn't we be just as able to bite the bullet and learn to love the wrongdoer? The argument for love of the wrongdoer, then, straightforwardly promotes the ethical salutariness of certain forms of self-deception, certain kinds of self-conscious attempts to con, rather than just constrain, the authentic self. Duping yourself into love of the wrongdoer thus requires something of the same self-deceptive skill as that required of Jesus' ideal (though hypothetical) almsgiver who gives with his right hand while keeping the transaction secret from the left one: "When thou doest alms, let not thy left hand know what thy right hand doeth."[59] Yet, lacking this overachieving almsgiver's ambition for fiercely competitive feats of virtue (an ambition, of course, that compounds the difficulties of keeping that left hand in the dark), why ever would the average victim of wrongdoing – or for that matter the average wrongdoer – be motivated to do the obviously gruelling work of self-deception necessary to generate brotherly love for the other?

To take stock, the argument here is simply this: that romantic passion is generated by, and is then buffeted about upon, the waves of fashion and caprice. Being such a fickle, changeable, and (in some important sense) easily led passion, it ought to be liable to be generated not just by force of fad, but by force of sheer willpower in opposition to our spontaneous inclinations. Thus, since something so personal, intimate, and immediate as romantic passion can be cultivated by force of will, surely this less passionate, less deeply personal, more emotionally detached brotherly love ought to be able to be called up to order as well.

And the argument might almost be persuasive were it not that we know it's major premises to be false. De Rougemont is simply wrong in saying that we can (and that we'd all be better off if we did) just arbitrarily pick some person – a creature of God like all the rest – and love him or her. It's just not possible. Or, if we are again confronting the limitations of my own moral mediocrity here, let me put it this way instead: There must be many of us for whom the cultivation of romantic passion in relation to the interchangeable other would be prohibitively difficult even if we wholeheartedly bought these arguments for trying to muster it.

But disposing of this argument does not bring us to the end of the matter. Comparisons to romantic and personal love in the context of the advocacy of universal love usually take the opposite and more beguiling tack. It is not through any notion of our imagined capacity to wilfully generate romantic or personal love that the advocates of universal agape try to persuade us of our potential competence as practitioners of love of our enemies. Instead, it is by describing spontaneous romantic love and universal brotherly love as wholly different kettles of fish that they hope to generate confidence in our competence for the latter. As we have already seen, the standard rhetorical device used to subdue our horror at the task of loving those who have seriously wronged us goes like this: "This universal love is nothing like your love for your parents or your siblings; it's nothing at all like the love you feel for lovers; nor is it anything like the love you feel for your friends or for any of the other familiar objects of your affection. You can relax because universal love doesn't mean you have to *really* love your enemy as you love your family and friends. The main thing about universal love is that it is *completely* different. It is *agape*; it is *caritas*; it's *brotherly* – but nothing like the love you feel for your brother. You have to make yourself feel *something*, but you certainly don't have to make yourself feel *that*." And we respond, "Oh! Okay. Phew! If universal brotherly love has nothing to do with any other sort of love I've ever experienced, well alright then, I'll sign up and quit worrying."

The hyperbole of this comparison between universal love and personal love actually lends an artificial aura of attainability to the fantasized love of the opponent. The characterization of love of the opponent as "something so completely different" distinguishes it from everything that has any meaning for us. So we are made to understand that nothing we understand is what is meant. And, astonishingly, we rejoice at having gotten the point so far. Yet, though our spirits are lifted by this little triumph and we are pleased the argument is at an end, we are still no further ahead with actually understanding the real content of that internal state of universal love extended to our enemy. But we know, nevertheless, that love of the enemy needs to be cultivated because it is not anything that we naturally feel.

Let's see what happens, however, if we shift our point of comparison. Rather than contrast universal love with spontaneous affectionate love of persons, why not try out this idea on something nice and easy, like a thing. Consider this beautiful snippet of dialogue spoken in a tête-à-tête between Catherine Morland and Henry Tilney in Jane Austen's *Northanger Abbey* and observe Mr. Tilney's wry celebration of the "teachableness" of a disposition to love:

> "What beautiful hyacinths! I have just learnt to love a hyacinth."
>
> "And how might you learn? By accident or argument?"
>
> "Your sister taught me; I cannot tell how. Mrs. Allen used to take pains, year after year, to make me like them; but I never could, till I saw them the other day in Milsom Street; I am naturally indifferent about flowers."
>
> "But now you love a hyacinth. So much the better. You have gained a new source of enjoyment, and it is well to have as many holds upon happiness as possible ... And though the love of a hyacinth may be rather domestic, who can tell, the sentiment once raised, but you may in time come to love a rose? ... At any rate, however, I am pleased that you have learnt to love a hyacinth. The mere habit of learning to love is the thing; and a teachableness of disposition in a young lady is a great blessing."[60]

Exactly so: The mere habit of learning to love is the thing. The seeming triviality the object of love – a hyacinth – is entirely beside the point.

It is the very possibility that Catherine could go from indifference – or even hostility – to love of something (anything) by dint of effort that is deserving of our attention.

Of course, this is also a flirtatious conversation, so the idea of cultivation of romantic love is sneaking back up on us. Tilney is insinuating that first coming to love a hyacinth and then perhaps, a rose, Catherine might also come to love him. Though his hopes for success with her seem to be wisely pinned not on his faith in this argument about the flowers, but on his sense that Catherine is likely to be charmed by his flawlessly decorous skill as a flirt and by the delightfully witty quality of the attention she is being paid. In any event, *we* know, and we know Tilney suspects, that Catherine is already crazy about him. We know too that, in a Jane Austen novel, love is (almost always) a matter of the unfolding of an irrepressible natural affinity and the fulfilment of the true species-being of each of the lovers. It is not something that needs to be, or can be, taught.[61]

However, the gender of the student of love is worthy of note. It is in the lady that we most value the schooled disposition to love. And it ought to be put on the record here that the demographics of restorative justice on the question of who is required to learn love of their victimizers will prove no exception to this rule: Women victims of domestic violence, sexual assault, and other crime will be overrepresented in the pool of victim participants in restorative justice programs.[62]

But Mr. Tilney and Miss Morland, like Zehr, are (though much more playfully) drawing our attention to the distinction between, on the one hand, love arrived at through pedagogical effort or cultivation and, on the other hand, spontaneous personal love. And like Zehr, Tilney and Morland affirm the possibility of actively cultivating such love. However, Tilney and Morland, unlike Zehr, are also pointing out the real delicacy and difficulty of such cultivation even in relation to such a thing as a hyacinth. And, inasmuch as we can identify with Tilney's expression of justifiable astonishment at a particular successful instance of someone learning love for *something*, I suggest that his speech reveals with greater immediacy the serious difficulties of willing oneself to love.

This quotation from Austen suggests to us – or I'm hoping that it can be looked at in a light that allows it to suggest – that our familiar drastic comparisons between agape and spontaneous love, rather than assisting us with gaining a realistic assessment of the difficulties of agape, merely snooker us into a muddle-headed enthusiasm for this fictitious kind of love. If, however, we compare cultivation of love for an enemy with the cultivation of love for a hyacinth (and if a hyacinth seems too easy for you, try a lungwort, a beard tongue, bladderwort, or the milk-vetch), the difficulty of cultivating love for the enemy actually becomes more vividly apparent. If you doubt your ability do it with the lungwort or the milkvetch (also creations of God), how are you going to do it with the drunk driver or the rapist?

We readily assent to the drastic distinction between love of our enemies and spontaneous personal love. But the difference between learning universal love for our enemies and learning love of a lungwort, or anything else to which we are by nature indifferent or hostile, is both less apparent and more troubling. And if we look into our heart of hearts and find a lurking doubt about our ability to do as well as Catherine did with learning to love a hyacinth, then perhaps we should be very slow to enthusiasm about a theory of justice grounded in optimism about the "teachableness" of a disposition to love between victims and wrongdoers.

The ethical salutariness of self-deception is all very well when we are speaking of simple striving for one's personal best in matters of virtue. The downside risk falls only on oneself. The failure of self-deception of the almsgiver about his true motives is no skin off the nose of the recipient of the alms. The recipient probably doesn't really care whether the giver's left hand knows about the gift or not. However, the ethical perils of the failure of self-deception in the realm of universal love as the foundation of justice are far more readily apparent. By falling for the rhetoric of universal love here, we lull ourselves and others into misguided reliance on the false but easy comfort of a love we are almost certain to be woefully unable to deliver. The mind reels at the host of betrayals, disappointments, and power plays that a system of justice based on optimism about our shared capacity for such love will yield.

3
Three Precarious Pillars of Restorative Optimism

The rhetoric of restorative justice is optimistic about the cultivation of brotherly love and compassion between victims, offenders, and their communities and about the possibility of harnessing such love in the service of justice as healing and right-relation. It promises that encounter, self-disclosure, and truth-telling between victims and offenders will do much of the pedagogical work necessary to teach each a compassionate, loving understanding of the other.[1] It rests on the expectation that an immediate and emotional encounter will generate a surge of affect between victims, offenders, and their communities, which will act as a booster rocket toward mutual benefit. This optimistic vision of mutual benefit is perched on three supporting pillars of optimism. First, we have the optimism that our associations between justice and the infliction of proportionate suffering can be debunked and replaced with stronger, more compelling associations between justice and the experience of mutual equality and respect. Justice can retain its essential connection to reciprocity, yet the form of that reciprocity can be transformed from reciprocal infliction of "pay-back" suffering to the establishment of reciprocal equality and respect. The second pillar of restorative optimism is its faith that encounter and participation in the restorative process will alter the offender such that he or she will become able and willing to engage in relations of respectful regard with the victim and community. The restorative process seeks to heal the wounds that cause offenders to offend. The third pillar of restorative optimism is its confidence that the process will also succeed in healing the victim's pain and anger and will bring the victim into renewed well-being, dignity, and secure membership in community. Restorative processes, guided by universal love, will heal both offender and victim and will radically transform our understanding of justice itself. It is to these three points of optimism that we now turn.

Malleability of the Meaning of Justice

> Who shall put his finger on the work of justice, and say, "It is
> there"? Justice is like the Kingdom of God – it is not without us
> as a fact, it is within us as a great yearning.

> – George Eliot, *Romola*

In common parlance, when we ask "Was justice done?" what we generally mean is "Was sufficient proportionate authoritative punishment
meted out by the state?" Failing that, we might mean "Did the victim
manage privately to stick it to the wrongdoer?" Failing *that*, we mean
"Did anything befall the offender that could be called poetic justice?" –
that magical kind of justice that sometimes surpasses both public punishment and private vengeance in terms of victim satisfaction, that perfectly delicious downfall cosmically attributable to some illusive blend of
God's wrath, the victim's indignation, and the offender's own stupidity.
Yet in each case we identify justice with some kind of counterbalancing
pain for the wrongdoer, with some power that delivers the offender's just
deserts.

Advocates of restorative justice are hoping that we can change this identification and come to see these connections between justice and the infliction of pain on the offender as arbitrary or at least inessential. To
return again to Llewellyn and Howse's formulation: "There is no positive
value for justice in the *very fact* of the perpetrator's suffering or sacrifice
of well-being."[2] Llewellyn and Howse see punishment as a practice artificially grafted onto the far more essential notion of justice as a rectification of the imbalance that the wrongdoing has created in the social
equilibrium.[3] Since, in their view, it is a *social* equilibrium we are concerned with re-establishing, punishments that isolate or alienate the
offender seem particularly inapt. They remove the offender from the community rather than requiring him to maintain contact with the victim
and others while doing what is possible to make things right. We can
restore the social equilibrium more effectively by actively involving the
offender in the project of repair of the harm he has done than we can
by casting him out of society. Restorative justice is optimistic that we can
reprogram ourselves to understand the collective effort toward relations
of equality and respect to be a "first-best" notion of justice.[4]

The theory behind the South African Truth and Reconciliation Commission, for example, is that punishment of the offenders of apartheid
simply will not do as a "stand-in" for justice in a new, equal South Africa.[5]

True postapartheid justice is to be found in a new world of relationships of equality and respect between South Africans of all races. Thus the atrocities of the past ought to be addressed not through a process of trials and punishment, but through a forward-looking process of encounter and disclosure between victims and wrongdoers that has as its goal the creation of respectful relationships for the future.

Restorative justice, therefore, rejects the idea that mercy is a corrective to the excesses of hard-hearted justice. Rather, justice itself is defined in terms of an active extension of mercy to, and between, victim, offender, and community, each helping the others through the process of making things right again. As Herman Bianchi puts it: "Mercy cannot replace justice. In a tsedeka model, justice *is* mercy, the two being completely interwoven, the one nonexistent without the other. Mercy is not the gentle and tender replacement of a harsh institution; there is no need for that ... It means the benevolent acknowledgement of a competence for renewal in every person, a willingness for human interaction ... Mercy ... is the restoration of right order ... The use of the maxim 'temper justice with mercy' is therefore nonsensical by implication. It should be replaced with 'show mercy through justice.' Mercy is just, and justice is merciful."[6]

The restorative rejection of a punitive understanding of justice has two related aspirations. First, it wants to debunk the age-old idea that rectification of the imbalance caused by wrongdoing requires that reciprocal suffering be inflicted on the offender. Second, it wants to take this reconceptualization of justice one step further, insisting that we cannot locate justice in *any* predetermined and external state of affairs. Justice is not to be found in second-best tokens such as punishment but in the first-best experiential quality of lived relationships of equality and respect. Justice inheres in the experience of right-relation.

Restorative justice, then, shares something with George Eliot's claim that justice "is not without us as a fact, it is within us as a great yearning."[7] Like Eliot, proponents of restorative justice claim that we cannot find justice in any of those external states of affairs to which we are accustomed to giving the stamp of justice, such as the enforcement of punishment or compensation. Yet they would reject Eliot's suggestion here that true justice is locked forever within – that it is trapped in the longings of our hearts. Restorative justice aspires to the fulfilment of our internal yearnings for the just. Yet it conceives of these longings in wholly beneficent terms. It privileges our longings for the frictionless harmonies of the kingdom of heaven and seeks to purify us of any hankerings we may have after the fiery justice of a punitive hell.

Of course, it is also impossible in respect of any particular wrongdoing to say in advance what will produce this experiential form of justice. The solution must emerge from the particularities and idiosyncrasies of encounter between *this* victim, *this* wrongdoer, and *this* community. Thus restorative justice sees itself as resolutely context-specific and as challenging participants to do the imaginative work of coming up with ways of inducing that shift from the I-it to the I-Thou relationship. There is a tremendous reluctance in the rhetoric of restorative justice to boil it all down to precise concrete remedies.[8] To do so would collapse restorative justice into just another form of tokenism. Thus both punishment and restitution are insufficient proxies for justice-as-repair. As Conrad Brunk puts it, "restitution itself does not achieve *restoration* of the relationship between the offender and the victim or the offender and the community. It does not deal with all the social and psychological aspects of the 'breach' represented by the offence."[9]

Thus restorative justice is not mere reparation or compensation for the harm done.[10] Michael Hadley, speaking about the ultimate aims of restorative justice, says: "One might very well ask what actually happens when restorative justice 'works.' As participants attest, it is something more easily experienced than defined. Some have spoken of the unexpected moment of peace, of calm and tranquillity, of self-assurance, of release."[11] Brunk again explains that "offenders, victims, families, mediators, judges and lawyers who participate all speak of the 'magic' or 'deeply spiritual' aspects of the events which take place when offenders come to terms with the pain they have inflicted on victims or their families and express repentance, or when victims experience personal healing from offenders' acts of repentance, and from their own ability to forgive."[12]

Inasmuch as restorative justice eschews reliance on external states of affairs as satisfying proxies for justice, its proponents have much in common with critical legal studies and feminist critiques of rights. Like the restorative critique of punishment, these critiques of rights maintain that we have settled for artifacts like rights and punishment as tokens of justice instead of holding out for the genuine experience of justice in our relationships. Valerie Kerruish in her book *Jurisprudence as Ideology* speaks in terms of rights fetishism. Rights, like the practice of punishment, teach us to focus on the artifact instead of the relationship; the shoe instead of the lover; the video recorder instead of the child.[13]

In elaborating this idea, Kerruish tells the story of a band of Australian Aborigines who obtained an injunction against a corporation to stop it from bulldozing a sacred burial site in the course of constructing a pipeline.[14] When Kerruish congratulated the chief on the court victory, he replied that, frankly, they considered it a defeat. They were unable to negotiate an amicable agreement with the corporation. Moreover, the victory had been won by reliance on the beneficence of a liberal white judge rather than through any autonomous exercise of power in the relationship. Kerruish took the chief to mean that what the band *really* wanted was "mutuality of understanding" and "respect for their beliefs" – neither of which was achieved. They were granted rights instead: mere tokens of respect that only pointed to, without delivering, what was genuinely desirable.[15] The sacred site was unscathed, but the relationship between the Aborigines and the corporation remained one of hostility and contempt. Rights did not, and could not, deliver the desired experience of mutuality and respect in the relationship. Kerruish writes: "There is a difference between being respected and winning a court case which establishes entitlement to respect in a specific instance."[16]

The restorative justice critique of punishment travels a similar path. The argument is grounded in a theory of the desirable and, more precisely, the *truly* desired. Punishment of the offender is not what the victim *really* wants. The victims' authentic longings for justice are better understood in terms of their desire for the experience of affirmation of their worth and secure membership in the community. What victims really want is for the offender to own responsibility for the harm, to shift his or her attitude from disrespect to respect for the victim and the norms of the community, and to feel and express genuine shame, remorse, and contrition. Victims want the shared feeling of letting go of the loss and sadness of the past harm through forgiveness and healing. They want the public vindication that is achieved through caring and authoritative acknowledgment of their suffering. Punishment does not deliver any of these outcomes. It is a mere token: an external fact that does not and cannot fulfill our internal longings for experiential justice.

Moreover, as tokens go, punishment is far more pernicious than are rights. Rights limit us more than they actively harm us. Rights strip life of the experiential richness it might otherwise have were we not so fixated on them. Yet they only prevent life from being as good as it might be if we could just get ourselves to stop paying attention to the shoe and attend, instead, to the lover. By contrast, alienating, isolating punishment – token though it is – has a burgeoning sinister life to it. Punishment doesn't merely deprive us of more fulfilling and meaningful responses to crime; it goes further, actively reproducing the lust for revenge. Moreover, it exacerbates harm done by making the offender angrier and more hostile to the community and its norms.[17]

So punishment is an even more destructive token for justice than are rights. What is more, it is easier to remedy the problem with punishment, easier to aim at the genuine article. While critics of rights such as Kerruish often concede that the law, in its present institutional structure, is not in much of a position to do anything about the shortcomings of rights (Kerruish asks "What more can the law do?" and her answer is "Nothing."),[18] institutions of restorative justice claim to be far more capable of shifting our focus off the token and onto living justice experienced as the personal achievement of relations of repair, accountability, healing, respect, and equality.

If restorative justice can give us an experience of the real thing, why then would we settle for ersatz tokens of justice? At first blush, the idea of lived experience of relational justice seems to be vastly more attractive than familiar token-based understandings of justice. However, once we delve a little deeper, reasons begin to emerge that justify a choice to settle for tokens instead of holding out for the real thing. The first reason for potentially doing so stems from a concern that if we give play to our true internal longings for justice, they may not turn out to be as respectful as restorative justice anticipates. We settle for tokens because they protect the perpetrator from the dark side of the victim's and community's internal longings for a lived experience of justice.

The second reason for settling for tokens is their very tangibility. Authentic respect is too intimate and too illusive a value to be demanded as a matter of justice at all, let alone by public institutions of justice amongst strangers or enemies. To aim directly at generating authentic respect as an element of justice is to lay ourselves open to all manner of fraudulent performances of respectful relation. Tangible tokens of justice protect us (and here I primarily mean the victim and community) from the risk of falling for a wrongdoer's phoney contrition, concern, respect, and regard. They protect us from the self-serving gamesmanship and power strategies that can underpin dramatic performances of remorse, contrition, apology, respect, and forgiveness by both the perpetrator and the victim of wrongdoing.

Tokens as a Buffer against Revenge

Tokens of justice protect offenders from the excesses of the nasty side of victims' internal longings for experiential justice. Our willingness to settle for lifeless, lacklustre tokens instead of holding out for this richer wish-fulfilment is motivated, to a considerable degree, by our anxiety about the dark side of those internal longings. Our institutions of retributive punishment put forward measured, state-administered punishment *precisely as a token* in order to prevent outraged victims and communities from going for what they *really* want. Retribution is a means of limiting the potentially limitless desire for revenge.[19] In the wake of wrongdoing, the not very lofty truth is that, more often than not, what we really want is "blood" – not relations of mutual respect.[20] State-inflicted punishment, in its capacity as a token, offers a buffer against the excess and violence of that desire. Thus, as Nietzsche puts it in *The Genealogy of Morals*, "punishment [serves] as payment of a fee stipulated by the power that protects the wrongdoer from the excesses of revenge. Punishment [stands] as a compromise with revenge in its natural state when the latter is still maintained and claimed as a privilege by powerful clans."[21]

Yet restorative justice eschews reliance on the limiting powers of such tokens of justice because it aspires to render victims' *true* desires for justice in wholly beneficent terms. It believes in its own institutional potential to help participants get in touch with their higher selves and thus to bring out the benign side of their desires for justice.[22] Nevertheless, restorative justice does see the need to make space for victims' anger and resentment in the course of the restorative encounter. Indeed, the affective momentum of the restorative encounter depends on the release and immediate expression of this anger within the constraints of equality and respect.[23] Yet the expression of anger is thought to lead inexorably toward resolution and reciprocal regard. Restorative justice hopes that, by making appropriate space for the controlled expression of mean-spirited desires, we can transform them into healthy desires for right-relation. By controlled examination of our mistaken desire for revenge, we unearth our true desire for reconciliation.

Consider the following case study described in restorative justice advocate Mark Umbreit's book *The Handbook of Victim Offender Mediation*. Bob and Anne were burgled by Jim. Though they were initially reluctant to participate in the victim-offender mediation process, they eventually agreed. Their agreement was motivated in large measure by their desire for an opportunity to "'let that punk know' how angry they were."[24] During the encounter, Bob, the victim, poured out his anger toward Jim, the perpetrator, telling him how furious he was with this kind of "crap." Fearing a "direct verbal attack" on Jim by Bob, the co-mediators were about to intervene when Jim himself stood up and said: "I'm not taking this crap any longer – I've had it. I'm leaving." A co-mediator responded by saying: "I'm sure it has been difficult listening to the anger expressed by Bob, but I know that he is interested in working out some kind of settlement. Could you just give it another ten minutes?" So Jim reluctantly agreed to stay. Umbreit explains: "The co-mediator's comment appeared to have validated some of Jim's concern that he was being 'dumped on.' The interaction between the mediator and Jim also evidently had a positive impact on Bob. From this point on, Bob's communication to Jim was far less emotional, and his body language slowly began to loosen up."[25]

Thus restorative justice provides space for the expression of vengeful anger within the norms of respect. It was important for the victim, Bob, to be heard in his feelings of outrage and to attempt to inflict suffering on Jim by expressing that anger, and it was also important to ensure that Jim not feel "dumped on."[26] This controlled release of anger led to a happy ending. The parties came to an agreement about how Jim could make things right by paying back some of what he stole over a period of months. But again, simple restitution is not enough for restorative justice. Thus the case study ends with that special "something more" by way of healed relations of reciprocal respect and regard. When the mediator suggested they meet again several months later to ensure that the agreement was working well for all concerned, Jim responded: "I'd really like to do that. Could we have it at my house? ... I'd like you to meet my wife and baby ... I'm not a criminal." Umbreit concludes by telling us that: "The meeting was scheduled two months later at Jim's home, with a mediator present. Jim offered to cook lasagna. Bob and Anne quickly indicated their interest." The momentary expression of the darker side of Bob's desire for an experience of justice-as-revenge ends in a more lasting experience of justice-as-reconciliation: the breaking of bread together, sharing, and reciprocal regard.

This reciprocity, according to restorative justice, is what victims really want. Bob's vengeful longings belied a mistaken understanding of his true best interests. Restorative justice helped him to find a way to a more elevated understanding of his more fully autonomous interest in achieving justice as the experience of respectful relation. Restorative justice claims to have obviated the need for precise and fixed limits on the desire for revenge because it claims to have the capacity to tame that desire through processes of respectful encounter.

Thus the restorative justice way of coping with the potentially unlimited desire for revenge is the inverse of that of retributive justice. Retributive justice aspires to bracket the desire for vengeance, to interpose the state between victim and offender, and evenhandedly to deal out proportionate allotments of punishment commensurate with the nature of the offence. Thus retribution confines the extent of comeuppance for the offender by claiming a monopoly on violence and insisting that the offender's suffering not extend beyond the token of punishment authorized and delivered by the state. At the same time, punishment stands in for vengeance and gives official, though circumscribed, acknowledgment and legitimacy to the victim's and community's sense of indignation.

Restorative justice, as demonstrated in the example of victim Bob and burglar Jim, has a very different relation to the animating force of the victim's desire for revenge. Instead of seeing a need to interpose the state between victim and offender in order to manage (and again, bracket) the force of that desire, restorative justice seeks to bring victim and perpetrator together in a more immediate encounter and, if necessary, to give play to the victim's wrath. It provides an opportunity for the victim to vent or blow off steam. It does not, however, validate or legitimize the victim's desire to see the perpetrator suffer. Retributive justice authoritatively validates, while authoritatively confining, the impulse to inflict suffering on the offender. Restorative justice humours the victim's anger while invalidating its central intuition: that the perpetrator deserves to suffer because of what he has done. Restorative justice gives dramatic space to the victim's vengeful longings, while at the same time denying the force of those longings as reasons for either state or private action. It admits entry to the victim's desire for revenge, while at the same time giving priority to the protection of the perpetrator's dignity and person. The perpetrator is to be protected not only from the actual infliction of any retributive suffering, but also from the potentially degrading experience of being "dumped on" by or having to "take crap from" the victim. The perpetrator is protected not by any authoritative *ex ante* limitation on revenge but by the assurance that victims and communities will be successfully cajoled into treating the perpetrator with respect.

This consideration for the perpetrator might seem to create the worst of both worlds for the victim but for the fact that restorative justice further promises that this method will purge the victim's desire for vengeance and restore the victim to a sense of dignity and well-being.[27] Restorative justice promises that encounter, disclosure, and the perpetrator's willingness to acknowledge responsibility for harm will lead the victim and perpetrator and their communities toward relations of mutual respect and regard. Further, it promises that these relations of mutual equality and respect will read as a robust conception of justice. Restorative justice is optimistic that the victim's, offender's, and community's experience of reconciliation and sharing – symbolized in Umbreit's example by the lasagna dinner – can come to be meaningfully understood as justice. Moreover, it is optimistic that fostering more and more of these restorative successes will help us collectively to shift our understanding of justice so that we come to understand it not in terms of the infliction of deserved hard treatment on an offender, but in terms of similar experiences of reciprocal respect and regard.[28]

Restorative justice is confident that we can do away with tokens of justice such as punishment because it is confident that the protection of the offender from the excesses of revenge can be achieved in other ways. The success of restorative justice will, therefore, be cumulative. The more we identify justice with the repair of right-relation, the more we will succeed in undermining the cultural legitimacy and vigour of the desire for revenge. Successful practices of justice-as-repair will ultimately lead to the withering away of the pernicious impulse to vengeance.

Restorative justice buttresses its claim that the desire for revenge is misguided (and, therefore, susceptible to being culturally erased) by pointing to the fact that within our traditional system of retribution, many victims do not experience the anticipated sense of closure or satisfaction when they see the offender punished. Our participation in practices of punishment is not meaningfully autonomous since it is grounded in an illusion that punishment will bring satisfaction and closure. Disappointment with punishment also belies that inner, and possibly even unconscious, *true* desire to be heard and respectfully listened to, the desire not for further wounds, but for mutual healing through the creation of relations of equality and respect.[29]

Yet one wonders whether the failure of punishment to satisfy the victim isn't necessarily inherent in cases of irrevocable serious harm. The failure of punishment to satisfy the victim points to the tragedy of crime. Nothing can make things better again. As Dan Markel writes: "To the extent that certain losses and grief are incompensable and inconsolable, it is uncertain – even improbable – that the suffering of another will serve as balm to the perturbed mind" of the victim.[30]

Moreover, when we turn our noses up at tokens such as rights and punishment, is it not also possible that what we really desire is not mutual respect but some more gruesome comeuppance for the wrongdoer than the justice system is able to deliver? Even in the case of the Aboriginal chief who calls the court victory a defeat, one wonders about the accuracy of Kerruish's sense of this reaction as a disappointed desire for relations of mutual understanding. Is there not an outside possibility that this chief was actually calling the victory a defeat because he was wishing they could have laid the corporation far lower still? The corporation represents a power that has come close to decimating Aboriginal culture. Is it not then possible that the victory felt hollow not because it failed to deliver relations of mutual respect, but because it was a relatively piddling shot back at an appalling bully that has been getting away with such wrongs for decades? The so-called victory did not deliver anything approaching reciprocity of insult and injury. Moreover, the shot back – such as it was – had to be delivered by an authority figure within the legal system constituted by the bully itself. Isn't it possible that what this chief *really* wanted was to see the band exercise independent power to bring this corporation painfully and meaningfully to its knees?

Yet, by daring to eschew tokens and pursue experiential justice directly, restorative justice must convince us that the nasty side of our experiential desires for justice can reliably be placated and transformed through the restorative process. Yet there is little basis, apart from restorative success stories, for us to be so sanguine about such a possibility. Indeed, when proponents of restorative justice such as Braithwaite, Llewellyn, Howse, and Bianchi claim that restorative justice has been the dominant mode of justice throughout history, they play down, even disown, the brutally violent side of these precedents.[31] Though tribal and traditional practices provide us with examples of restorative justicelike peacemaking, most historical and anthropological analyses of these cultures show peacemaking to be born of a recognition that one was up against the wall. Peacemaking was one side of a coin whose other side was war. The potentially mandatory nature of the infliction of reciprocal suffering, injury, and insult was absolutely central to the concept of justice in the cultures restorative justice looks to as its predecessors.[32] The inducement to make peace and to keep it was the fear of the feud. Certainly, a conception of respect for one's opponent was involved here. But it was a respect born of the recognition that your opponent was capable of thoroughly thrashing you if you got out of line.

The Fakability of Justice-as-Respect

Our willingness to settle for tokens is also motivated by the impossibility of commanding, and possibility of faking, these inner states of mutual understanding and respect. The kind of respect that rights critics like Kerruish and advocates of restorative justice are talking about is not a respect primarily grounded in fear; nor is it mere respect-as-toleration: an overcoming of inner contempt and hostility at the level only of outward speech and action. Nor is it the respect that inheres in a commitment to resist the impulse to mock. It is no negative, minimalist, liberal willingness to leave others alone. It is an authentic regard that surpasses, and preempts even the need for, toleration. It is the genuine – even spiritual – appreciation of the inherent worth and dignity of the other, an appreciation that extinguishes even the inclination to mock or contemn. It is an active recognition of the inestimable value of the other.

Indeed, the "respect" of restorative justice approaches something very much like love in the form of a personal and immediate form of agape. John Braithwaite consistently speaks of restorative justice as "maintaining bonds of respect or love" for the offender while inducing appropriate shame.[33] In Hadley's book on *The Spiritual Roots of Restorative Justice*, the entry for respect in the index reads: "see also compassion, ... love."[34] The love that restorative justice relates to respect has all the piety, vagueness, and need for devout cultivation of that universal love discussed at length in the previous chapter.[35] Moreover, this sort of respect as true appreciation and esteem of the other is as difficult to command as that universal love. It is conceivable to command a respect grounded in fear, possible even to command a respect primarily understood in terms of toleration, show of deference, or forbearance from public mockery.[36] What we can't command is that people feel this sort of authentic esteem for others' very beings or for the substance of others' beliefs. As William Ian Miller puts it, "the problem is that real people and their assaults on one's senses and sensibilities get in the way of loftier ideals."[37]

Authentic respect in the form of appreciation and esteem is a very delicate, and profoundly personal and private, inner state. We extend our respect as esteem when we are convinced that others have earned it. Indeed, one of the most significant exercises of autonomy and self-definition must surely lie in our unfettered ability to decide when to give and when to withhold respect. Judgments about when and why to confer respect as authentic esteem form the essence of our individual and group sensibilities. Moreover, autonomy around the decision to give or withhold respect is one of the few arenas in which we genuinely enjoy fundamental equality. We are each equally free to feel either contempt, respect, or indifference in our relations no matter how they are structured on lines of race, class, education, gender, sexual orientation, and the like.[38]

Institutions of restorative justice cannot, realistically, presume to generate authentic respect. What they can (and do) provide, however, are the conditions under which participants will be given clear cues and scripts for how to perform respect. Such shows of respect, however, are ultimately just another token. Moreover, as tokens go, they lack the sort of tangible, identifiable concreteness and specificity that, at the end of the day, most commend our more familiar tokens like punishment and rights. As Richard Delgado puts it, "offenders ... play along with what is desired, while the victim and middle-class mediator participate in a paroxysm of righteousness. In such a setting the offender is apt to grow even more cynical than before and learn what to say the next time to please the mediator, pacify the victim, and receive the lightest restitution agreement possible."[39]

In the context of a conception of justice that puts so much store in respect, we must be concerned with the difference between genuine respect and this cynical parroting of what one knows is going to satisfy others as a performance of respect. Consider again the Aboriginal chief and the corporation. What is the interplay between the aspiration to genuine respect in this relationship and the possibility of the corporate executive's cynical performance of what will likely satisfy by way of a show of respect? Further, let's also inquire as to whether the chief, in all fairness, was entitled to ask for genuine mutuality of understanding and respect for the substance of the beliefs of the band? According to Kerruish what he wanted was respect for the Aborigine belief that the Waugal water snake moved throughout the sacred area, creating a dreaming track.[40] But should others who do not hold this belief not be free to feel contempt for it, even as they ought also to be required to reroute their pipeline? Moreover, before asking for respect for this belief, the chief might first have asked how many of the executives of this corporation had genuine respect even for their own religious beliefs, how many had authentic respect for the belief that the bread and wine of the eucharist are the body and blood of Christ, or that one must not look at the Kohanim as they are chanting the priestly blessing on Rosh Hashana. In our highly secularized culture, the average person may well not have authentic respect and esteem even for their own sacraments and observances.[41] A religious belief or ritual that has all the awe-generating assistance of having been ingrained since childhood can often only muster within us a bemused toleration and an occasional begrudging willingness to bite the bullet and fake reverence for it.[42] Thus the absolute maximum the chief can be asking for from his corporate opponents here (in addition to a detour for the pipeline) is a polite performance of respect for their belief in the Waugal water snake.

Let me give another example. At various legal gatherings involving Aboriginal issues in Canada, such as judicial training seminars, Aboriginal perspectives days in law schools, and even some land claims trials, it has become customary to open the proceedings with traditional Aboriginal ceremonies, including prayers by Aboriginal elders and the burning of sweet grass. Inevitably, non-Aboriginal participants (judges, lawyers, law students, and so forth) looked on in reverence, some to the point of putting on a show of gravity they would have thought completely unnecessary for their own traditions. A tremendous crisis of political correctness sometimes ensues when the Aboriginal sacrament requires a prayer over tobacco, which is often brought out in the form of a bag of Drum tobacco and sometimes even as a pack of Player's Light cigarettes. What is a conscientious white yuppie lawyer, law student, or judge to do? She can't show disrespect to the Aboriginal practice; on the other hand, how can she possibly even feign to go along with veneration of the spiritual powers of the filthy, stinky carcinogen? Generally, the crisis is resolved in favour of an outward public show of respect for the tobacco ceremony followed by furtive, embarrassed, and semiapologetic mutterings to other non-Aboriginal people about how unseemly it seems to have a prayer over a pack of cigarettes. Nevertheless, non-Aboriginal lawyers, judges, and students, though they may grumble expressions of disdain or contempt to themselves under their breath, invariably muster their best and most respectful manners during the ceremony itself.

Now, these ceremonies certainly show some degree of progress in the form of increased standing and power for Aboriginal peoples in Canada. There is no way that such a ritual would have been allowed in a courtroom, or at a law school, or at a conference of judges twenty years ago; nor would all the white lawyers and judges and law students have trotted out their best manners in observance of it. But, clearly, the currency here is not one of authentic respect. At stake is the ability to demand that others knuckle under and pretend to pay homage to your traditions – however much they may consider them at best quaint, possibly silly, or even downright offensive.

William Ian Miller, referring to Stephen Greenblatt's discussion of power and ritual, articulates our deference to ritual as follows:

"The point," Greenblatt says, "is not that anyone is deceived by the charade, but that everyone is forced either to participate in it or watch it silently." The more you can make people swallow, the "more outrageous the fiction, the more impressive the manifestation of power." The claim apparently is that these rituals are so fake that they constitute an in-your-face challenge to hoot them down. When those in attendance fail to do so, they then have to accept themselves as cowards or, if not quite broken in spirit, at least safely docile in the face of the usurping authority.[43]

The ritual, then, may simply be a demonstration of power relations. One tests one's power over others by creating conditions under which they will almost certainly feel like "hooting it down" and then seeing if one can successfully prohibit them from doing so. Thus authenticity of respect may be beside the point. The ritual succeeds, or we know that the respect that counts is present, when participants are motivated to make the effort not to sneer openly. It may be, then, that the goal for Aboriginal people is achieved merely by getting these self-satisfied (and possibly racist) lawyers and judges in a position of having to stuff whatever it was they were really thinking about the ritual and act respectfully. The recent acquisition of the power to determine the aesthetic of ritual in these arenas of white authority – the courtroom, the classroom, and the conference room – may then be an important victory, in and of itself, for Aboriginal people.

Of course, it may also be a convenient sop to Aboriginal people inspired by liberal guilt. And it may be that, by granting this virtually costless-to-the-whites perk, whites find it easier to avoid having to cough up more tangible and useful rights. But whether getting white people to behave here is more of a gain for Aboriginals than it is a balm for white guilt or the window-dressing of esteem – either way – a white show of obeisance to Aboriginal ritual is not, and cannot be required to entail, authentic respect. It is a performance of respect and thus remains a mere token – once again pointing to, but not delivering, mutuality of understanding and respect for the belief.

The same problems arise in the restorative encounter. Restorative justice wants to posit respectful relations as the essence of justice. Yet we may ask again whether victim and offender are entitled to demand authentic respect of one another, though they are unquestionably entitled to demand nonviolation or restitution as matters of justice. Further, we need to ask what the relation is between "real" respect in the restorative encounter and cynically feigned respect inspired by an awareness that it is in one's best interests to perform docility in the face of the authority of the mediator and victim. The victim's dignity is supposedly restored when the offender is motivated to make the effort not to scoff. But, again, we know that the offender has a host of self-interested reasons for doing so. The offender's performance of respect is motivated by the real threat of punishment in the event of the failure of the victim-offender mediation.

Yet even in the face of these difficulties surrounding respect as an element of justice, restorative justice aspires to the real thing. It is confident that the revelations made during the course of the restorative encounter tend to lead the participants toward authentic respect. It is this authentic respect that represents the fruition of the restorative vision of justice. Though we know such inner states cannot be coercively commanded, restorative justice seeks to put in play an affective momentum pulling participants toward this reciprocal respect, understanding, healing, and regard.

Transformability of the Wrongdoer's Character

> The judge he felt kind of sore. He said he reckoned a body
> could reform the old man with a shotgun, maybe, but he didn't
> know no other way.
>
> Mark Twain, *The Adventures of Huckleberry Finn*

The criminal law has long acknowledged the possibility that a wrongdoer may successfully turn over a new leaf. The rules of evidence prohibiting the admission of proof of past wrongdoing as proof of the present offence acknowledge (among other things) the outside chance of radical change for the better. You can't prove that Mr. X committed an armed robbery today by proving that he committed one yesterday.[44] Evidence of a propensity for wrongdoing is excluded, however, not because it is not probative but because its prejudicial effect is overwhelming. When the jury spies the prior wrong, they leap at once to a conclusion of guilt. They shirk their civic duty of putting the prosecution to the strict proof of *this* offence.

Yet it is not because they are unfair or stupid that they make this leap. Rather, they are likely to make it because, in our day-to-day common sense judgments about others, nothing is more ubiquitous than our reliance on "similar fact evidence." We reason from past conduct, propensity, and character of others to reach conclusions about their probable actions in specific instances, as well as to predict their conduct in the future. We do so with our co-workers, our neighbours, our lovers, and our loved ones (and even with our pets). However, the particularities of the criminal trial – our concern to keep the coercive power of the state in check, our concern with safeguarding the liberty of the individual and so forth, combined with the possibility that the offender *might* just have transcended his criminal inclinations this time – urge us to forgo our familiar recourse to propensity reasoning in this narrow context.

The law's perceived need for an abundance of caution here springs from the overwhelming force of our habit of reasoning inductively about people's behaviour. To counteract the force of our habitual cynicism about wrongdoers, we set up procedural protections to acknowledge the optimistic off-chance that perhaps the accused did not stay in bad character this time. Restorative justice – instead of placing such optimism as a cautious corrective to our commonsensical cynicism – asks us for a complete inversion of these assumptions. Optimism about offenders' capacity for radical change becomes a foundational premise of the restorative approach.[45] Punishment is no longer necessary because restorative justice presumes to be able to offer something better: a healing process that will morph the offender into someone capable of mutual relations of respect and accountability. Restorative justice asks us to will away at the outset our overwhelming inductive pessimism about the possibility of radical transformation.

As John Braithwaite puts it: "The job of citizens in a restorative process is to treat offenders as worthy of trust."[46] Restorative justice advocates seek to support this pillar of optimism with empirical data about success in reducing rates of recidivism. However, the evidence about the effectiveness of restorative justice in reducing repeat offending is equivocal. Empirical research on restorative justice and recidivism has found that repeat offending was lower for violent offenders, higher for drunk drivers, and the same for property offenders who participated in restorative processes in comparison to those who went through the court system.[47] Nevertheless, restorative justice rests on the hope of bringing about dramatic positive transformation in the life of the offender. Contrasting the limited ability of punishment to change the offender with the allegedly more expansive ability of restorative justice to effect change, Braithwaite writes: "Where punishment is thrust into the foreground even by implied threats, other-regarding deliberation is made difficult because the offender is invited to deliberate in a self-regarding way – out of concern to protect the self from punishment. This is not the way to engender empathy with the victim, internalization of the values of the law and the values of restorative justice, the sequences of remorse, apology, and forgiveness that I will argue can transform lives in permanent ways. In contrast, contingent threats at best could only change lives in immediately contingent ways."[48]

This faith that the restorative encounter sets up optimal psychological conditions to transform the offender is coupled with two fundamental shifts in the way that restorative justice positions and relates to the offender. The first is the practical and dramatic shift wherein the offender goes from being a silent denier of responsibility to a loquacious confessor of guilt. The second is the shift in theoretical or spiritual focus away from the offender's crime and onto his humanity, holistically conceived.

Let's look at the first shift. In a world obsessed with extracting confession, our typical criminal accused's surly stance of silent but implicit denial is more a crime than the crime itself.[49] In our tell-all, talk-show era, nothing is more despicable than remaining silent. Yet the most we usually hear from an accused is a defiant "not guilty." The media strains to pick up clues of affect in the accused's countenance. But, for the most part, the accused quietly sits back and watches the rest of us expend energy and resources scurrying around trying to sort out what to do about him.[50] And this silence, in itself, annoys us.

Restorative justice provides the opportunity and the inducement for offenders to come out and speak up. It deals only with offenders who "admit it."[51] Though our traditional rules of evidence distrust and discourage confessions induced by offers of advantage, the recruiting of offenders into restorative justice programs is based squarely on such incentives. Restorative justice exchanges mercy for conversation. Though the accused is motivated by the hope of escaping punishment, the effect that his coming-out has on us is dramatic. He has rejoined our world of confessors. And this sign that his antisocial will has been broken itself inspires the spirit of optimism and forgiveness. We are delighted, even fascinated, by an offender who is willing to talk, to participate, to engage, to connect.

His willingness to face the music and publicly own up to having committed the crime astonishes us. So taken aback are we by the offender's shift from denial to confession, from silent recalcitrance to willingness to behave nicely and "encounter," that we are swept up into the further assumption that this shift will parlay into lasting change. The spectacle of the wrongdoer's self-accusation stands in for, and appears to obviate, the need for punishment.

The second shift is primarily about taking a wider angle on our view of offenders. We no longer look at offenders as merely criminal; we go on now to look at offenders in the fullness of their humanity. We are to stop looking at them as monsters and to start looking at them as people who have likes and dislikes, people who care about others, assume responsibilities, and are, in all things other than the offence, pretty much regular sort of people just like "you and me."[52] Though restorative justice does not want us to reason from character evidence of prior wrongdoing to a conclusion that the offender is incorrigibly criminal, it does want us to reason from character evidence of the offender's being a "regular guy" to a conclusion that he will be willing and able to repent and change. Restorative justice asks us to identify with the offender. It asks us to resist the impulse to demonize him. It seeks to "put a human face on crime."[53]

Consider the words of James Scott, project coordinator of the Collaborative Justice Project in Ottawa, a project that uses restorative justice techniques in cases of serious crime. The project deals with offences such as "robbery, robbery with a weapon, weapons offences, break and enter, theft over $5,000, fraud, assault, assault causing bodily harm, impaired driving causing bodily harm or death, and careless driving or dangerous driving causing bodily harm or death."[54] In pursuit of this shift in attitude toward the offender, Scott asks us to imagine how we would respond to a drunk driver who kills someone by driving down the wrong side of an expressway: "We might have one answer if we didn't know the driver, and another if the driver was our father, our grandfather or a friend. The difference, of course, is that we have intimate knowledge of our relatives and friends. We know that their acts may cause serious harm to others, and that they should be held responsible for their actions, but they are not bad people."[55] Likewise, Scott notes, our sense of the appropriate response to an armed robber would be different if we were married to the robber or if he were our best friend.

Thus restorative justice now asks us to view the offender through the eyes of personal love.[56] And, so seeing him, to hold out hope for the possibility of his taking responsibility and making good. Shifting from an impersonal universal conception of love as agape, restorative justice here seeks to access our personal feelings of love for our family and friends and to transfer hypothetically and imaginatively those intimate and affectionate feelings onto the offender.

But this is a complicated request. Scott assumes, without argument, that we would want clemency for the serious wrongs committed by our loved ones. The reason we would want a merciful restorative approach is because, viewing the wrongdoer as though he were one of our loved ones, we will then not view him as an inveterate criminal. It is clear, however, that Scott is not addressing a gathering of the spouses or children of armed robbers and drunken drivers here (and he certainly is not addressing the spouses of batterers or the children of child abusers). If he were, he might not be as confident about the persuasive force of this rhetorical device. He is assuming that he's talking to people whose loved ones are not criminal wrongdoers. He is asking us here to think about how we would react to evidence of terrible wrongdoing by a person for whom such acts would be anathema, how we would react to seriously harmful conduct in someone of generally law-abiding character. It is in relation to those whom we cannot imagine doing wrong – those whom, if they did wrong, we would assume *must* have some justification or excuse – that we would want to extend clemency and the chance to make amends.

But is this necessarily the case? Historically, it doesn't stand to reason. People in feuding cultures generally knew their enemies extremely well, and the intimacy between them did nothing to quell their passion for revenge.[57] Moreover, in a more personal vein, one's own love for a person does not generally count as a reason for others to extend clemency to him when he does serious wrong. The film *The Music Box* provides an interesting illustration that this is so. Jessica Lange plays Ann Talbot, a lawyer defending her father Michael J. Lazlo against charges of Nazi war crimes committed in Hungary. As long as Ann Talbot believes her father to be innocent, we approve of her stalwart defence of him. Even as her cross-examination of the victim witnesses appears to us to be verging on the inhumane, we endorse her zealous advocacy in protection of her father. But when she discovers that he is guilty, we also endorse her repudiation of him and her decision to turn against him by anonymously delivering proof of his guilt to the authorities to secure his punishment. We affirm her sense that her love of him does not carry justice value and is not an argument capable of answering the claims of his victims. Even though she knows him in the fullness of his humanity and trusts him as a loving father and grandfather, she considers his crimes against others to be simultaneously a betrayal of her.[58] She places her commitment to public justice above her private desire to see her father treated mercifully.

To examine a little further Scott's claim that we do not want to see our loved ones punished, let's take a look at Plato's *Euthyphro*.[59] It's not like Socrates to back down from an argument. Nor is it like him to hedge his position. But this is what he does in his discussion with Euthyphro about the justice of Euthyphro's prosecuting his own father for murder. Euthyphro says that one has a duty to seek impartial justice for any offender irrespective of whether the offender is kin. Love must yield to justice. But Socrates expresses doubts about whether this is so. Euthyphro replies to Socrates' misgivings thus: "I am amused, Socrates, at your making a distinction between one who is a relation and one who is not a relation; for surely the pollution is the same in either case, if you knowingly associate with the murderer when you ought to clear yourself and him by proceeding against him. The real question is whether the murdered man has been justly slain. If justly, then your duty is to let the matter alone; but if unjustly, then even if the murderer lives under the same roof with you and eats at the same table, proceed against him."[60]

Euthyphro's position seems reasonable. And Socrates doesn't really press the matter too far. He insinuates his disapproval of Euthyrpho's betrayal of his father, and we end up going along with Socrates. But, as usual, the deck is stacked in Socrates' favour. When Euthyphro tells the story of his father's wrongdoing, it becomes clear that there are tremendous doubts about the father's culpability. It appears that the victim was himself a murderer and that he died accidentally while the father was seeking advice from a diviner as to what to do with him. Moreover, the really provoking thing about Euthyphro is that he *delights* in the prospect of seeing his father punished. It causes him no pain whatsoever. The disgrace to himself and his family doesn't even register with him, which is where we begin to distrust his motives. Unlike Ann Talbot, who agonizes over the conflict between her civic duty to participate in her father's prosecution and her love for him, Euthyphro thrills to the idea of skewering his father. Moreover, what completely pushes us over the edge is that Euthyphro casts his prosecution of his father in the most self-congratulatory of terms. Euthyphro superciliously sets up his actions as the very essence of piety (the definition of which soon becomes the actual substance of the dialogue). So we reject Euthyphro's argument about impartiality taking precedence over kinship and love not so much because he is wrong in principle but because he's disingenuously standing on a principle that does not apply to his case in an attempt to convince others of his moral superiority. Euthyphro appears to be dressing up his desire to see his father suffer in the guise of impartiality.

But if Euthyphro had been genuinely grappling with how to respond to serious wrongdoing by a loved one, then Socrates would surely have lost the argument.[61] Indeed, Socrates' criticisms of Euthyphro are centred primarily around his sense that Euthyphro has not put careful moral thought into his decision to prosecute his father. Even at that, it is clear that Socrates' countervailing concern is one of loyalty rather than one of justice. Allegiance to family ought to trump justice.[62] It is a counter-pull to justice; it is not justice itself.[63]

James Scott asks us to personalize the question, to imagine how one would respond if the offender were his father, grandfather, or a friend. So let me try the imaginative experiment he invites. If you were to prove to me, beyond any whisper of a doubt, that my mild-mannered, cautious-Casper, hyperlaw-abiding father, who hasn't even had a speeding ticket in the past thirty years – nay, who hasn't so much as forgotten a single garbage day – had held up a bank with a shotgun, I would be, above all, utterly flabbergasted. I would be thrown into a speechless state of astonishment and horror from which I would *never* recover (less so, actually, if it were my mother – then I would see shades of *Thelma and Louise*). Yet, if I were faced with incontrovertible evidence of my father's wrongdoing, I would not necessarily believe that he ought to be treated with greater leniency than I would accord the stranger. I would still see the value of impartiality. I would not assume that he ought not to be punished simply because he is someone I love. His punishment would cause me excruciating vicarious pain, and my own first-order humiliation would be unendurable, but I would not count my personal concern for either his or my own pain and humiliation as reasons for not punishing him. Of course, I would want to be able to help him avoid punishment, but I would have to acknowledge that my reasons for so wanting were not justice-based. The situation would set up within me a direct internal conflict between love and justice.

Fortuitously, I happen to be in a position to follow Scott's challenge a little further. As it happens, one of my best friends from childhood did grow up to become a serial armed robber.[64] And neither the fact that he robbed once, nor that he went on to do it repeatedly, surprised me a bit. Everything about Hughy had "wrongdoer" written all over it, from his attempts to tell me that only *he* could eat the raspberries in *my* yard because I was only five and you had to be six like him to eat them, to the sinister way he used to climb the back fence to peer over at me in my paddling pool, to the way he would hit me if I wouldn't do what he wanted, to his noon-hour threats of "Egghead Acorn, you die aster skewel" and the follow-up thrashings I got from him on the way home. (Okay, he wasn't *that* great of a friend – but I knew him very well.) Everything about Hughy, from the time he was three, spelled trouble. And knowing him well, in the fullness of his humanity, only made me more certain of the justice of the punishment he received when he hit the big time.

As anecdotes, these stories prove absolutely nothing about the propensity of prudent people to stay prudent or about the propensity of bad actors to keep on being bad. Criminologically speaking they are worse than worthless. I offer them, however, not to demonstrate any such thing but rather to respond to Scott's challenge by suggesting that intimate, and even loving, acquaintance with an offender, of either habitually good or habitually bad character, does not necessarily lead one to a conclusion that punishment is an inappropriate response. The point of these anecdotes is to question the assumption that if I think of the offender as an intimate acquaintance, I will necessarily eschew punishment and search for gentler ways to remedy the wrong.

Let's get back now to the central issue here. I'm suggesting that the restorative justice request that we view the offender as though he were someone we love is a rhetorical device intended to bolster optimism that the offender is, or will become, someone capable of respectful relations as well as someone capable of resisting the impulse to reoffend. If I think of the offender as my father, then I am more inclined to believe that he would *never* rob a bank again (and, of course, I believe this because I can't imagine him having done it in the first place.) If I think of the offender as my father, I feel confident that the offender would be eager conscientiously to re-establish relations of respect. If the offender were my father, there *would* be a quick and easy way to get him to stop offending immediately and start behaving respectfully because the conduct would have been wildly aberrational given the whole of who he is as a human being.

By thinking of the offender as someone we love, restorative justice asks us to think of him as capable of responding to an invitation to caring connection and through the support of that connection of changing into someone capable of relations of mutual respect.

Certainly the idea that loving connection can heal the brokenness that leads to wrongdoing is a soothing one. It is part of a larger spiritual tradition and mythology about the power of love as hope for change, and it inspires in many a deep spiritual belief. Yet skepticism about the possibility for radical change runs deep as well. Both personal experience and the teachings of literature affirm the intuition that, for the most part, people remain "in character." The compelling novel is most often one that depicts the layers and consequences of character rather than its radical reform. Moreover, our sense of story generally confirms the idea that change of character for the better is a delicate and precarious process dependent upon the assistance of compelling and consistent forces of willpower, external pressure, support, and desire. Thus the optimistic presumptions of restorative justice have as their formidable opponent the savvy sense that dramatic catharsis and momentary performance and embrace of the aspiration to turn over a new leaf are rarely sufficient to effect stable and lasting change from nasty to nice. Speaking in the context of restorative justice for young offenders, Richard Delgado notes that "a forty-five minute meeting is unlikely to have a lasting effect ... If the offender-victim encounter is brief and perfunctory, and the ensuing punishment demeaning or menial, young offenders will learn to factor the cost of restitution into their practical calculus the next time they are tempted to commit a crime and to parrot what is expected of them when caught."[65]

Consider now an old and venerated story that ridicules the optimistic premises of restorative justice about the likelihood of radical change: *The Adventures of Huckleberry Finn*. Huck's father was an alcoholic reprobate. Pap, as Huck called him, was a violent man whose sole interest in his son was to prevent him from getting any further ahead in the world or, failing that, to exploit any good fortune his son might gain. Huck had come into some money, and Pap was trying to steal it from him so that he could spend it on drink. The new judge in town took a restorative approach to the case, believing that through caring and compassion he might help the miserable man find a way to repair relations with his son and get his life back on the straight and narrow. So the judge took Huck's father home to his family and gave him new clothes, good food, and a comfortable place to stay.

> And after supper he talked to him about temperance and such things till the old man cried, and said he'd been a fool, and fooled away his life; but now he was a-going to turn over a new leaf and be a man nobody

wouldn't be ashamed of, and he hoped the judge would help him and not look down on him. The judge said he could hug him for them words; so he cried, and his wife she cried again; pap said he'd been a man that had always been misunderstood before, and the judge said he believed it. The old man said that what a man wanted that was down was sympathy, and the judge said it was so; so they cried again. And when it was bedtime the old man rose up and held out his hand, and says:

"Look at it, gentlemen and ladies all; take a-hold of it; shake it. There's a hand that was the hand of a hog; but it ain't so no more; it's the hand of a man that's started in on a new life, and 'll die before he'll go back. You mark them words – don't forget I said them. It's a clean hand now; shake it – don't be afeard."

So they shook it, one after the other, all around, and cried. The judge's wife she kissed it. Then the old man he signed a pledge – made his mark. The judge said it was the holiest time on record, or something like that.[66]

But after the judge and his wife lovingly tuck in Pap for the night he sneaks out, trades in his new clothes for liquor, gets drunk again, and ends up with a broken arm lying in the ditch. And, in reaction, "the judge he felt kind of sore. He said he reckoned a body could reform the old man with a shotgun, maybe, but he didn't know no other way."[67] We anticipate Pap's backslide. And we fear – even as the judge and Pap are rapt in restorative euphoria – that the judge's optimism about Pap's future self is a betrayal of Huck. The judge, by trusting Pap in an emotional moment of remorse and forgiveness, withdraws the protection of Huck that we anxiously seek from him. Thus Twain tells us that replacing retributive feeling with naive optimism about the offender's capacity for right-relation is a trap not only for this judge, but also, and more importantly, for the victim, Huck, whom the judge was responsible to protect. Nevertheless, restorative justice bravely goes hand in hand with our new-found faith in therapy and our confidence in the power of twelve-step transformation to arrive at the conclusion that we can safely dismiss such cautionary tales of doomed, though ever-so-earnest, attempts to turn over a new leaf.

Now it is true that the judge's handling of Pap's case does not fulfill many of the core requirements of a restorative process. Huck was never given the opportunity to confront Pap and explain the details of the way Pap had harmed him. (And perhaps thankfully so, since such a scene would be very un-Hucklike.) But I suspect that had Huck been there and done that, Pap would have put on the very same show he put on for the judge. Moreover, had the cathartic encounter been between Pap, Huck, and the townspeople, the collective optimism about the possibility of Pap turning over a new leaf would likely have been even more intense – even more in the mode of the old tent-show revival. And the intensity of that euphoric optimism would not have enhanced the sincerity of Pap's performance at all, except perhaps negatively. Nor would the intensity of that optimism have increased the likelihood that Pap's forecasts of self-improvement would be accurate.

Before leaving this issue of the restorative optimism about the malleability of the offender's character, let us make one further observation about the story of Huck's father, Pap (and thereby bring the discussion back around to the first point about the power of confession to shift our view of the offender). The euphoria of the offender's repentance – his dramatic acceptance of the invitation to connection, his giving up of the stance of silence and denial – is absolutely central to the restorative process. As we saw in the previous section, proponents of restorative justice tell us that when it works, it delivers that shared sense of peace, harmony, healing, and magic.[68] The moment of shared tears and shared hope between the judge, his wife, and Pap is the very cornerstone of restorative justice. While optimism that henceforward the offender will wise up is a necessary condition of a restorative conception of success, it is not sufficient. Mere change for the better would not be enough to displace the need for punishment. The exultant moment of shared joy over the sinner's repentance is a necessary and even more central condition of the restorative triumph. It is this euphoria, and not the assurance that the offender will change, that occupies the energetic space of punishment, and appears to obviate the need for it.

Transcendability of the Victim's Loss

> They were too hopelessly alienated in their inner life ever to have that contest which is an effort towards agreement.
>
> – George Eliot, *Romola*

Restorative justice is also optimistic about its power to assist the victim to transcend pain, bitterness, and resentment.[69] It is confident that it will be able to do so by means other than the infliction of proportionate suffering on the wrongdoer. Healing is what is on offer for the victim. Indeed, "healing" is probably the most emotively powerful word in the restorative vocabulary.[70] The offender's motivations to engage in the restorative process are obvious: He avoids prison. The victim's motivations for signing up, however, lie primarily in the lure of these more illusive promises.[71] No punitive system would presume to promise "healing" to victims. Yet restorative justice entices victims with precisely such hopes. Concern for consumer protection seems to have been overlooked. There is no money-back guarantee if the healing doesn't happen. While restorative justice insists that the victim's participation be fully voluntary (it would of course be unconscionable were it coerced), its insistence on consent does not let restorative justice off the hook of having to answer for the ethics of the tactics it uses to secure the victim's participation.

Restorative justice advocates seek to support this pillar of optimism again with empirical data documenting "victim satisfaction." However, as with rates of recidivism, examination of the statistical evidence on victims' experience of the process once again leaves us with some troubling questions. For example, a study done by Gerard Palk, Hennessey Hayes, and Timothy Prenzler found that victims are the least satisfied of participants in restorative justice processes.[72] Likewise, a study done by David Miers, Mike Maguire, and Shelagh Goldie found that victims were less satisfied with the process than were offenders.[73] Yet restorative justice advocates still hope to craft victim satisfaction surveys that will yield favourable results so as to justify the allocation of greater resources to restorative justice programs.[74] Though restorative justice promotes itself with the rhetoric of healing, questions about whether victims experienced healing are rarely present on victim satisfaction surveys intended for use in promoting restorative justice. Instead, typical questions include: "Was it helpful to be able to talk directly with the offender about the impact of the crime?" or "Did participation in the victim-offender mediation program make the criminal justice process more responsive to your needs as a victim?"

Healing, of course, is a dangerous thing to promise and a difficult thing to assess. And it is dangerous and difficult since – though healing does happen – its processes are prohibitively mysterious.[75] The idea of "healing" elicits a complex interplay between our literal and metaphorical understandings. Its association with cure and recovery from physical wounds is soothing. It is also problematically inscrutable. We know that as far as the healing of cuts and gashes goes, first the blood clots, then scabs form, later they fall off (or get picked off), and eventually the wound heals – though scars may remain. But we don't have much of a conscious hand in making this healing happen. We can do things to either promote or hinder healing. But ultimately healing happens by the grace of the body and through no merit or action of our own. The idea that justice might be about "getting well" or "feeling better" is comforting. But healing is always somewhat miraculous. That's why it made sense for Jesus to stake his credibility as a messiah primarily on his talent as a healer.[76] But, without preternatural assistance, healing on command is beyond us.

The Christian interweaving of instantaneous physical healing and spiritual renewal gives multiple and rich resonances to talk of healing in the context of crime. Nevertheless, healing as a notion of justice is suspiciously sentimental.[77] Justice as healing evokes a fantasy of "no more pain," a new state of wholeness, happiness, and connection. And it tacitly assumes that we will have a smooth and incrementally less and less painful transition into this better space. But it does not give us a precise prescription for bringing that transition about. In keeping with the new-age optimism about the transformative power of "positive self-talk," it hopes, perhaps, that talk about healing will do the trick on its own. In any event, it anticipates that we will transcend injustice and morph into healing somehow. Indeed, the very idea that spiritual, emotional, and existential pain can be healed like a cut or a broken bone can evoke a tremendous surge of optimism and even an immediate sense of relief in a sufferer of injustice.

Perhaps the most dramatic and famous example of a victim who embraced restorative justice as being fully and even miraculously healing is found in the story of Lucas Baba Sikwepere, who was blinded when a South African police officer shot him in the face while he was in custody. After telling his story in front of the South African Truth and Reconciliation Commission, Sikwepere said: "What has brought my sight back, my eyesight back, is to come back here and tell my story. But I feel what has been making me sick all the time is the fact that I couldn't tell my story. But now it feels like I got my sight back by coming here and telling you the story."[78] Sikwepere plays with the metaphor in a way that is both moving and troubling. Of course, his blindness wasn't really healed, and though we celebrate the benefits he has obtained through the opportunity to tell his story, we can't help feeling some anxiety around his own dramatic exaggeration of the salutary effect.[79]

Yet restorative justice uses talk of healing as a means of enticing victims to participate. The promise of healing puts the victim in the mood to try to reconnect with the wrongdoer in an emotionally responsive way. It is meant to prevent that internal shift in the victim toward a fixed unwillingness to engage with the wrongdoer. It preserves (though potentially quite artificially) the emotional suppleness necessary for repair of relations. The victim (enticed with promises of healing) and the perpetrator (drawn in by promises of mercy) conquer, for the moment at least, overt mutual contempt.

The primary remedies in the restorative medicine cabinet are apology and forgiveness. Restorative justice has tremendous faith that the offender's outward performance of an inner state of contrition will smooth the way to a revival of the victim's sense of honour and well-being, thus releasing the victim into the liberation of forgiveness. Apology and forgiveness are healing; they promote reconciliation and repair.[80]

Take, for example, the South African Truth and Reconciliation Commission. The legal framework of the commission required that perpetrators disclose politically motivated wrongdoing and encounter their victims.

Amnesty would follow if disclosure was complete and political purpose could be shown. The creation of an accurate public record of the atrocities of apartheid, and the opportunity for victims to face their perpetrators, would be two of the major benefits of the process that would help move the country into a new era of racial equality and respect. Apology was not required – nor, *a fortiori*, were inner states of contrition or remorse. The facts of disclosure, political motive, and willingness to face the victims were legally sufficient for amnesty. However, Archbishop Desmond Tutu – with his dramatically spiritual style of leadership and sensing that simple disclosure would not effect the needful shift toward meaningful healing – urged the further extra-legal steps of apology and forgiveness.[81] Something more powerful than matter-of-fact disclosure seemed to be necessary.

Consider Tutu's urging of apology in his forward to the proceedings of the commission: "When a husband wants to make up with his wife, he does not say, 'I'm sorry, please forgive me, but darling of course you too have done so and so!' That is not the way to reach reconciliation. That is why I still hope that there will be a white leader who will say, 'We had an evil system with awful consequences. Please forgive us.' Without qualification. If that were to happen, we would all be amazed at the response."[82] Tutu romanticizes the relationship between victims and offenders under apartheid, analogizing it to a marriage and likening the goal of the process to loving reconciliation and erotic embrace between husband and wife. Aptly, Tutu casts the perpetrator as the offending husband and the victim as the injured wife. In urging apology as the way toward healing, he papers over any details of wrongdoing; is it a near fatal beating or a rape this husband is apologizing for, or a sideways glance at another woman? He constructs the matter as one of getting the querulous wife to relent. To that end, he counsels the wrongdoer to offer a clean and complete emotional and symbolic self-lowering – an unreserved assumption and performance of the perpetrator's one-down-and-in-the-wrong-position in relation to the victim. His expectations about the returns of such an apology are high. We expect nothing less than joy when the sinner repents.[83] Tutu anticipates and desires an amazing euphoric catharsis.[84] The result of this unconditional and symbolic repentance is not a state of mere "cantankerous co-existence"[85] within formal equality.[86] It is a transformative state of mutual acceptance and embrace. Tutu's words resonate with a prevalent sentiment that apology and forgiveness are the most effective and most benign means of overcoming cycles of violent revenge and moving into relations of equality and respect.

Tutu's marriage analogy presupposes two things. First, it presupposes that the process of apology, forgiveness, and reconciliation as effected between husband and wife returns the couple to an *ex ante* state of conjugal equality and harmony. Second, it presupposes a victim/wife who is willing and able to reconnect with the wrongdoer husband in an emotionally responsive way. Both these premises require an idealized notion of marriage. A brief consideration of marriage as a site of chronic hostility and oppression gives us some sense of how troubling the analogy is.

First, Tutu relies on our willingness to assume that, between husband and wife, apology, forgiveness, and "making up" are good things. Rifts are healed, resentments are ended, and the couple returns to a desirable state of loving embrace. We may remind ourselves here, however, that practices of apology and forgiveness within marriage are often beguiling and dangerous for victims of intimate violence. Moreover, they are effective tactics for enforcing patriarchal oppression within the family. The role that apology and forgiveness play in perpetuating the cycle of domestic violence is well documented.[87] The skill of contrite apology is routinely practised by abusers in violent intimate relationships. A battered woman herself is also likely to be an expert at apology as a means of appeasing her spouse, of quieting his insecurities and his anger, of assuring him that she is not trying to exercise undue power in their relationship, of demonstrating her willingness to wear responsibility for every unpleasant aspect of life. When her apologies are unsuccessful in appeasing his wrath, he beats her.

Now it is his turn to apologize. He is passionately, even desperately, contrite and apologetic, swearing that he will never do it again. This display of remorse, as Tutu's advice anticipates, leads her to forgiveness, and they reconcile. The reconciliation is followed by a new buildup of tension in the relationship, followed by another violent episode, followed by another apology, and so on and so on. What is noteworthy about the batterer's apologies, is that as apologies they are often flawless; they lack none of the essential elements one would desire in an apology. Consider the following very demanding and extensive list of necessary conditions for a satisfying apology. An apology:

- should be an acknowledgment of responsibility for wrongdoing;
- should be reflective of a deeply felt inner state of remorse;
- should be a product of the free autonomous action of the wrongdoer and should not be externally coerced;
- should identify and name the precise wrong to which it refers;
- should affirm the value of the victim and the significance of the wrong as a violation of the victim;
- should be motivated by a valuation of the relationship with the victim and a desire to restore that relationship; and should not be motivated by external or instrumental goals;
- should not attempt to displace that responsibility onto any other person or influence;

- should acknowledge the need for change in the future and propose a plan for that change.[88]

The apologies of batterers in the honeymoon phase of the cycle of violence often exhibit all these qualities yet they are both impotent and destructive. They prolong the psychological hold of the batterer on the victim.[89] Moreover, what makes them irresistible to the victim is the shift in power relations that they seem to promise. The victim, who habitually apologizes for everything, finds tremendous gratification when the tables are turned and the batterer is sorry. Yet, while the batterer's apology is a momentary reversal of the *posture* of the one-down position, and while it promises a shift toward equality and respect, the apology actually reinforces and maintains inequality and abuse.

It is therefore perplexing that conventional wisdom regards apology and forgiveness, in contrast to revenge and reprisal, as precisely what is needed to heal the wounds of wrongdoing and to break out of a cycle of violence.[90] In the family context (and in many other contexts as well), unequal and violent relations are often maintained by processes of apology and forgiveness that occasionally give the one-down party the illusion that there is, or soon will be, an equal sharing of power in the relationship.[91] The lure of apology and forgiveness saps the victim's energy and resolve to move toward some more radical transformation of, or break with, the relationship.[92] Apology and forgiveness, the primary method of restorative repair, can often be anything but healing. They can be essential weapons for placing an offender in a position to inflict new wounds and reopen old ones.

Consider now the second premise of Tutu's analogy. Tutu's reference to marriage is meant to evoke a sense of openness on the part of both parties to reconnect and repair. In an ideal sense, marriage simply means the perpetual willingness to come together to attempt to repair, restore, and reconcile. Yet less utopian pictures of marriage may put us, just as vividly, in mind of emotional states of utter inflexibility and unwillingness to engage in any efforts toward repair.

I began this section with a quotation from George Eliot's *Romola*, in which she describes the marriage between Tito and Romola Melema. Eliot writes: "They were too hopelessly alienated in their inner life ever to have that contest which is an effort towards agreement."[93] We recognize the emotional state Eliot describes: one in which we would not only see no hope of reconciliation, but also regard any attempt toward reconciliation as a serious self-betrayal. It is an emotional state governed by an inflexible conviction that the other's wrongdoing has caused an irredeemable breach. Our mistrust of the other creates a duty to our self to refuse engagement. One has a fixed notion of the wrongdoer as incapable of making meaningful, satisfying efforts toward repair. One is committed to protecting oneself from the dangers of further engagement.

Restorative justice is optimistic that this state of hopeless alienation can be avoided or overcome. It seeks to persuade victims to retain the emotional pliability necessary to the work of repair in their relations with offenders. But how does it answer the persuasive force of our recognition of and respect for the staunch rejection of the possibility of justice-as-repair that Eliot describes here? Proponents of restorative justice acknowledge this attitude of resolute disengagement.[94] They recognize that the victim's impulse is often simply to say: "No. I don't want to deal with you. I'm not interested in respectful relations with you. I'll do my healing on my own. And I'm especially not interested in helping you feel better about the wrong you have committed." Recognizing this state, how then can restorative justice also be so sunny and evangelical about a conception of justice that expects, requires, cajoles, and coaxes the opposite stance, an ever-enduring willingness to engage in that perilous contest toward respectful accord?

Restorative justice acknowledges but frowns upon an unwillingness to engage toward repair. It takes it to be a repudiation of the inherent worth of the offender as a fellow human being and a repudiation of the moral bonds of community – which, of course, it is. More to the point, however, restorative justice also paternalistically views this state to be contrary to the victim's best interests, inimical to the victim's legitimate hopes for justice as healing. Such brittleness isolates both the victim and the wrongdoer. It prevents both of them from "getting over it." It is the victim's melodramatic, and possibly self-indulgent, clinging to the wrong. She wants to further punish him by withholding the possibility of his making amends. She clings to the moral superiority of her victim status. She exaggerates the wrongdoing by making out as though absolutely nothing can repair it, when probably there is something that can. The wrongdoing is cherished as a means of stigmatizing the wrongdoer. And thus it retains a sinister power and intensity in all parties' psyches. The possibility of true healing for both victim and offender is destroyed.

Restorative justice earnestly seeks to help the victim overcome this alienation. It promises to protect the victim. It promises that the perpetrator will come to share a common moral ground with the victim and will acknowledge and remedy the harm done. It tells the victim that she can safely emerge from the prison of her distrust. It is confident that it can put effective institutional pressures and supports in place to bring about a crucial shift in the inner life of the wrongdoer. For this reason, it is confident that, through extension of the combination of loving kindness and measured reproach, it can access genuineness and bona fides in the offender. His truthfulness and willingness to be accountable for harm will prove the victim wrong in her cynicism and in her sense that the project of repair is futile. Restorative justice trusts its emotional hold on the offender and is thus confident that it can make good on the promise to protect the victim from further harm or humiliation in the process of working toward agreement.

This promise (along with the caveat that restorative encounter must always be voluntarily entered into) is the restorative response to the hopelessly alienated victim. It recognizes this victim's desire for disengagement but promises to deliver what she really needs to transcend the self-protective impulse that keeps her aloof. It promises that the restorative encounter has the power to bring the offender to his knees with grief for the damage he has done, to make him long for the opportunity to make things right again.[95] Restorative justice disqualifies alienated disengagement as a sensible position because it anticipates meaningful moral access to the inner life of the offender. Confidence that it can get a hook into the offender's soul makes a victim's stance of resentful detachment both unreasonable and unjust.

However, one brush with a perpetrator whose inner life truly is inaccessible to us, whose conscience is beyond our reach, who is either smugly self-excusing and self-justifying or, more likely, smugly (if secretly) aware that his self-interest is promoted by performances of contrition, and the lustre of restorative justice fades; the reasonableness of the position of detached disengagement resurfaces. Restorative justice provides no protection against the offender who has us pegged as suckers for performances of contrition and remorse. To promise relational healing with such an offender seems to be culpably naive and unconcerned with the interests of the victim.

Consider Eliot's further description of Tito Melema in his relation with Romola, his wife: "There was no possibility of an easy relation between them without genuineness on his part. Genuineness implied confession of the past, and confession involved a change of purpose. But Tito had as little bent that way as a leopard has to lap milk when its teeth are grown. From all relations that were not easy and agreeable, we know that Tito shrank: why should he cling to them?"[96] Eliot agrees with the restorative assumption that genuineness and confession on the part of an offender can lead to repair of marital or other relations. She is not cynical about this possibility when we have an offender who is genuine and able to change his purpose. Yet she depicts Tito as incapable of such change. She demonstrates the radical inaccessibility of his conscience and, in so doing, justifies Romola's (very-long-in-coming) rigid refusal to entertain the possibility of repair.

Let's recapitulate. Enthusiasm about restorative justice rests primarily on three great expectations. The first is that we will be able to uncouple justice and punishment and create new, equally strong couplings between justice and right-relation. The second is that the restorative encounter will be a moment of significant moral growth for the offender, that he will emerge from the encounter with new motivation and capacity to behave toward others in respectful and healthy ways. The restorative encounter will heal the causes of criminal behaviour in the offender. The third is that the restorative encounter will help victims to recover both materially and psychologically from the crime.

Much of the momentum behind this optimistic vision comes from our desire to believe it. We'd rather conceive a softer understanding of justice that didn't have any disreputable associations with revenge and the deliberate infliction of pain. We'd like to believe that we have found the secret to inspiring moral conversion in offenders. And, most of all, we'd like to believe that the harm inflicted by crime and violation can be put right and that we have found the secret to soothing victims' suffering. Yet these desires are suspect inasmuch as they deny the complexity of human relations, the concrete reality of some offenders' delight in violating others, and the permanence of the loss suffered by many victims of crime. We might say, indeed, that there is a troubling strain of sentimentality in these desires, and it is to that strain that we now turn.

4

Sentimental Justice: The Unearned Emotions of Restorative Catharsis

> This is the inevitable fate of the sentimentalist. All his opinions
> change into their opposites at the first brush of reality.
>
> – George Orwell, *The Road to Wigan Pier*

> Love must be regarded as the final flower and fruit of
> justice. When it is substituted for justice it degenerates into
> sentimentality and may become the accomplice of tyranny.
>
> – Reinhold Niebuhr, *Love and Justice*

> If we begin by acknowledging disproportionality, how can we
> avoid falling into one or other of the dangers mentioned above,
> exaltation or emotional platitudes? In other words, unthinking
> sentimentality.
>
> – Paul Ricoeur, "Love and Justice"

Some scorn for restorative justice is simple anxiety about the sentimental. Of course, when I say sentimental here I mean it as a term of derision. I don't mean it the way Schiller uses it in "On Naive and Sentimental Poetry" as a superrefined capacity for subtle reflection such that "sentimental" can be an adjective capable of modifying "genius": one able to "climb up to the level of ideas and control his material freely and spontaneously."[1] I am talking about sentimentality as a pollutant, as that which induces the cringe, as an experience of the emotional that, even when powerful (perhaps chiefly when powerful), embarrasses even as it compels.

The restorative aspiration to reconcile love and justice, its vision of cathartic encounter followed by harmonious embrace between victim and offender, even its habitual reliance on the resounding success story, can cause the nonbeliever (and sometimes even the believer) to wince with embarrassment. At its mildest, this cringe is something like the one you get from bad schlock, the kind you're immune to – say Bette Midler's *Beaches*. At its most intense, it is more like the cringe you get from brilliant shlock, the kind you're susceptible to, the shlock that pulls you into its melodramatic world against your aesthetic better judgment – like the death of Little Eva in *Uncle Tom's Cabin*[2] or the last thoughts of Sydney Carton as he goes to the guillotine in *A Tale of Two Cities*.

If we allow that a considerable amount of animosity to restorative justice is sheer fear of, and disgust with, the sentimental, we have to ask what the appropriate status of that animosity is. What, after all, is really wrong with a sentimental theory of justice? Perhaps hypervigilance around the sentimental here unjustifiably promotes aesthetic concerns to the level of ethics. Moreover, since restorative justice smacks of the new-age, feel-good, self-help genre, perhaps academics' rejection of it in turn smacks of elitism. Detractors of restorative justice are perhaps uptight about, and embarrassed by, the proliferation of touchy-feely, pop-psychological inspirations for, and the absence of high cultural tropes in which to ground, restorative justice.[3] We need to guard against the undue influence of such intellectual and cultural snobbery in our evaluation of restorative justice as an ethical theory.

But it is a delicate matter to determine whether judgments about sentimentality have normative value or not. The core case of the sentimental is found in art. We may have good aesthetic reasons to object to sentimental art: Its pitch to our emotions is too direct; it lacks nuance, skill, or subtlety. Or perhaps it is skilful enough, but the emotions it seeks to evoke are too commonplace. The sentimental artist makes things both easier and harder for himself by choosing to draw his material from predictable scenes that will reliably make us all feel the same thing at the same time and in the same way.[4] Typically he chooses the death of the completely loveable child or the death of the parents of the lovable child: Little Eva, Little Nell, Little Orphan Annie, or Oliver Twist. Like the death of the sweet, dear, innocent, and vulnerable, the death of the big, great, glorious, and heroically self-sacrificing also takes us into sentimental territory.[5] Any protracted death scene tends toward sentimentality as well: Who could not harbour a secret wish for Aschenbach to hurry up and die in Venice?

And, though we may go along with George Orwell to conclude that there is good bad art and bad bad art, these trappings of the sentimental generally lead us to conclude that it is bad art.[6] But this does not mean that these purely aesthetic judgments have any moral or ethical weight. The death of the child or her parents *is* just sad.[7] The sentimental exploitation of sadness can disqualify the art as good, but it can't disqualify the death of children or their parents as genuinely sad or potentially ethically and morally significant. The greatest risk is that suffering that ought to be accorded moral significance becomes trivialized in our perception by its distasteful associations with kitsch. But again, permitting this trivialization is a wrong-headed elevation of aesthetic concerns to the level of ethics.

Nevertheless, aesthetic condemnations of the sentimental are tricky because they do read as having – and are usually intended to have – moral or ethical punch. Orwell's critique of Charles Dickens as sentimental *is* an ethical critique.[8] As is Reinhold Neibuhr's critique of Martin Luther King, Jr., as sentimental.[9] But are such aesthetic concerns ever relevant in our evaluation of a theory of justice and, if so, why? At first blush it would seem not. In evaluating a theory or practice of justice, surely such stylistic concerns ought to take a back seat to questions about its concrete effectiveness in meeting the needs of the victim, preventing recidivism, inspiring a sense of dignity and closure, and, beyond these utilitarian concerns, satisfying us as a viable conception of *justice*.[10] If restorative justice can point to such concrete advantages; if it can commend itself as a superior notion of justice, surely squeamishness about its touchy-feeliness ought to be dismissed. Yet, for many, it is the sentimental feel to restorative justice that makes it unpalatable.

We need then to look a little closer at the ethical foundation of our rejection of the sentimental. "Sentimental" tends to be an all-purpose term of derision. Thus we ought to suspect it of carrying potentially ethically unexamined anxieties. Most particularly, the devaluing of the sentimental may primarily belie simple anxiety around feeling, affect, or emotion. By denouncing even *oneself* as "sentimental" – ridiculing or disqualifying one's *own* feelings as mere sentimentality – one gains protective distance from those feelings as well as a ready means of dismissing them as reasons for action. Some distaste for the sentimental is surely rooted, therefore, in stiff-upper-lip, WASP-type anxieties about feeling itself. We ought not to be governed by this kind of concern since our aesthetic sense about the unseemliness of emotions may have damaging ethical consequences – especially when applied to our practices and institutions of justice.

Robert Solomon in *A Passion for Justice* mounts a defence of the sentimental along these lines.[11] He argues that even classically "manipulative" sentimentality promotes empathic identification with the suffering of others and is, therefore, a good thing: "If this is sentimentality then surely we need much more of it in morals and social philosophy."[12] And he rightly points out that: "The manipulative sentimentality of a novel such as *Uncle Tom's Cabin* turned a morally flawed country around when it became a best seller back in the mid-nineteenth century."[13]

Solomon dismisses various objections to the sentimental that purport to be grounded in ethical concerns. He first addresses Kant's denunciation of the sentimental as privileging emotion over argument. Solomon retorts that while emotions *can* intrude inappropriately in our thinking, "the real worry is morality and theories of justice devoid of feeling."[14] He then takes on Oscar Wilde's quip that "a sentimentalist is simply one who desires to have the luxury of an emotion without paying for it."[15] (Wilde repeatedly contrasted the cold, hard realities of the market with the devalued sentimental. He also called the sentimentalist "a man who sees an absurd value in everything and doesn't know the market value of a single thing.")[16] Solomon rejects these commercial metaphors as inapt. He argues that the notion of paying for or earning emotion is simply meaningless and, moreover, that there is absolutely nothing wrong with being naturally, spontaneously compassionate even if the impulses to that compassion are at surface level.[17]

He then rejects Mary Midgley's concern that sentimentality as idealization invites "flight from, and contempt for, real people"[18] and diminishes our ability to "deal with the real world." Solomon argues rather that sentimentality "activates our sensitivity to actual tragedies."[19] He also rejects Michael Tanner's concern that indulgence in the sentimental breeds all sentiment and no action. Here again Solomon argues that sentimentality may not lead to heroic action but can lead, nonetheless, to actions "even so simple as firing off a letter to one's congressman or dropping a check in the mail."[20]

But these answers seem a little too hasty. Few today would buy into Kant's stuffed-shirt paranoia around the contaminating effects of emotion. Nevertheless, emotions cannot, on their own, lead us to justice. As we will discuss at further length in Chapter 6, even compassion is an unreliable guide toward justice inasmuch as it tends to spring from arbitrary and irrational forces.[21] Sentimentality packages and prettifies just the sort of suffering Aristotle identifies as giving rise to compassion: the undeserved suffering of the innocent, with whose vulnerability we identify.[22] Sentimentality does not engage with the suffering of the repulsive, the annoying, the smelly, the guilty. Neither does it concern itself with those too far away for us to care about or too close and familiar for us to idealize.[23] Sentimentality teaches compassion for the endearing, not for the unprepossessing: the wide-eyed, meek, and starving child in Africa but not the ugly, middle-aged, equally starving father; the delightful Anne Frank but not the sullen, complaining, old orthodox Jew; the Christ-like Uncle Tom but not the scary-looking black teenagers on the subway. Thus compassion inspired by sentimentality is subject to and dependent upon manoeuvres not grounded in legitimate justice concerns.

Likewise, Solomon's dismissal of Wilde's notion of earned emotion as meaningless seems to gloss over Wilde's insight too quickly. Surely we earn emotion by enduring all the complicating, uglifying mess of life and managing to feel the feelings anyway. The sentimental neatly packages emotional stimuli – stripping them of all the qualifying baggage that, in life, leads inevitably to emotional ambivalence. We can watch a sentimental film and have pure, intense, memorable experiences of love, joy, anger, fear, longing, or sadness. The scenes are so moving because they are airbrushed from life, with the life taken out of them: There is no stench, the person dying is not annoying us, nor are we thinking of inheriting from them; the children are perfectly sweet and don't whine about being bored; the lover is perfectly appealing and doesn't have smelly socks or one eye on the TV, checking the score. Sentimentality gives us an experience of the emotional while releasing us from the work of overcoming all the usually occurring distractions and detractions that alloy our feelings. The sentimental produces pure emotion without the complicating qualifications of real life.

This aspect of the sentimental, of course, leads to Mary Midgley's point that the sentimental teaches contempt for real people. By celebrating the pleasurable and intense emotional experiences that it produces, sentimentality teaches us to be dissatisfied with our necessarily more qualified, ambivalent, muddled experiences of life. Sentimental perfection in art inspires the desire for sentimental perfection in life and disgruntlement at everything else. We feel disappointment escalating to contempt when the soundtrack isn't right, the lover *is* checking the score, or the kid *is* whining. Our experiences of love as intermittent – as little emotional flickers between long periods of boredom, annoyance, and the desire to escape the whole situation – seem to disqualify our feelings as love at all.[24] We feel disappointment escalating to contempt for the real people who inevitably bungle our magic moments. Of course, some thoroughgoing sentimentalists can salvage real life through *post facto* airbrushing. Some are able to reconstruct memory to meet the sentimental specs – hence the relation between sentimentality and nostalgia. But in so doing they again show contempt for the real people who failed in the first instance to get the scene right.

In life it is very difficult to solve the coordination problems of sentimentality and get everyone together on the same sentimental page. Christmas, birthdays, marriage proposals, weddings, a woman telling her lover she is pregnant, and anniversaries are prime occasions for collective collusion but (I suspect) more often for failed collective collusion in sentimental scripts. Even where there is agreement that all should be doing their bit to make the magic moment happen, there is still the problem of whose sentimental vision is to govern. Who gets to direct the scene? Is it the most sentimental person, the most powerful, or the one who is going to be most disappointed if they lose? Turf wars over directorial authority here have great comic potential. Even a flicker of disagreement over how the scene should go destroys everything. Thus sentimentality is deeply totalitarian. Deferring to someone else's vision of the sentimental is as bad as abandoning sentimental hope entirely. Botched performances are an offence. The sentimentalist presumes others' incompetence or insufficient zeal in faking pure contentment or wonder or joy to be an indication of malicious intention to wreck the moment.

Thus many a hapless villain has "ruined Christmas" by failing in those roles he or she ought rightly to have had down cold: the beneficent, all-providing father; the wide-eyed, delighted, and appreciative child; the serene, selfless, and contented mother; or the jolly and unconditionally loving grandparents.

This totalitarian aspect of sentimentality leads me to Tanner's point that sentimentality encourages all feeling and no action, and allows the supreme sentimental narrative to dominate all other concerns. Solomon attempts to dismiss this problem by pointing out that sentimentality does urge us to action; it urges us to send letters to politicians and to put checks in the mail and so forth. Yet is this really true? *Uncle Tom's Cabin* is a rare instance of politically motivated and motivating sentimentality, but it's difficult to think of other sentimental art or literature that has a politically radical purpose.[25] Sentimentality is enlisted in the service of conservatism, bourgeois domesticity, and the status quo far more than in the service of equality-seeking political change. However, though Solomon's refutation of him is unconvincing, Tanner's point about sentimentality and inaction also fails to convince. Sentimentality inspires all kinds of action in the pursuit of that longed for perfection. It dissipates our energy for efforts toward more attainable, more provisional "goods." The sentimentalist strives to emulate that purity of moment and feeling. In so striving, she commits herself to a practice of ignoring or denying most of what is actually going on. Sentimentality is studied insensitivity to life in the pursuit of imaginary purity. Great art can teach us to pay attention to life. By astute and subtle observation it can encourage us to own up to our authentic experience. As Emerson puts it: "In every work of genius we recognize our own rejected thoughts: they come back to us with a certain alienated majesty. Great works of art have no more affecting lesson for us than this. They teach us to abide by our spontaneous impression with good-humoured inflexibility then most when the whole cry of voices is on the other side."[26] Sentimental art, by contrast, teaches us to want those airbrushed moments and then to go after them by airbrushing out of our conscious awareness offending experiences and observations. It teaches us to reject all those aspects of experience that contradict the sentimental ideal. Finally, it teaches us to mobilize our energy in pursuit of those prettified goals. The most common struggle in which it enlists our energy is, of course, the quest for perfect, harmonious, bourgeois domesticity, or, as Orwell puts it in his critique of Dickens, "radiant idleness."[27]

Thus, while the emotions of the sentimental are unearned, the price paid for uncritical participation in them is potentially very high. I will discuss the obvious significance of this point to the role of sentimentality in restorative justice soon. But first, let me consider an element of the defence of the sentimental I have so far shirked. The politics of who gets reviled as sentimental are significant. Every time "sentimental" is used as an insult, it carries with it a supplemental charge of surfeit of the feminine. Even my "special occasion" examples are obviously gendered and vaguely misogynist. The director of the magic moment – say, the fairytale wedding, the euphoric Christmas morning, the perfectly popped question, or the joyous anniversary – is stereotypically female, and the culprit who ruins it is stereotypically male. Thus sentimentality – both in art and in life – is close to being coterminous with the sappily womanish as a devalued category.

Consider, for example, Ann Douglas's discussion of the sentimental as degenerately feminine in *The Feminization of American Culture*. For Douglas, muddling of the boundaries between private and public is what sets off the alarm; it is the exhibitionist exposure of the private in the public that sullies and sentimentalizes: "Sentimentalism is a cluster of ostensibly private feelings that always attains public and conspicuous expression. Privacy functions in the rituals of sentimentalism only for the sake of titillation, as a convention to be violated. Involved as it is with the exhibition and commercialization of the self, sentimentalism cannot exist without an audience. It has no content but its own exposure, and it invests exposure with a kind of final significance."[28] This indignation over the unseemly intrusion by the private into the public maps directly onto the polluting intrusion of the devalued and insignificant feminine into the valuable, significant masculine realm. Douglas's definition of the sentimental, along with her sense that respect of the boundaries between public and private is the way to purge the sentimental, looks like a cure worse than the illness.[29] To avoid the sentimental we are supposed fastidiously to keep the private/feminine hidden. The consequence of this kind of hyperdecorous and misogynist denunciation of the sentimental in relation to institutions of *justice* in particular is certainly politically and ethically pernicious. The aesthetic sense that the fundamentally private ought not to be exposed in public is, as has been demonstrated by countless feminists, a tremendously powerful tool in securing men's freedom to commit sexual and violent crime against women and children in private with impunity. We ought not to shame public expression of the private feelings to which crime gives rise. If we sneer at the public exposure of private matters as exhibitionism, then how are we to give public consequence to private wrongs?

Further, our vigilantly proper and lawyerly attempts to keep all displays of private feeling to a minimum in our courts of law can itself be seen as a failing of our institutions of justice inspired by the antisentimentalist sensibility typified by Douglas. When injustice engages the innermost private, how can we create effective institutions if we posit as a virtue their capacity to cleanse the proceedings of the exposure of private emotion in public?[30] Consider how well we recognize the feelings expressed by Saul Bellow in his novel *Herzog* describing the courts' capacity to drain of emotion even that stand-by of a sentimental trope: the death of a child. Moses Herzog witnesses the trial of a young woman charged with murdering her infant son. As Herzog listens to the blandly delivered testimony of the witnesses describing the habitually filthy condition of the deceased child, the mother's destitution, the child's bruised corpse, he is overcome by the incongruousness between the heartrending events and the emotionally indifferent manner in which they are being related: "All this seemed to Herzog exceptionally low-pitched. All – the lawyers, the jury, the mother, her tough friend, the judge – behaved with much restraint, extremely well controlled and quiet spoken. Such calm – inversely proportionate to the murder? he was thinking. Judge, jury, lawyers, and the accused, all looked utterly unemotional."[31]

The legal system grinds even the most horrifying of crimes and violations down into ho-hum business as usual. The art of lawyering in part entails the deflation of the profusely emotional and resolutely private stuff of crime, reconstituting it for unsentimental, desiccated, masculinized presentation in the public space of the courtroom. The good lawyer coaches the client to keep it short and simple so as to shield him from the risk of disgusting the judge as judicious spectator.[32] The aesthetic of the legal process by and large pays homage to precisely Ann Douglas's brand of distaste for the sentimental by managing and confining the affective and private lives of the parties for suitable public presentation.

Distaste for the feminine surfaces in Herzog himself, who is aware that any expression of his own emotion would be girlish, awkward, and dissonant with the firmly established masculine tenor of the proceedings. He has an impulse to respond emotionally, to do something to snap the others out of their zombielike vacantness. At the same time, he fears that an emotive response would be pointless. It would be mere sentimentality that wouldn't lead anywhere.[33]

> With all his might – mind and heart – he tried to obtain something for the murdered child. But what? How? He pressed himself with intensity, but "all his might" could get nothing for the buried boy. Herzog experienced nothing but his own *human feelings*, in which he found nothing of use. What if he felt moved to cry? Or to pray? He pressed hand to hand. And what did he feel? Why he felt himself – his own trembling hands, and eyes that stung. And what was there in modern, post ... post-Christian America to pray for? Justice – justice and mercy? And pray away the monstrousness of life, the wicked dream it was?[34]

An institutional structure that makes no space for the emotionality of wrongdoing can offer only an emaciated conception of justice. The law's ability to get at justice is hamstrung by its concern with purging the emotional.[35] Certainly one of the main strengths of restorative justice lies in its aspiration to make dignified space for – to foster true freedom of expression in relation to – the emotionality of injustice.[36] Restorative justice recognizes that justice is importantly connected to emotional satisfaction and a restored sense of emotional security. In this respect, restorative justice is an important corrective to the emotional desiccation of our present system. The troubling sentimentality of restorative justice lies, rather, in its vision of the end goal of justice as an idealized relationship between victim, offender, and community. It is the understanding of justice in terms of an idealized notion of wholeness, healing, equality, respect, and connection, coupled with the promotion of restorative justice primarily by way of grand success stories, that creates legitimate anxieties around the sentimental. It is the too abundant, too easy, too harmonious comfort at the end of the restorative justice rainbow that gives rise to legitimate anxieties about its sentimentality.

In this light, then, let me venture a definition of the sentimental: Sentimentality seeks, in a simplistic way, to evoke feelings of harmony, wholeness, and connection, and it portrays the means of arriving at those feelings as magical and/or easy. Sentimental momentum is propelled by the desire to feel these pleasing emotions. It asks us to buy into an illusory and fictitious method of achieving that comfort. The anxiety around the sentimental here lies in the awareness of a delusional quality. If we are ashamed to feel sentimental emotions, it is because we are aware that such feeling requires complicity in its fictions.

But this definition is incomplete. Sentimentality is about perfectly harmonious connection, to be sure. But it is also about indulgence in woe, despair, despondency, sadness, grief, lamentation.[37] The most potent strain of sentimentality is, therefore, found in the quick flip between these two sets of sentimental emotions. It is typified by the facile movement from lugubrious to joyful, from unrestrained woe to complete fulfilment and happiness. Sentimentality teaches us to overlook the inadequacy of the mechanism of its shift from misery to bliss. It teaches us to exaggerate and languish in our woes while, at the same time, we dissipate our energies in delusional plans to transcend them. It habituates us to falling for the quick fix, the shallow and ephemeral hit of joy.

Consider the sentimental classic Little Orphan Annie.[38] Clearly the story of Little Orphan Annie works both sides of this sentimental street. It is the easy play between the surfeits of wholly innocent sorrow and wholly wholesome happiness that drive its sentimental appeal. The adorable Annie's misery in the orphanage is paired with the ultrajoyful jackpot of

Daddy Warbucks and his millions. The story asks us to adore Annie as ideally loveable, pity her suffering, and rejoice in her supergood fortune. It asks us to indulge in enjoyment of a magical shift from woe to elation, wholeness, happiness, and connection. It seduces us toward a simplistic account of the way from A to B. The lugubrious balances off the joyous and vice versa. Each makes the excess of the other possible. We can wallow in Annie's misfortune with so much abandon in part because we know that we will soon be celebrating her happy destiny. With this understanding of sentimentality in hand, let's proceed to the role of sentimentality in restorative justice.

Restorative Justice and the Sentimental Success Story
Restorative justice is torn between marketing and disclaiming its own sentimentality. Many of the success stories that constitute so much of the advocacy for restorative justice have an undeniable sentimental cast. At the same time, proponents of restorative justice are at pains to refute charges of sentimentality and to contend that restorative justice, while grounded in an ethic of compassion, is not naively optimistic. Some proponents of restorative justice, such as Dutch criminologist Herman Bianchi, are at pains to convince us that to place affective inner states like remorse and forgiveness at the core of our understanding of justice is not sentimental at all.[39] Indeed, giving due space to the lived reality of these emotions of justice and structuring our institutions of justice such that they respect and reflect that reality, rather than deny and repress it, is a step in the right direction. Far from being sentimental shlock, these processes effect a shift toward institutions of justice that make possible the authentic experience of healing, closure, and repair of the damage done by crime. They give space to the "human side" of wrongdoing such that the real needs of the parties and the underlying causes of crime can be meaningfully addressed. Bianchi writes: "These concepts as I propose them are by no means soft, naive or sentimental. They are hard, real, and tangible."[40]

Yet consider the following transcript of a radio interview in which Bianchi tells a story meant as a set piece to demonstrate the superiority of justice-as-repair:

A friend of mine – was an attorney – an advocate in Amsterdam ... And one day he told me his story. He had two sons. His eldest son had fallen in love with a girl. But there was another lover. And the lover killed the son of the attorney. It was what the French call a *crime passionel*. And the attorney told me what happened.

He said: "the same evening after that happened, my other son said. 'I am going to kill that man.'... And I realized that the lover had not only killed my son he was killing all of us because of our vengeance feelings ... that's fatal to your soul."

And he thought: "How can I find a solution? How can I find a solution?"

Well the next day or two days later after two sleepless nights he said "I have the solution. I must speak to that lover."

So he contacted the public prosecutor and he said: "Can I see that boy who killed my son?" "Well," said the public prosecutor, "You are crazy but I can't stop you. Do what you want."

He said: "I went to the cell where that boy was sitting – the lover. I didn't know what to say. Neither did he. We had been sitting there for half an hour without speaking. I left. Then a few days later I said: I will go again. Then the lover – the criminal – said: 'I feel so sorry.' He said that and we both wept."

I am almost weeping now myself. This is how it should be, you know, but it never happens.

He said then "my wife, my daughter, my other son also visited him. We all prayed together."

You see? This is the solution. Even if the lover would be in prison for a couple of years that won't do harm to his soul. Then it is good punishment. Better would be if he said "Alright I will join the Flying Doctors in Africa. I will go to do a lot of good things to plague sufferers in Africa" – that would be better – that would be better. Exposing himself to the plague. That's penitence. Not sitting in the cell and quarrelling with the other prisoners.[41]

Of course, as we see it here on paper, the story is deprived of much of the persuasive power it derives from Bianchi's charm and his impassioned and colourful telling. Bianchi dramatically evokes the brother's tortured passion for revenge, the father's grief and desperation in search of a better resolution to the loss of his son, and a murderer's terrible sense of remorse before the father of his victim. Bianchi himself is overcome with tearful emotion in the moment of healing connection between surviving victims and murderer and their shared journey into right-relation.[42]

Embedded in the story one finds many of the foundational assumptions of restorative justice. First, we have the idea that retributive understandings of justice inflict hidden but serious additional harms on victims. The longing for vengeance conscripts the victim into a soul-destroying quest to inflict suffering on the wrongdoer. The father in the story realizes that the desire for revenge is, in this figurative sense, "killing" his entire family. The murderer inflicts one harm by killing their son. Over this harm, the family has had no control. But he inflicts another harm on the family by poisoning their lives with the desire for revenge. Over this aspect of the loss, the victims do have some control.[43] The father is motivated, therefore, by a desire to protect himself and his family from the deadly trap of toxic vengeance.

Next, the story presumes that the bad guy is not a bad guy through and through. He is not evil, nor is he a danger to the community. He is a lover, a boy, someone who has committed a grievous act but who remains, and should be acknowledged as, a fully human being capable of compassion, integrity, and, most importantly, good-faith action.

Third, the restorative solution is found through an intimate and emotionally cathartic encounter between victim and perpetrator. The tears shared by the victim and perpetrator are offered as the beginnings of a lived experience of justice in the relationship. The victim and perpetrator are locked in a darkly intimate and exclusive relationship in which each is the source of the other's pain but is also the only hope for a way out of the other's misery. The shared experience of profuse feeling – in which both victim and offender show compassion and respect for the feelings of the other – provides the energy through which victim and offender can move toward repair. The victim respects and does not reject the offender's remorse. Likewise, the offender honours the victim's grief and despair.

Fourth, God has an important hand in the restoration. The ultimate moment of reconciliation comes when the victims and offender join in prayer. Together they concede their own inability to heal the wrong. They defer to God, asking for his assistance in making things right. This moment of shared prayer is even more intimate than the moments of shared grief, confusion, and remorse. It assumes an incredible amount of common cultural and moral ground between the victim and the offender. The victim and offender are each willing to be vulnerable supplicants to God in the presence of the other. Both appear to trust that neither are praying to God to strike the other down with revenge.[44] God is a force to be appealed to for assistance in reconciliation and shared healing. He is not, as he often can be, sought as a source of divine retribution for the enemy.

Finally, there is a poetic affinity between the crime and the efforts at repair. The perpetrator is given an opportunity to honour the victim symbolically through heroic self-sacrifice and thereby to restore the balance of justice. The murderer has taken the life of another, and, therefore, in order to right the balance, it would be best if he risked his life for the sake of others by going to help the sick in Africa. His remorse is a necessary but not sufficient condition for restorative justice. He must also desire to act so as to give concrete confirmation to that remorse.

By concurring in the strangely happy ending of this story – concurring in Bianchi's sentiment that "this is how it should be" – we show our willingness to be converted from a punitive to a restorative understanding of justice. Only the most hard-hearted of retributivists could suggest that the vision of justice offered by Bianchi here would be deficient because of the absence of state-inflicted suffering on this murderer/boy/lover as he goes off, in Bianchi's speculation, to Africa to do penance for his crime by ministering to the dying.

But at least part of the problem with reading this kind of story as legitimately persuasive of the conclusion that we ought to adopt a restorative model of justice is that the story – and the understanding of justice it recommends – may be grounded in indulgence of unearned, easy, airbrushed emotions. If the story is seductive, it is so, in large measure, because it convinces us of the possibility of a miraculous shift from the terrible to the joyous. On the one hand, it is clear that the story is one of extreme woe. Though the characters in the story do not engage in sorrowful expositions of their losses or grief, the story does, in a very short space of time, evoke extravagant grief. We begin, of course, with the primary grief of the father and brother of the murder victim. But the extent of the grief goes far beyond this. We have the grief of the girl who was the beloved of both the murder victim and the murderer. Interestingly she is absent from Bianchi's telling of the story, or at least she is absent as a participant in the healing and reconciliation. Yet the story derives a good measure of its pathos from the rich mix of romantic misery swirling around the girl. The murderer has failed in his aspirations to find romantic happiness by rubbing out his competitor. We are given to understand that the murderer's sorrow authentically springs from his compassion for the pain of the deceased's family and his guilt over the death itself. Yet the depth of his grief must in some measure also be bound up with his failure to secure the desired union with his beloved. His sorrow is perhaps also fuelled by a sense of his own public humiliation. It may now be painfully clear to him that this was a spectacularly stupid plan. Thus there is a kind of superabundance of woe here embroiled not so much in ideals about innocence but in romantic intrigue.

What then of joy and harmony? The ending of this story is oddly yet abundantly joyful. We close with the intimacy of shared prayer. The scene is one of harmonious unification and reconciliation. Bianchi envisions the murderer's departure on an exotic quest to help the miserable victims of the plague (presumably a euphemism for AIDS or ebola virus – yet we imagine something more romantic). We are asked to envision his transformation from miserable prisoner to gallant and selfless giver of aid to the destitute. The boy/lover/murderer starts out as our villain and ends up as our hero – a drastic shift for even the most sentimental of stories.

Much of the joy here, however, springs from Bianchi's own joy in the telling. The sense of happy closure arises out of Bianchi's impassioned conviction that here we have found "the solution." We have arrived at the long-lost and now-found happy ending to injustice. The story ends not merely on behalf of the characters themselves, but on behalf of all those searching for better, healthier ways to cope with crime.

Of course, even the very notion of "solution" in such a context carries a sentimental charge. The belief that tension may be resolved, complexity simplified, and suffering brought to an end is fundamental to sentimental joy. Further, skepticism about the foundations of such a belief again fuel our anxiety about the risks of getting sucked in. In Bianchi's story the shift from terrible trouble to perfect solution is effected with characteristic sentimental ease. Indeed, the time frame of events appears to be astonishingly short. The father is overwhelmed by his need to find release for his grief and goes to the prison only two days after the killing. The breakthrough occurs but one day after that. All is concluded within the week.

The mechanism effecting the shift is typically mysterious and magical. The encounter is what sparks the change, but a full understanding of how it takes place remains elusive. The moment of face-to-face encounter between victim and offender magically effects the shift from agony to joyful release. Thus Bianchi offers us precisely that which we ought to be wary of in the sentimental: a misery-to-miracle story with a facile account of the transition from A to B. The reason this narrative ought to alarm us in the context of justice is that it threatens to draw us into a practice of responding to wrongdoing with the sentimentalist's desire for, and optimism about, the possibility of purely harmonious closure and contentment. Bianchi, albeit in all good faith, is advocating for a transfer of resources and for the diversion of people's energies toward a conception of justice that promises sumptuously happy endings it is unlikely to be able to deliver.

Restorative Justice and the Sentimental Reading of Literature: A Restorative Encounter between Priam and Achilles?

Some proponents of restorative justice also cite classical literature as authority for the restorative approach. Van Ness and Strong, for example, offer a reading of Homer's *The Iliad* as a precedent for restorative justice.[45] They posit the encounter between Priam and Achilles at the end of *The Iliad* as epitomizing the fundamentals of restorative justice. While they concede that the encounter does not put an end to the Trojan war, they place significance on Homer's choice to end *The Iliad* with negotiation and rapprochement between the two men: the breaking of bread together, the pity for and commiseration with each other's losses, the shared tears, and the reluctant but authentic according of mutual respect.[46] Homer, they argue, has set out for us the essential elements of restorative encounter:

The first, of course, was that the two men actually met ... Priam came to Achilles' tent for the *meeting,* and the two men talked and ate together. The second is that they spoke personally; they told the story from their own perspective. This admittedly personalized approach has been called *narrative.* They did not attempt to generalize or universalize, but instead spoke with feeling about the particulars of the decade-long conflict that concerned them most. The third is related; they exhibited *emotion* in their communication. They wept as they considered their own losses; they wept as they identified with those of the other ... A fourth element is *understanding.* They listened as well as spoke, and they listened with understanding, and that helped them acquire a degree of empathy for the other. Fifth they came to an *agreement* that was particular and achievable. Achilles agreed to turn over Hector's body for burial and in addition agreed to give the Trojans time to conduct Hector's funeral.[47]

I see this as a culpably sentimental reading of Homer. Van Ness and Strong read the story as though it were about caring and empathic identification and accord. They employ the usual sentimental modus operandi of not paying attention to the nuances of what is going on, replacing such attention with a simplistic story about the smooth ride from woe to harmonious, caring connection. Moreover, Van Ness and Strong paper over blatant sentimentality that *is* present in the story: the sentimental glorification of grand enemies' admiration for each other's ability to inflict harm. Homer's undeniably sentimental glorification of the mutual admiration felt between heroic warriors completely disqualifies the story as a precedent for restorative justice between victim and wrongdoer.

Of course, that Van Ness and Strong misread *The Iliad* does not, in itself, discredit restorative justice. Both the theory and practice of restorative justice perhaps remain, in a sense, independent of the errors of its individual proponents. But what is of significance here is that Van Ness and Strong have both misread *and* misappropriated *The Iliad*, presenting it as an authoritative source that supports the claims of restorative justice. They attempt to seduce us to enthusiasm about restorative justice by evoking the venerable Homer as a fellow booster of their agenda. There is a quackery here – a kind of false advertising – that we ought not to overlook. So let us now take the trouble to examine the story carefully and see whether it really gives support to the claims of restorative justice.

Let us deal first with Van Ness and Strong's sentimental simplification of the story. To do so we must back up and remind ourselves that, for the whole of *The Iliad*, Achilles has been petulantly refusing to fight on the side of the Achaeans. He has been refusing to enter the battle in order to make King Agamemnon pay for injuring and insulting him by taking away his prize girl, Briseis. Eventually Agamemnon and the Achaeans recognize their dependence on Achilles. In what is, in many senses, a more interesting (though failed) example of restorative justice, they attempt to make amends for the wrong done to Achilles and to reintegrate him into the community of Achaean soldiers. Agamemnon expresses remorse for failing to give him appropriate honour and offers him more than adequate compensation, including the return of the "untouched" Briseis. But this attempt at restorative justice – that is apology, compensation, acknowledgment of wrongdoing, forgiveness, and the restoration of community – fails. Achilles angrily rebuffs Agamemnon's offers and sticks to his stance of resentment and alienation.

Finally, in the face of terrible losses by the Achaeans, Achilles' best friend Patroclus convinces Achilles at least to allow *him* to go into battle. He borrows Achilles' armour and joins the battle on the side of the Achaeans. But Patroclus is killed by the great Trojan warrior Hector. The victorious Hector then attempts to behead Patroclus's corpse. However, before Hector is able to defile the body, the Achaeans manage to get it back. Enraged by the death of his friend, Achilles finally makes up with the Achaeans and enters the battle himself. Yet he is prompted more by his passion to avenge Patroclus's death than by any concern to win the war for his fellow Achaeans.

Achilles does kill Hector. Book 24 of *The Iliad*, the one Van Ness and Strong focus on, opens with the now-insomniac Achilles tossing and turning all night with enduring grief over Patroclus's death and continued fury at the dead Hector. Achilles ends his sleepless nights by getting up at dawn to drag Hector's body behind the horses in circles around Patroclus's barrow. This gratuitous defiling of Hector's corpse is seen by virtually everybody as a war crime. The gods themselves take extreme offence at it. Indeed, Apollo has been protecting Hector's body with his golden aegis. At a meeting of the gods, it is decided that Achilles must be stopped. Zeus summons Thetis to go and tell her son Achilles that he has offended Zeus and the rest of the gods and that he must accept a ransom for the return of Hector's body to the Trojans. The messenger goddess, Iris, tells King Priam, Hector's father, that she has come with a message from Zeus that Priam should take treasures to Achilles, and that as a suppliant to Achilles he will be safe. Against the advice of his wife, but with these assurances from Iris and the protection of Hermes, Priam proceeds to Achilles' camp to offer him riches in return for his son's body.

With the help of the gods, Priam makes it to Achilles' tent, approaching him thus: "'It is to get him back that I have come to the Achaean ships, bringing this princely ransom with me. Achilles, fear the gods and be merciful to me, remembering your own father, though I am even more entitled to compassion since I have brought myself to do a thing that no one else on earth has done – I have raised to my lips the hand of the man who killed my son.'"[48] Priam makes a number of moves here. First, he offers gifts. Then he reminds Achilles of the threat of punishment by the gods. Next, he asks for Achilles' mercy and tries to put Achilles in mind of his feelings for his own aging father. Finally, he emphasizes and acknowledges the extent of his self-humiliation in coming *as a suppliant* and kissing the hand of a man who has killed his son. And, indeed, as Achilles points out, he has killed *many* of Priam's sons. So, yes, Priam is asking for pity. But he positions his request for pity in third place after the offer of gifts and the reminder of Zeus's wrath and follows it up immediately with a posture of submission to Achilles' greater power. All these moves are most immediately directed toward preventing Achilles from killing Priam on the spot. Priam has the protection of the gods, but given Achilles' temper he has still placed himself in an incredibly vulnerable position by going into the enemy camp alone.

Priam, the victim, is supplicating and bribing Achilles, the wrongdoer, at the same time as he is reminding him of the threat of punishment by the gods. This is not a case of the wrongdoer accepting accountability for his actions and seeking forgiveness. It is the victim who is seeking kindness from the wrongdoer, and the only thing putting him in a position to do so is the power of the gods. Achilles, as wrongdoer, is being appeased by his victim, and no small part of that appeasement is accomplished through Priam's humiliation at having to talk nicely to the man who has killed so many of his sons. Yes, there is a meeting, narrative, emotion, understanding, and agreement here, but these elements of the encounter are mixed with other motivations that have nothing to do with accountability for wrongdoing. Achilles does respond hospitably. The two do weep over their respective losses. And Achilles does indeed acknowledge the extent of the harm he has inflicted on Priam – though in acknowledging Priam's losses, it is clear that Achilles is also boasting about his own prowess in having inflicted those losses. It is true that they come to an agreement that the body will be returned and that time will be given for the funeral of Hector. But it is also true that the agreement was dictated in advance by Zeus and the rest of the gods.

When Achilles doesn't immediately kill Priam, Priam's sense of relief leads him to become ever so slightly overconfident. He moves just a hair out of his submissive stance and presumes to attempt gently to persuade Achilles to return the body. He almost has the effrontery to suggest to Achilles that the return of the body is due to him as a matter of justice. Achilles reacts by immediately threatening Priam with death. Watch where Priam, ever so subtly, oversteps himself:

"Do not ask me to sit down, your highness," said the venerable Priam, "while Hector lies neglected in your huts, but give him back to me without delay and let me set my eyes on him. Accept the splendid ransom that I bring. I hope you will enjoy it and get safely home, because you spared me when I first appeared."[49]

The ever-sensitive Achilles immediately jumps on this impertinence. Priam is presuming to ask for delivery of the body; he is commending the value of his own offering; and he is arrogating to himself the authority to extend fatherly approval to Achilles: in all, a cluster of imprudently brash assumptions on Priam's part that he is in a secure enough position to presume to persuade. Achilles will not suffer even this subtle attempt by Priam to exercise power and comes down on him thus:

> "Old man, do not drive me too hard," said the swift Achilles frowning at Priam. "I have made up my mind without your help to give Hector back to you. My own Mother, the Daughter of the Old Man of the Sea, has brought me word from Zeus. Moreover, I have seen through *you* Priam. You cannot hide the fact that some god brought you to the Achaean ships. Nobody, not even a young man at his best, would venture by himself into our camp ... So do not exasperate me now, sir, when I have enough already on my mind, or I may break the laws of Zeus and, suppliant though you are, show you as little consideration as I showed Hector in my huts."[50]

Achilles makes it clear that he is acting in response to a threat of punishment by Zeus and that he is not moved by Priam's initiation of the meeting or by his narrative of sorrow. In the course of reaching the agreement, Achilles' primary concern is to ensure that the inequality between him and Priam – that Achilles retains almost all of the power in the situation – is kept front and centre in the course of their encounter. Achilles is humouring Priam. He is being polite because Priam is being protected. But he will not suffer Priam to pretend to courage or independent power in the bid to convince Achilles to hand over the body. Achilles is going to hand it over, but he is going to do so because of his prior meeting with his mother, Thetis, and her reports of Zeus's disapprobation.

This is hardly the kind of emotion and understanding that Van Ness and Strong want us to see in the story. Achilles' reminder to Priam that he is acting purely in deference to Zeus does not conform to their sentimental conclusion that "stirred by pity Achilles agrees to return the body."[51] Van Ness and Strong are asking us to read the encounter as a move from enmity and wrongdoing to harmonious emotional connection and right-relation — when, in fact, Achilles' primary objective in the encounter is to make Priam feel his humiliation. Achilles is giving moderate concessions to Priam not as a result of his empathic understanding of Priam's emotive narratives of loss, but in response to overwhelming pressure from the gods, backed by their coercive power. He can, if he decides he wants to, still incur the wrath of the gods by murdering Priam on the spot and going back to defiling Hector's corpse. And, it matters to Achilles that Priam see it this way. It matters to Achilles that his position of power over Priam in the encounter be acknowledged and maintained. Like much of the rest of *The Iliad*, the encounter is primarily about Achilles' distinctive blend of petulant prima donna-ism and realpolitik. It is difficult to read the encounter as one that establishes equality when so many aspects of it show us Achilles' skill in maintaining power over his victim even as he makes concessions to him in the face of a threat of serious retributive punishment by the gods.

Moreover, Van Ness and Strong appear to be offering the story as an example of restorative *justice*. Yet it is difficult to know where the justice is in this agreement. Achilles, the wrongdoer, is being bought off by Priam, the victim. Furthermore, Priam is well aware that he can't as much as whisper an accusation against Achilles of anything. If he tries to bring justice into the discussion at all, he is a dead man. The agreement is reached only because Achilles is treated with kid gloves throughout and Priam is scrupulously careful never to mention Achilles' having violated Hector's corpse. Even *Achilles* knows enough to protect himself from his own reactivity to being told he's in the wrong. Achilles knows that if Priam for one second steps out of the role of flatterer and suppliant, he, Achilles, will lose his temper, kill Priam, and thereby harm himself by incurring the wrath of Zeus. Achilles anticipates and avoids the risk that Priam will be overcome with rage at the sight of Hector's body:

> The prince then called some women-servants out and told them to wash and anoint the body, but in another part of the house so Priam should not see his son. (Achilles was afraid that Priam, if he saw him, might in the bitterness of grief be unable to restrain his wrath and that he himself might fly into a rage and kill the old man thereby sinning against Zeus.)[52]

It is a delicate negotiation. The main concern is not to ruffle Achilles' feathers because Achilles is the one who has the power – both in the sense that he has what Priam wants and in the sense that Priam is isolated in enemy territory. This aspect of the story hardly inspires optimism about justice as reconciliation. Priam gets the body back, but he pays for it and needs the coercive assistance of the gods to accomplish his purpose.

Thus the details of the encounter between Priam and Achilles do not bear out Van Ness and Strong's sentimental reading of it as the achievement of a reconciliatory agreement through empathic identification via emotionally present narrative. However, *another* deeply sentimental element of the story, one that Van Ness and Strong ignore, serves to further undermine the encounter as an authoritative precedent for restorative justice. I have been referring to Achilles as a wrongdoer and Priam as a victim; Achilles' wrongdoing in the desecration of Hector's corpse is the immediate wrongdoing that has prompted the intervention of the gods and made the meeting possible. However, in the broader context of the relationship, these two men are warriors whose extravagant harms to one another are grounds for mutual respect. The story partakes of the sentimental trope of heroic acknowledgment of the true greatness and glory of one's adversary. The story is primarily one of maintaining inequality until it shifts toward this sentimental connection between two famous people admiring their own celebrity. Each affirms his own magnificent strength and capacity for destructive aggression by paying homage to the similar might of the other. After concluding the agreement, Priam and Achilles share a patently sentimental, dewy-eyed moment together:

> Their thirst and hunger satisfied, Dardanian Priam let his eyes dwell on Achilles, and saw with admiration how big and beautiful he was, the very image of a god. And Achilles noted with equal admiration the noble looks and utterance of Dardanian Priam. It gave them pleasure thus to look each other over.[53]

The moment of mutual respect and affirmation of the other's dignity is directed to the other as formidable adversary and worthy warrior. They do not respect each other as vulnerable human beings with an inherent right to dignity. Though Priam is an old man, he is a great and powerful king – someone in relation to whom ten years' worth of attempts at decimation could be seen as well spent. The two men admire each other as exemplars of a military honour and greatness. If either saw the other as vulnerable victim rather than as mighty opponent they would never extend this mutual admiration. Again, the relationship is one in which the lament for the other's losses is simultaneously a form of bragging. Achilles says to Priam:

> "They say there was none to compare with you for wealth and splendid sons in all the lands that are contained by Lesbos in the sea, where Macar reigned, and Upper Phrygia and the boundless Hellespont. But ever since the Heavenly Ones brought me here to be a thorn in your side, there has been nothing but battle and slaughter around your city. You must endure and not be broken-hearted. Lamenting your son will do no good at all."[54]

Achilles' pity for Priam's loss is inseparable from his pride at having inflicted Priam's loss. He advises Priam that the code of honour onto which they both have signed demands Priam to buck up and take it like a man. It is impossible to transpose this kind of sentimental mutuality between warlike foes to the relationships, say, between a burglar and a home owner, a drunk driver and the family of his victims, a batterer and his spouse, a rapist and rape victim, or perpetrators and victims of the atrocities of apartheid.

Moreover, as Van Ness and Strong concede, the moment of mutuality occurs simultaneously with (and, I would add, is completely dependent upon) the absolute intention of both to go back to war against the other immediately after Hector's funeral. Van Ness and Strong brush this fact aside as irrelevant to the larger restorative justice point. The important thing, they argue, is that Homer sees fit to end the story with the moment of agreement and accord.[55] That the fighting resumes immediately thereafter, however, cannot be dismissed so quickly. The agreement is a "time out" in a relationship of continuing hostility and destruction. If we can posit this agreement as an important example of restorative justice, then a momentary reconciliation and embrace between a violent husband and his wife could equally be touted as a model of restorative justice, even though the husband went on to brutally beat her the next day. If we are free to stop the story wherever we want, there is no end of examples of fleeting rapprochement that can serve as authoritative precedents for justice-as-repair.

5
"Lovemaking Is Justice-Making": The Idealization of Eros and the Eroticization of Justice

There can be a strong undercurrent of eroticism in the notion of right-relation. And some proponents of justice as right-relation explicitly make the erotic connection. Lesbian, feminist theologian Carter Heyward, for example, theorizing about justice as relations of mutual empowerment and respect, has adopted the slogan "lovemaking is justice-making." Heyward places a notion of mutuality at the core of both her conception of the erotic and her conception of justice. She sees the erotic impulse as fundamentally an impulse toward, or longing for, mutuality and sees mutuality as the organizing aim of justice. The erotic impulse, by inspiring us toward greater mutuality and by giving us an intense experiential understanding of mutuality, helps us to transcend patterns of injustice.[1]

Martha Nussbaum has also argued for sexual desire as a morally significant force.[2] Like Heyward, Nussbaum commends the heightened affect of desire and romantic love as a catalyst to greater ethical sensitivity and attentiveness to the other. Thus, according to Nussbaum, the romantically desiring point of view leads toward "a most truly human morality and [morality's] fitting completion."[3] The fulfilling and passionate erotic relationship provides the most highly idealized vision of right-relation. And Nussbaum's discussion points toward not only a confluence of desire and morality, but also the most lavish vision of a confluence of love and justice. Close to Heyward's claim that lovemaking is justice-making, Nussbaum claims that there is romance in morality and morality in romance.[4]

In this chapter, I will explore in greater detail both Nussbaum's and Heyward's attempts to relate the erotic to justice and morality.[5] Neither Nussbaum nor Heyward are explicit proponents of restorative justice (though Heyward's extensive engagement with the notion of right-relation gives her closer associations with the movement itself). However, the attempts of each to relate desire to right-relation are of interest to us as efforts to strengthen the connections between positive affective concern for individuals and the struggle toward justice. They attempt to read the loving and desiring point of view as inspirations to intense states of mutual and respectful connection. They attempt to see desiring relation as offering the most intense experience of willingness to work toward repair, toward eliminating suffering and fostering renewal. Erotic relation is a metaphor for right-relation and hence for justice. In this chapter, then, I will examine both Nussbaum's and Heyward's discussion of the connections between sexual desire and romantic love, on the one hand, and justice, morality, and right-relation, on the other.

Nussbuam, Steerforth, and Adam Smith: The Conflict between Desire and Morality

Martha Nussbaum, in an essay entitled "Steerforth's Arm: Love and the Moral Point of View," takes aim at Adam Smith's discussion of romantic love and sexual desire in *A Theory of Moral Sentiments*. In talking about romantic love and sexual desire, Smith claims that we do not feel sympathy for the sexual desire or romantic love of others because we cannot imaginatively "enter in" to those passions. Nussbaum reads this claim by Smith as a sweeping dismissal of these feelings from the moral realm. Indeed, Nussbaum reads Smith as viewing love and desire as morally suspect feelings and inherently inappropriate states. Describing what she takes to be Smith's position, Nussbaum writes: "The spectator's responses are themselves constitutive of what is and is not morally appropriate. The fact that he cannot enter into love is not a sign that points beyond itself to some independently existing inappropriateness in the relation. It is the very fact that he cannot enter in that *makes* the passion inappropriate."[6]

Nussbaum turns to Charles Dickens's novel *David Copperfield* to frame her rejoinder to what she takes to be Smith's rejection of romantic love and sexual desire as moral forces. Nussbaum sees the novel as one that masterfully opposes and explores the tension between the desiring point of view and the conventionally moral point of view. She confesses to being sexually aroused by Dickens's rakish character James Steerforth. Nussbaum argues that the erotic desire Dickens inspires her to feel for Steerforth illustrates the superiority of a life-affirming morality grounded in, and enlivened by, eros. She commends this fully engaged sexual state of being as a better foundation for morality than any dour and deadening morality governed by prohibitions and prudent nay-saying.[7]

In what follows, I shall examine first whether Smith really does see love and desire as morally inappropriate feelings. I will then go on to look in more detail at Nussbaum's discussion of the romantic feelings Steerforth inspires and at her argument as to how those feelings demonstrate to us the greater richness of morality animated by desire. Finally, I shall try to show that Nussbaum and, ironically, Smith as well, miss some of the more important (but actually also more typically cited) reasons for having qualms about the moral validity of the romantic and desiring point of view.

Adam Smith and the Queasy Spectator of Sexual Love

As Nussbaum points out, Adam Smith was famously uneasy about the relationship between love and desire, on the one hand, and sympathy or compassion, on the other. Sexual desire and romantic love, according to Smith, posed prohibitively vexing problems for the judicious, impartial, and empathic spectator. The problem with both desire and love for Smith is that the spectator cannot "enter into" them. Other people's sexual desires are too physical – too decisively located in the body – and their loves too particular for us to enter into them as judicious spectators. Consider sexual desire first. Smith rejects sexual desire as the sort of thing the spectator can enter into because of its immediate location in the body. Smith argues that bodily states, including hunger, pain, and sexual desire, are problematic not because we share them with the brutes, but because the spectator cannot vicariously feel the participants' *very feelings* by observing their experience of those feelings. Smith writes:

> Such is our aversion for all the appetites which take their origin from the body: all strong expressions of them are loathsome and disagreeable. According to some ancient philosophers, these are the passions which we share in common with the brutes, and which having no connexion with the characteristical qualities of human nature, are upon that account beneath its dignity. But there are many other passions which we share in common with the brutes, such as resentment, natural affection, even gratitude, which do not, upon that account, appear to be so brutal. The true cause of the peculiar disgust which we conceive for the appetites of the body when we see them in other men, is that we cannot enter into them.[8]

This basic failure of the possibility of empathy results in the spectator perceiving the participants' feelings as disgusting and, in that sense, improper.[9]

Feelings that the spectator *can* easily go along with, according to Smith, are those arising out of some particular imaginative activity on the part of the "person principally concerned."[10] Smith sees fear as the paradigmatic instance of this sort of feeling. Fear, as Aristotle notes, is "a kind of pain or disturbance resulting from the imagination of impending danger, either destructive or painful."[11] Because fear is itself an imaginative, rather than a bodily, state, the spectator can join in vicariously by imagining the frightening thing. Hunger, physical pain, and sexual desire, because they are themselves purely bodily, are not states that the judicious spectator can feel on behalf of the persons principally concerned. William Ian Miller, in an interesting discussion of the place of disgust in the judicious spectator's moral sensibility, goes along with Smith's position on the difficulty that sexual desire poses: "Smith's observation is compelling even when the specter of pornography is raised as proof against it. Pornography does not work by vicarious emotion, but by instilling a first order passion."[12] Thus, even though one may become sexually aroused by watching another's desire and imagining its object, one becomes aroused on one's own behalf, as it were, and not on behalf of the other whom one observes.

This distinction seems reasonable enough. But let's consider whether Smith is really creating a tenable distinction here between fear as a condition springing from the imagination and sexual desire as a purely bodily condition. Surely the mind/body distinction is unstable here. First, consider the resolutely bodily aspects of the experience of fear: the racing of the heart, the quickening of the breath, or even the gasp, the rush of adrenaline, the sweat and so forth. Next, consider the necessity of imagination to sexual arousal. A compelling fantasy of a desirable sexual object and experience is precisely what engages the sexual response. Finally, consider whether the fear one experiences as the spectator of another's fear, say in the case of a very scary and suspenseful film, is any more or less a first-order passion than the sexual desire one experiences watching pornography. In both cases, it is because I enter into a vivid imagining of that which either scares or arouses the other that I too come to feel either fear or arousal. Consider the failure of either the scary or the pornographic film. If I do not, on my own behalf, think that what is being depicted is frightening or arousing, I will not be able to enter into the other's fear or desire.

We can see then, at least, that these distinctions between vicarious and first-order feelings, and between feelings generated by the imagination and bodily feelings, are very tricky indeed. Thus we already have reason to be skeptical about Smith's categories and their consequences for sympathetic response. But, before we go on to Smith's rejection of romantic love as capable of eliciting empathic response in the judicious spectator, we must consider what Smith's rejection of desire was in aid of. Recall that Smith rejects sexual desire *along with* hunger and physical pain and *for the same reason.* This move is truly astonishing. If the judicious spectator seriously has a problem of a ruffled sense of propriety when faced with the sight of another's hunger or physical pain, then one really has to wonder what possible relation the sympathy of such a spectator could have to justice or morality. Such a spectator would seem to be an absolute nightmare of hard-heartedness in relation to the worst of privations. And certainly such an understanding of the limits of sympathy would preclude it from having any relation at all to morality or justice.

But we must be careful not to leap too quickly to the conclusion that Smith means to say that the judicious spectator properly feels no sympathy for hunger, pain, or desire. In fact, Smith notes that he does not mean that there is *no* sympathy for these things.[13] Rather, I would argue that what he means to say is, first, that because the thing being felt by the person principally concerned is a bodily thing, whereas the sympathy of the other is an imaginative thing, there will be a basic and insurmountable incongruence between what the person principally concerned feels and what the spectator feels. This incongruence will always create a huge disparity between the feelings of the one and the sympathy of the other. Second, he seems to be pointing out that the loud or impassioned performance of bodily feelings does absolutely nothing to help the spectator to enter in. Such "strong expressions" of bodily feelings are repulsive to the spectator and interpose powerful feelings of disgust between the spectator and his sympathy, which in turn make it difficult for the spectator to view the other as deserving of moral attention and concern.

The problem, then, is with bodily states. While the spectator experiences some sympathy with them, the intensity of this sympathy is disproportionately slight relative to what is felt by the person principally concerned. This gap tends to alienate the spectator, making it more difficult for him to feel the moral pull of sympathy. Moreover, strong expressions of the feelings that spring from the body, instead of making identification easier for the spectator, actually make matters worse by disgusting him. Smith's reasoning here seems, then, not an attempt to dismiss the bodily feelings from the realm of the morally relevant or to call bodily feelings, in any moral sense, improper. Rather, he seems to be giving advice about the many impediments to successfully enlisting the compassion of the spectator in relation to these bodily states. Thus Smith's advice is this: If you are in physical agony, you can be reasonably confident that the spectator is likely to feel at least *some* sympathy for your physical pain (however disproportionately slight it is to what you are actually going through). But you will do yourself no good and much harm in attempting to elicit his compassion by screaming or crying out. Such a display will read as improper and will put him off. Smith writes: "To cry out with bodily pain, how intolerable soever, appears always unmanly and unbecoming."[14] Indeed, it would seem that Smith regards understatement as sympathy's steadfast ally:[15] "We are disgusted with that clamorous grief, which, without any delicacy, calls upon our compassion with sighs and tears and importunate lamentations. But we reverence that reserved, that silent and majestic, sorrow, which discovers itself only in the swelling of the eyes, in the quivering of the lips and cheeks, and in the distant, but affecting, coldness of the whole behaviour."[16]

Before dismissing Smith's advice here as outrageously prudish, we should observe that it is taken seriously by empathy-seeking advertisers all the time. Oxfam and Save the Children do not run ads depicting starving children crying out or screaming or writhing (or even whining) in the pain of their hunger. Their ads convey information about the bodily state of hunger, depicting the distended belly and the emaciated limbs and so forth. But the children themselves are just what the judicious spectator would want them to be: serene and controlled in their bodily suffering, supplicating but not accusing, wide-eyed and sorrowful but never given to "violent out-cry." And surely this strategy is taken, at least in part, because it addresses precisely the concern that Smith identifies: the likelihood that the spectator, if faced with a too demonstrative exhibition of hunger, *will* react to it as imprudent and unbecoming and *will* withdraw rather than extend his sympathy. So Smith's point about bodily conditions seems to be not that they should be rejected from the morally relevant sphere of sympathy, but that they pose particularly difficult problems for eliciting sympathy and hence for commanding moral attention. Most importantly, one's strategies with the spectator in relation to this category of feeling have to be subtle and controlled and must make compelling appeals to other, more imaginatively based feelings that the spectator will not find improper and will be inclined to go along with.

Still Nussbaum takes Smith to mean that the spectator's disgust is an indication that bodily feelings such as hunger, physical pain, and sexual desire are in some sense morally inappropriate feelings. Recall Nussbaum's conclusion: "The spectator's responses are themselves constitutive of what is and is not morally appropriate. The fact that he cannot enter into love is not a sign that points beyond itself to some independently existing inappropriateness in the relation. It is the very fact that he cannot enter in that *makes* the passion inappropriate."[17] Thus, according to Nussbaum, Smith is saying that the spectator's inability to enter into erotic desire makes that desire morally problematic. I hesitate to adopt this interpretation of Smith, recalling that whatever Smith is saying about desire, he is also, according to the structure of his argument, saying it about hunger and physical pain and *for the very same reasons*. It would seem again that this absurd result would militate against this interpretation. Smith can't possibly mean that the victim is behaving inappropriately insofar as he is starving to death or having his leg cut off or that hunger or physical anguish are "morally inappropriate passions." Nevertheless, Nussbaum takes Smith to mean that these feelings themselves are inappropriate and thus without a proper place in the field of moral sentiments.

Nussbaum also takes Smith to be making the same negative moral judgment about romantic love. Certainly Smith warrants that the judicious spectator will not easily accept an invitation to enter into the romantic loves of others.[18] Although love is no mere bodily feeling and springs sufficiently from the imagination of the person principally concerned, it is too particular, too idiosyncratic, to be felt vicariously by others. The spectator just "doesn't get it." The spectator can't see what is so enthralling about the beloved. Therefore, Smith argues, the spectator is always going to see romantic love as an irrational and possibly comical overvaluation of the beloved far out of proportion with his or her actual worth. Thus George Bernard Shaw's insufferably sexist quip that "love consists in overestimating the differences between one woman and another" points to the precise blind spot that renders Smith's spectator incapable of sympathizing.[19] The lover focuses on and values those adorable little particulars of the beloved that, for any impartial observer, remain undistinguished. The road that the lover's imagination must travel in order to arrive at love for another is far too long and narrow for the spectator to follow: "Our imagination not having run in the same channel with that of the lover, we cannot enter into the eagerness of his emotions."[20]

Interestingly, it is not the same with the *loss* of a love. Smith says that grief at the loss of a mistress is in fact easier for the judicious spectator to enter into than is physical anguish at the loss of a leg![21] The loss of a leg is one of those bodily pains that the spectator has trouble with, whereas the loss of the mistress is one with which he can readily, imaginatively identify. Likewise, the "expectations of romantic happiness" arising out of romantic love *are* feelings that the judicious spectator can enter into, these again not being contingent upon an understanding of the particular attachment. Inasmuch as we recognize that we ourselves are subject to states of romantic love, we can sympathize with the hopes and disappointments springing from that condition. "But though we feel no proper sympathy with an attachment of this kind, though we never approach even in imagination towards conceiving a passion for that particular person, yet as we either have conceived, or may be disposed to conceive, passions of the same kind, we readily enter into those high hopes of happiness which are proposed from its gratification as well as into that exquisite distress which is feared from its disappointment."[22]

Now, once again, Smith's discussion here is open to the interpretation that it is merely advice to seekers of the judicious spectator's sympathy as to when and why they are going to run into trouble in getting him on board. Perhaps, then, like his discussion of desire, Smith's discussion of romantic love is less a judgment about the appropriateness of love than it is an account of the barriers to enlisting the spectator's sympathy for the particular loves of others. It is an explanation of why the spectator's sympathy for love (like his sympathy for desire) will be – however regrettably – weak. Smith's discussion of both sexual desire and romantic love seems, then, to be a description of some limits of spontaneous sympathy – a caution to lovers that they are faced with serious difficulties in getting the spectator's sympathy – rather than a rejection of either bodily states or romantic love as feelings morally deserving of sympathetic identification.

However, the matter does not end here because Nussbaum also supports her interpretation of Smith as disapproving of love and desire on the grounds of their moral insignificance by highlighting a subtler aspect of Smith's discussion. She suggests that Smith's misgivings about romantic love and desire stem from his conclusion that they – being emotions that others can't enter into – do not contribute in helpful ways to the creation of a moral community. Love and desire work to isolate the lovers from the rest of the community in a relation of intimacy, exclusivity of communication, and privateness of feeling that is unintelligible to the rest of us. Being so thoroughly relational, private, individualized, and exclusive, love and desire, though they are experiences we all participate in, do not contribute to the ways in which we, as members of moral communities, are able to join together in collective judgments about moral value.

William Ian Miller takes up this point when he contrasts the potential for love and disgust to arouse collective or communal feelings around agreed-upon moral judgments. Following Smith, Miller writes: "I would suggest that the reason love lamentably has not had much historical success as the sentiment upon which a moral community can be built is that it cannot be readily entered into by third parties. We can, for instance, readily enter into disgust on someone's behalf for their having been defiled or indignation for their having been wronged or harmed, but we cannot readily feel the love or jealousy another enjoys or suffers; those feelings are always personal, *sui generis,* and somewhat incommunicable."[23] Thus, while we can all join in a communal experience of disgust at the violation of agreed-upon moral norms, and while this collective experience of disgust will perhaps strengthen both those norms and the community, we can't have the same kind of simultaneous, spontaneous, and morally significant experience when it comes to love. And this deficiency of love – its being too private to form the foundation of moral consensus – ousts it, however lamentably, from the arena of moral sentiment. No matter how much we might like to be able to, no matter how much morally better human life might be if we could, we simply can't bond as a community of spectators of others' experiences of love; thus we must set love aside as a foundation for moral thinking.

Recall that Nussbaum's purpose here is to refute this view of love. She is arguing in support of the importance of participation in loving-relation as a morally significant activity, as well as claiming the significance of the particular love relation to the moral point of view. I will try to show now that while Nussbaum does not convincingly demonstrate how romantic love and desire contribute to morality, her discussion of James Steerforth unintentionally disproves Smith's and Miller's contention that we do not, as spectators, vicariously enter into other people's romantic love. Nussbaum's discussion shows that we do this all the time as spectators of other people's love and, what is more, that our judgments about the romantically loveable are not at all idiosyncratic or particular. In fact, we have every bit as much communal convergence around those judgments as we do around our judgments about the disgusting. Moreover, in pointing this out, Nussbaum, though clearly inadvertently, points to reasons not identified by Smith at all for viewing love and desire as morally suspect, as passions unable to ground moral community.

Nussbaum, in arguing for the moral significance of the loving point of view, uses the example of the mass wave of romantic love and erotic desire for the fictional character James Steerforth in Charles Dickens's novel *David Copperfield*. Nussbaum opens her discussion of the novel by telling the story of her own teenage daughter falling in love with Steerforth. She reports her initial, purely judgmental reaction to both Steerforth and her daughter's enchantment. However, despite all Steerforth's evildoing, upon rereading the novel, Nussbaum confesses to falling in love too. Nussbaum's initial schoolmarmish disapproval was no doubt inspired by the fact that Steerforth is both insufferably conceited and breathtakingly inconsiderate of others. Steerforth is guilty of numerous malicious and harmful acts, most notably his deliberate humiliation and ruination of the school teacher, Mr. Mell, and his heartless seduction of Em'ly and subsequent refusal to marry her because she is too far beneath him in social standing.[24] Yet, despite this conduct, Nussbaum responds gleefully, doing precisely what Smith says we don't do – that is, "entering into" the romantic love for Steerforth that is felt by so many characters in the novel, from David himself[25] to Em'ly, Rosa Dartle, Steerforth's mother, and even the lugubrious Mrs. Gummidge. Nussbaum describes her seduction by Steerforth's character: "I felt my heart quite suddenly take itself off, rushing happily from the firmness of judgment to the eager volatility of desire."[26]

Nussbaum's main point is that this space of desire and abandonment to romantic love is, indeed, morally significant. It is from this space of desire that we become full participants and not mere spectators. The novel that "beckons to us erotically" and seduces us to full participation in human "being" is not morally suspect for having done so. It is in the unreserved relationality of romantic love that we find the most active moral stance toward the other. Thus, Nussbaum writes, "the posture of the heart that is best for morality – most vivid, most gentle and generous, most active in sympathy – is also more susceptible and less judgmental ... and is bound, in its mobile attention to particulars, to fall in love, and to feel for the object that it loves a non-judgmental loyalty that no moral authority, however judicious, can dislodge."[27]

Further, Nussbaum argues that the sort of love for fictional characters that we experience as readers of novels is one that interacts with and enhances the sort of directly participatory love that we experience in our relationships. In a rich and complex passage, Nussbaum writes:

> Here David shows that love in life interacts in complicated ways with fantasy, memory and projection. That, indeed, insofar as it involves endowing a perceived form with a mind and heart, in this way going beyond the evidence, it is always a kind of generous fiction-making. All love is, in that sense, love of fictional characters; and literature trains us for that element in love. This fiction-making, we clearly see here, need not be pernicious or self-deceptive. His fantasy has led David outside himself to see Steerforth with love and to focus generously on his actual presence. Fantasy and a genuine relatedness are mutually supportive, as the imagining of the play makes him more keenly aware of what is outside him and prompts a generous outpouring of feeling.[28]

There is much of interest here. We are being asked to conclude that David is able – as a participatory novel reader himself and as a result of his passionate and emotionally active relation to fictional characters – to endow another person before him with the qualities of mind and heart. Others, on the evidence (that evidence being our sensory perception of body and voice), have nothing much going on inside. But fiction fills us in on what is not obvious from just looking at and listening to those around us – that is, the richness of their inner lives. So in life, when we are faced with others, fiction helps us make the imaginative effort to attribute these things to them and thereby to come to the kind of particular understanding of others that will support love toward them. All of this is convincing. Literature helps us to an awareness of the existence of the complex inner workings of the minds and lives of others and in this sense educates the compassionate moral sensibility.[29]

Yet, while we can readily go along with these observations, we should stop short of following Nussbaum to conclude that all love is in this sense fiction-making and that one's attribution of a mind and heart to the other is a form of fantasy. In loving-relation, although one most generously trusts in and feels from an awareness of the existence and immediacy of the other's mind and heart, one also ideally looks for authentic evidence *from the other* about what is going on in his or her inner life of mind and heart. The task of the lover is surely to pay attention to the beloved and to search for evidence of their inner state. The lover makes space for disclosure of the reality of the other's inner life and – ever aware of the dangers of his or her own incomplete understandings of the other – is eager for correction. The lover doesn't merely make up his or her own sense of the beloved's inner life as a playful activity of loving fiction-making. Further, the lover must, first and foremost, seek conversation precisely to ensure that his or her sense of the subjectivity of the other, and the enlivened understanding of the other's inner life, is not based on his or her own projections, either wholly made up or inspired by fiction.

This point is significant and directs us to a larger problem with Nussbaum's argument. Nussbaum points to David's love for Steerforth as an example of a sort of romantic and loving fiction-making that is neither "pernicious [n]or self-deceptive." According to Nussbaum, David's love for Steerforth is one where "fantasy and a genuine relatedness are mutually supportive." Yet, as we see in the unfolding of the novel, David's love for Steerforth is both self-deceptive *and* pernicious. David's romantic, fictional attribution of qualities of *noble* heart and mind to Steerforth is inaccurate. David's, Em'ly's, Nussbaum's, and our own love for Steerforth, although it disproves Smith's contention that we do not enter into romantic love of others as spectators, reveals some genuinely morally problematic aspects of romantic love that Smith does not mention. Though we enter into love of Steerforth, though we are charmed by his good looks, charisma, quick wit, vitality, and masterful engagement with the world, Steerforth is, nevertheless, a seriously harmful person. What this awareness, which Nussbaum largely glosses over, leads us to recognize is, first, that romantic love – especially insofar as it is inspired by and enmeshed with romantic fiction and cultural tropes of romantic heroes and heroines – mixes up the idealized fantasy of the romantic hero with the flesh and blood beloved. In so doing, the lover mistakenly attributes qualities of mind and heart to the beloved that he or she may well not have. The romantic lover gets caught up in an unsubstantiated fantasy of the beloved as conforming to a romantic ideal. For this reason romantic love (famously) has the capacity to be both dangerous and fickle. Relying on their fictional romantic projections, as David and Em'ly do, lovers do not protect themselves from the consequences of the potential gap between the cluster of good qualities they project onto the beloved and the reality of the beloved's character. Therein lies the danger. Moreover, after getting a good look at this gap, the lover is often quite likely to respond to the now former beloved (and often to him- or herself as well) with disgust rather than with love. Therein lies the fickleness.

David's love for Steerforth is obviously morally problematic in this sense. David is drawn in by Steerforth's power, his wealth, his good looks, and his enjoyment of and attention to David. But, in his enchantment, David mistakenly attributes to Steerforth a large number of positive characteristics (like honour, kindness, honesty, and, most important, indifference to class distinction) that Steerforth absolutely doesn't have. This self-delusion leads David to trust Steerforth in ways that he shouldn't, and this trust subsequently leads to serious damage to other people, particularly to Em'ly and her Uncle Peggotty. The romantic mistake doesn't lead to excessive damage for David himself. Luckily for David, Steerforth dies in a storm at sea before David has to confront his error in his relationship with Steerforth. Indeed, both of David's romantic errors – his first wife Dora Spenlow and Steerforth – die before David ever has to really confront the gap between the qualities he projected onto them and the reality of who they were. David loves Dora for her beauty and lightness of spirit and, in his romantic zeal, attributes to her even earnestness, which she clearly does not possess.[30] The point at which David reconciles himself to her shallowness is precisely the point at which Dora becomes ill – and, very soon thereafter, she dies. Thus David is spared from having to tough it out in a relationship after romantic disillusionment.

David isn't called upon to stick it out with Steerforth either. Love might have served as an energy holding David and Steerforth in relation and assisting them in dealing with each other as equals.[31] But one suspects that if David were no longer a star-crossed admirer, Steerforth would no longer find any charm in David's company. Thus, while romantic love *can* be an energy that propels the sort of authentic and vital engagement that Nussbaum wants us to view as having moral significance, the romantic love that we are seduced to enter into for Steerforth proves, more than anything, romantic love's notorious capacity for moral blindness and mischief.

The second morally problematic aspect of romantic love, which Steerforth also demonstrates, is that rather than being overly particular (as Smith suggests it is), romantic love tends to conform, all too predictably, to communally agreed-upon standards about what is and isn't romantically desirable. And, while we take these attributes to be largely morally irrelevant, we are ever so willing to go along with – to enter into – romantic love as spectators when the beloved possesses characteristics that conform to these quite predictable and culturally agreed-upon notions of the loveable.

We must concede Smith's point that we don't, as spectators, enter into love of the run-of-the-mill beloved whose particular charms, though captivating enough for the lover, leave the rest of us cold. But Steerforth is not an idiosyncratic taste. Thus, while Dickens has an easy time seducing us to enter into romantic love for Steerforth, he would have had quite an uphill battle had he attempted (which he wouldn't have) to get us to enter into the faithful old nurse Clara Peggotty's romantic love for the aging driver Mr. Barkas, or Mrs. Micawber's long-suffering and steadfast romantic love for her ever-insolvent and loquacious husband, Mr. Micawber. So, while the communally-entered-into love for Steerforth proves Adam Smith wrong in his conclusion that we don't, in our capacity as spectators, enter into other people's love, the novel as a whole also proves

Smith partially right: insofar as we do consider romantic love to be idiosyncratic, we react to the sight of it with, at worst, disgust and, at best, a mystified sense of it as basically comical.

Evidence abounds, however, that we do enter into love as spectators all the time *and* that we enter into it as communities of judgment about the loveable. Consider our celebrity culture. As spectators, we gleefully enter into Billy Crystal's love for Meg Ryan, Meg's love for Tom Hanks and so forth. And we enter precisely in the vicarious sense to which Smith accords moral significance; that is, we don't love Meg Ryan on our own behalf, but we are willing to enter into a feeling of love for her *on behalf of* Billy or Tom or whomever. But, at the same time as we have well-defined and communally agreed-upon standards of who is and isn't a credible object of romantic love, we are also aware that the characteristics that qualify someone as a credible romantic hero or heroine are not morally significant. Thus it seems clear that the second problem with romantic love is this: to the extent that we are inclined to enter into romantic love, we do so not at all idiosyncratically but as cultural communities and, in so doing, we elevate as loveable people with characteristics that we know have no particular moral value.

Thus Miller's point that we have an easier time entering into disgust than into love on someone else's behalf perhaps needs qualification. It is not that we don't enter into love either as willingly or as communally as we enter into disgust. Rather, to the extent that we are eager to enter into love as spectators, we do so on the basis of judgments and standards that – though widely agreed upon – are, in our better judgment, morally ridiculous. So we enter into love in precisely the same way that we enter into disgust – that is, when we agree about the judgments behind it, when we collectively see the object as either loveable or disgusting. It would be difficult to try to show that we have more agreement as spectators about what is loveable than about what is disgusting. Indeed, our agreement about one often stems from and arises out of our agreement about the other. The moral problem, then, with love as a basis for moral community is not that it is too particular but rather that its very well-settled norms are not morally grounded – and perhaps also that we cannot take morally seriously the communities of consensus to which it gives rise. For example, we hardly consider the community of North American teenage girls who as spectators enter into love for Josh Hartnet an important moral community. Here it may be not merely that we trivialize the community because its members are young and female, but that groups of such teenage girls who share this emotion do not constitute or function as communities at all; they are merely disconnected groups of people with similar tastes. While the problem with disgust as a foundation for moral community is perhaps that it is a little too promiscuous – in other words, that it doesn't reliably attach to valuable moral norms – the problem with love as a foundation for moral community is that we just can't get it to be promiscuous enough; it sticks too closely to our widely agreed-upon standards of the lovable, which have no meaningful relation to morality.[32]

It is difficult in the end to know how to respond to Nussbaum's claims about the connection between eros and morality, or eros and right-relation, as it is depicted in *David Copperfield*. Much of the difficulty stems from the fact that it is not at all clear what she means to say. She simply can't be saying that David's love for Steerforth is a force that pulls him into relations of equality and respect with Steerforth. The novel consistently reveals David's love as a force that urges him to accept a one-down, less-than position in relation to Steerforth, to forsake his own better judgment, and to sacrifice himself for the sake of Steerforth's ego time and again. So Nussbaum can't be making any claims about the capacity for romantic love to lead people into relations of equality and respect.

What Nussbaum must be presenting as morally commendable, rather, is the sensibility willing to venture an abandonment of self to the excitement and risk of romantic idealization of another. And she is arguing that this sensibility is morally preferable to that which cautiously withholds adoration with an eye to the potential negative consequences of indulgence. The more sophisticated the romantic sensibility – that is, the more it incorporates the sublime literary expressions of desire into its state of entrancement – the more morally significant it will be. It is the willingness to see a beloved other as worthy of almost infinite attention that, for Nussbaum, defines the heightened affective state in which the lover is more fully present to another and, hence, closest in perspective to the most fully human moral point of view.

Yet in *David Copperfield* admixtures of other baser motives routinely take the edge off of whatever moral quality can be attributed to romantic fascination. David's and Em'ly's loves for Steerforth are mixed with, and motivated by, social ambition. Steerforth's love for David is mixed with and motivated by the desire for a disciple. His love for Em'ly is mixed with lust and an exploitive fascination with innocence. David's romantic love for Dora Spendlow is mixed with and motivated by astonishment at the possibility of his sexual success. Her love for him is mixed with and motivated by the desire for secure bourgeois respectability.

Thus again there are all kinds of reasons to distrust romantic passion as a moral force. Indeed, the romantic passion that has the best chance of being morally significant is that idiosyncratic unenter-into-able sort that attends to and attributes a transcendent value to the particulars of one who would otherwise seem nondescript. Mr. Barkas's love for Clara Peggotty, the middle-aged, portly, kind-hearted nurse, is touching precisely because Barkas is enlivened by his awareness of a transcendent precious-ness in her. His love resists direction from the morally irrelevant cultural consensus about the desirable. Ironically, then, we have turned Smith's intuition on its head. While we have what amounts to a cultural obses-sion with entering into romantic passion for the predictable objects of desire, this romantic love into which we so readily enter on behalf of others has very little to say for itself morally. By contrast, the love that is singular to the point of being unintelligible to the spectator has far greater potential as a force that might enable us, by focusing on the dis-tinctiveness of the individual beloved, to do what we ought to do, but can't, in all our relationships – that is, to view the other as a miraculous human original.

Carter Heyward and Lovemaking as Justice-Making: Eroticizing Justice and Making the Erotic Just

Lesbian, feminist theologian Carter Heyward goes much further than Nussbaum in theorizing eros as a force toward right-relation. Heyward sees the erotic impulse as a longing for mutuality. And she sees mutual-ity as the essence of justice.[33] In Heyward's terminology, then, "love-making is justice-making."[34] Eros and justice share an elemental bond to mutuality that links and reconciles the two: "Justice, the actualization of love among us, is the making of right, or mutual, relation."[35] Heyward relates and entwines love and justice through the idea of right-relation. Her discussion is essentially an eroticized version of Christopher Mar-shall's claim that love and justice are reconcilable if we view "justice in relational and liberationist terms, justice as the existence of right-relationships, where there is no exploitation, and all parties exercise appropriate power."[36] Heyward makes this idea sexual. She explains her project as follows: "I am reflecting on the erotic as our embodied yearn-ing for mutuality ... In these pages, with Audre Lorde, I want 'to write fire,' to be erotic – touching, pressing, making connections, contributing what I can to the forging of that mutuality which characterizes right-relation or justice."[37]

Heyward relates mutuality to equality, relationality, and mutual em-powerment through relation. The erotic mutuality Heyward envisions is unreserved intersubjective engagement: abandonment to trust, open-heartedness, and empathic presence to the other. It connotes a shared and ultimate good in the relation that transcends but enhances the indi-vidual benefit of each. It connotes both superabundance and insatiabil-ity. Heyward draws on and eroticizes Martin Buber's understanding of the "I-Thou" as opposed to the "I-It" relation. For both Buber and Heyward, this idealized sense of relationality is about total presence to the other. Heyward writes:

> But what is justice? I invite you to think beyond the images of jurispru-
> dence and legalism often associated with justice in patriarchal, andro-
> centric society into a realm of radical relationality. In this realm, justice
> is right-relation and right-relation is mutual relation. In a mutual rela-
> tionship both (or all) people are empowered to experience one another
> as intrinsically valuable, irreplaceable earthcreatures, sources of joy and
> love and respect in relation to one another. To experience ourselves gen-
> uinely as friends: This is justice.[38]

For Heyward, the yearning for mutuality as unreserved engagement, a
yearning most immediately felt in the erotic impulse, is the most significant power source available in the struggle toward justice. Like Audre Lorde,
Heyward sees the erotic as a tremendously positive source of strength.[39]
Heyward does not deny, however, that the erotic impulse may also long
to dominate and humiliate. She concedes that the erotic is not a force
that necessarily enures to justice. Yet Heyward envisages a sort of primal,
pre-patriarchal erotic drive latent within us all that can be nurtured and
cultivated toward the creation of both fulfilling erotic connections and
just relationships in all other contexts of life.

As Heyward infuses her conception of justice with a positive erotic connotation, so does she negatively eroticize injustice. She identifies a poi-
sonous eros inherent in all wrongdoing. Heyward thus refers to relations
of unequal power, where the parties are not engaged in the project of
struggling toward equality as sadomasochistic:[40] "Few people in Euro-
american culture are strangers to feelings of sadomasochism in our social
relations, including our sexual relationships, regardless of how we may act.
Ours is a society focused on the dynamics of control and subjugation.
None can escape the psychosexual or spiritual fallout of such a system."[41]
Nevertheless, Heyward is optimistic that the erotic impulse toward mutuality can find its beginnings within sadomasochistic relationships of all kinds:
"Can sadomasochistic eroticism be a relational conduit through which
we move toward mutuality ...? The answer is that it *must* be. Because we
can reach each other and God only from where we are here and now."[42]

For Heyward, absence of mutuality is the source of all injustice, and
the pull toward mutuality is the way out of all injustice. Sex is relevant
because mutuality is most vividly conceived in its most embodied, hence
its erotic, form. Heyward has (at least) two concurrent aims. The first is
to give us a richer, more lavish, and unbounded (and, well, yes, a sexier)
understanding of justice. Her second aim is to give erotic desire (and especially lesbian desire) greater public or civic legitimacy and significance by
casting it as inextricably related to justice.

Heyward's discussion of justice as right- or mutual-relation is directed
to social justice and the struggle for equality for the dispossessed. She sees

the end goal of that struggle as a world in which there is a web of mutual (right and just) relations. Though many will not be sexual, all will partake of that virtue of mutuality most vividly present in the paradigm case: the happy sexual connection. Good sex propels us toward that more mutual world,[43] says Heyward, "Good sex involves us more fully in the struggle for justice – as, or with, people of color, women, differently-abled people, ethnic and religious minorities, elderly people and other earth-creatures."[44]

Though Heyward does not explicitly theorize mutual eros in the context of the victim-offender encounter, it is not unusual to see practitioners of restorative justice going so far as to eroticize right-relation as the end goal of justice. Recall, for example, from Chapter 3, Archbishop Desmond Tutu's analogies to lovers' quarrels in the context of the proceedings of the South African Truth and Reconciliation Commission. Tutu speaks of the process of dealing with the atrocities of apartheid as akin to husband and wife making up after a fight. The route is apology and forgiveness. The destination is loving erotic embrace.

One obvious problem with viewing justice in these terms is that it virtually obliterates the possibility of justice for victims of sexual assault. Let's take an example. Joe adores Susan. He longs for oceanic, erotic mutuality with her. She finds Joe repulsive and doesn't want to have anything to do with him. Giving too much ground to his longing for mutuality (again a longing we are supposed to understand as having a strong relation to justice), Joe rapes Susan.[45] Now Susan wants justice. But what do we have to offer her if our paradigm of justice is mutual embrace? Susan didn't want mutual embrace, and Joe violated her right to refuse it. When justice has been defined in such perilous proximity to the wrongdoing itself, how do we separate the two?

Moreover, is there any way of promoting restorative justice here that doesn't re-eroticize the relationship between Joe and Susan? How can we think of justice in these terms without betraying Susan's desire for sexual integrity, her right to be left alone, her right to reciprocal noninterference and emotional disengagement from Joe?[46] The erotic resonances of right-relation tell Joe that justice will be done when his victim comes around or at least when the two have reconciled somehow. To use Heyward's terminology, the sadomasochism of Joe's violent desire may be a "relational conduit" through which victim and offender can "move toward mutuality." But if mutual embrace is the goal of justice, this goal leaves very little conceptual space for justice as the strict enforcement of personal boundaries. If justice is "to experience ourselves genuinely as friends," it is difficult to know what justice has to offer Susan when she doesn't want to be friends with Joe.

We don't even have to look to sexual assault to see how frightening it is to adopt a conception of justice that by definition encourages engagement and mutual embrace. For any kind of violation, robbery, assault, murder, fraud, or what have you, to orient ourselves toward an ideal of justice as mutual embrace is invariably to ask the victim to let go of her desire for and right to noninterference, her right resolutely to exclude the wrongdoer from her field of vision and her circle of concern. If justice *is* mutual embrace, justice can't rule out mutual embrace.

And a justice that can't rule out mutual embrace is unhelpful in the context of violence against women. What women often need and want *(and they want it as a matter of justice)* is freedom from an unwanted relation.[47] They don't want right-relation. They want no relation. And they want to be able to look to a powerful and trustworthy state capable of effectively prohibiting relation. And they want this to be a justice-based entitlement due them as citizens. What they do not want (though throughout history this is what they have most often gotten) is a "supportive" community bent on cajoling them into the project of repair of relations.

How then can we endorse a conception of justice that by definition always sees absence of mutual relation as a failure of justice? Consider domestic violence. Can justice as mutuality in this context be anything other than a trendy version of the age-old advice to the battered woman to keep trying to make it work, to keep hoping that love and the erotic connection between victim and offender will work itself pure to a better, happier, more mutual relation? Could a battered woman ever demand *as a matter of justice* the right to rid herself of all connection with a violent spouse if justice means mutuality best understood as eros or embrace? It would seem that Heyward thinks not: "The fear of mutuality is the fear of our intrinsic interrelatedness, the fact that literally I am nobody without you ... This fear is so deeply structured into our social organization and psyches that we have learned not only to accept it as normal but also to affirm it as a good sign of the healthy self, separate and independent ... In this milieu, white middle-strata women's quest for independence is a slippery slope ... Coming out from under we must be careful not to set ourselves against the realization that we need one another."[48]

Yet doesn't the fear Heyward describes seem well founded? Shouldn't we fear a conception of justice that says that I am literally nobody without the thief who stole my bike? Shouldn't we fear more deeply still a conception of justice that says that Susan is literally nobody without Joe, and yet more deeply a conception of justice that says the black victims of apartheid are literally nobody without the white perpetrators of apartheid's atrocities?[49] Most of the time victims don't need wrongdoers, and they are more happily themselves without them. Heyward's notion of mutuality is self-avowedly at cross purposes with an insistence on disengagement. But justice has to be able to honour the right to refuse mutuality, to insist on noninterference and resist all connection with the wrong-doer. Yet, if we accept right-relation as the core of justice, unless we say that right-relation sometimes means no relation, which is basically to strip the idea of right-relation of any meaning whatsoever, breaking relations is always counter to justice.

Yet many restorative success stories, while stopping short of seeing justice in terms of erotic embrace, posit mutually emotionally present and affirming embrace as the ruling idea of justice-as-repair. The ultimate postrestoration goal is empathic embrace between victim and offender. Consider, for example, a story told by restorative justice advocate and Watergate convict Charles Colson about a prisoner, Ron Flowers, and his victim's mother, an African-American woman named Mrs. Washington. Flowers shot and killed Mrs. Washington's daughter. As a result of the daughter's death, both Mrs. Washington's son and her husband also died, leaving Mrs. Washington completely alone. After fourteen years in prison, Flowers agreed to participate in a restorative justice program. During the encounter with Mrs. Washington, Flowers, after years of denial, confessed his crime, apologized, and promised to change. And Mrs. Washington forgave Ron. But this was not all: "During the graduation [apparently there was a ceremony for people who had successfully participated in the process] ... Mrs Washington walked over and embraced him. She then turned to the crowd of volunteers, mentors, inmates, and corrections officials, announcing that Ron Flowers was now her adopted son."[50]

Unreserved emotional loving embrace is the ultimate for restorative justice. Colson goes on to tell us that someone had donated $10,000 to help Mrs. Washington and that she in turn had used half the money to help Flowers adjust to life outside of prison. The two then met every Sunday. Colson tells the story as a moving testimonial to the wonderful possibilities of restorative justice.

But can we unreservedly celebrate this mutual emotional embrace, and, more importantly, can we call it justice? He kills her daughter, and she makes him her son and gives him the money that was intended to help her. No matter how healing it may be for Mrs. Washington and Ron Flowers to be together now as mother and adopted son, there is no way that we can see this situation as one where a fair balance has been struck, no way that we can, from a position of authority, make this situation normative (in the sense of either normal or good) for victims of crime. We can, however, see Mrs. Washington as someone so desperate for mutuality, and so destitute of other opportunities for it, that she is willing to reach out to and connect with the only person available for intense relation – who, sadly, happens to be the man who killed her daughter. We can also see Mrs. Washington as a saint. Either way Ron Flowers is the beneficiary of her almost pathological kindness. But to allow this emotional mutuality, which is supported entirely by the gross supererogation of the victim, to become our standard for justice is to abandon the commitment to fairness altogether. Certainly we are fascinated, amazed, and horrified by stories of such drastic turnings of the other cheek. We are irresistibly drawn to their drama. But if we design our institutions of justice with an intention to set the stage for this genre of self-sacrificial play, we will eventually breed ever greater anger, resentment, and violence.

The theatrical moment of mutual embrace looks like a resolution. But let's ask what happens later when Mrs. Washington begins to wonder how her daughter would feel about having been sold out so cheaply, when Ron Flowers doesn't show up for his Sunday afternoon visit to Mrs. Washington for weeks in a row, and when Mrs. Washington desperately needs the money that she gave to him? How then is she going to keep on validating her choice to embrace him as her son, and how is she going to hold on to an understanding of that choice as an instance of justice? The moment of cathartic embrace is, indeed, the least demanding. In that moment she becomes an instant hero and celebrity. But much greater and less glamorous supererogation will be required, and many more serious risks will be run, in the months and years to come when the mutuality of this relation is put to the test. And here we need to ask ourselves why – when we are finite beings with limited opportunities to create mutuality in our relations and when real emotional mutuality is so rare and so fragile – we would ever commit to a conception of criminal justice that points us toward this goal in the context of the victim-offender relation.

My guess is that for Heyward the answer is an instrumental one. She defines justice in terms of embrace primarily as a strategy for valorizing lesbian sex. But surely she is being irresponsible here. Surely there are ways of celebrating and legitimating lesbian desire that don't do quite so much damage to the notion of justice. To be fair to Heyward, however, her slogan is "lovemaking is justice-making" and not the reverse. Her claim is that by having (good) sex we are creating more justice in the world. "Doing it" (well) creates a bigger pie of the mutuality that defines justice. Her primary aim, then, is to give sex justice value. But this is evidently a self-interested aim driven by the desire to tie lesbian eroticism to other social values and virtues. Certainly we have for centuries sold ourselves a line about how heterosexual sex within marriage is linked to all kinds of other social values and virtues such as loyalty, industry, procreation, stability, and so forth.[51] And heterosexual guilt and embarrassment about sex has for centuries been assuaged by this insistence on the instrumental value of sex in reproducing not just the species, but also these other public virtues. Of course, few queer theorists would ever want to link up queer sex and the sort of traditional family values that have vindicated conventional married heterosexual sex, nor could they link it to the (dubious) good of reproduction.[52] Indeed, Heyward's queer commitments require that she include even the most ephemeral and nonmonogamous erotic relations as potentially partaking of the mutuality she relates so strongly to justice.[53] Thus, in casting around for high-minded but less stuffily bourgeois values to associate with lesbian sex, right-relation presents itself as an attractive alternative. It is a public social good that can be tied to lesbian sex while also honouring other lesbian commitments to resisting conventionality.

However, I think we should question this whole project of linking sex to other virtues. Sex is sex. It isn't stability, loyalty, industry, creativity, or justice. Sometimes people who have sex a lot are also just, or creative, or loyal, or industrious, or stable. And sometimes they're not any of these things. And sometimes people who don't have sex at all are stable, or loyal, or creative, or industrious, and/or just. And sometimes they're not any of these either. Of course, if people like to think about justice when they are having sex, there is no reason whatever to stop them. But there is a reason to resist this proposed equivocation between private sex and public justice since, in many circumstances, justice – to be justice at all – must be free of connotations of embrace, erotic or otherwise. And we have reason to resist this attempt to persuade us to redirect public resources *away from* the struggle to create institutions of justice that credibly and coercively back the victim's desire to erase an unwanted connection with the wrongdoer *and toward* institutions that attempt to promote and facilitate justice as mutual embrace. We have a reason to oppose any channeling of resources away from institutions that at least try, as a matter of justice, to put an end to the relation between victim and wrongdoer. And we have reason to oppose the diverting of those resources to institutions that understand justice "to be a *mutual* relation that generates joy and justice and a desire for more of the relation."[54]

6
Compulsory Compassion: Justice, Fellow-Feeling, and the Restorative Encounter

"Oh, poor mother, poor father!" said Mary, her eyes filling with tears, and a little sob rising which she tried to repress. She looked straight before her and took no notice of Fred, all the consequences at home becoming present to her. He too remained silent for some moments, feeling more miserable than ever. "I wouldn't have hurt you for the world, Mary," he said at last. "You can never forgive me."

"What does it matter whether I forgive you?" said Mary, passionately. "Would that make it any better for my mother to lose the money she has been earning by lessons for four years, that she might send Alfred to Mr. Hanmer's? Should you think all that pleasant enough if I forgave you?"

"Say what you like, Mary. I deserve it all."

"I don't want to say anything," said Mary, more quietly; "my anger is of no use ..."

"I do care about your mother's money going," he said, when she was seated again and sewing quickly." ...

"I am so miserable, Mary – if you knew how miserable I am, you would be sorry for me."

"There are other things to be more sorry for than that. But selfish people always think their own discomfort of more importance than anything else in the world. I see enough of that every day."

"It is hardly fair to call me selfish. If you knew what things other young men do, you would think me a good way off the worst."

– George Eliot, *Middlemarch*

I have been approaching restorative justice primarily at its most spiritually ambitious: its aspiration to reconcile love and justice. Though I maintain that this aspiration, and the force of this longing, are at the foundation of much of the persuasive pull of restorative justice, it is also clear that some restorative justice thinkers would repudiate such a lofty and abstract aim. They would argue that to view restorative justice in terms of such an extravagantly idealistic and transcendental claim is to caricature restorative justice and thereby to obscure its considerable strengths. A more moderate and accurate claim, they might say, would be that restorative justice aspires to an easier, more immediate, though always partial and provisional, relation between compassion and fellow-feeling, on the one hand, and justice and accountability, on the other. We ought not, therefore, to dismiss restorative justice on the basis of these grandiose spiritual versions of it while ignoring its more modest and commonsensical claims. To do so would be to throw the baby out with the holy water.

The procedural structure and personal intimacy of restorative justice, it is claimed, allow us to conceive in new and more promising ways the relation not necessarily between love itself and justice, but between compassion or fellow-feeling and justice. The adversarial system of adjudication has certain structural barriers to giving compassion a prominent role in the struggle for just resolution to conflict. Restorative justice hopes to clear away these barriers and make way for closer interconnections between fellow-feeling and justice.

This chapter, therefore, examines the relation between compassion and justice in order to test the restorative justice claim that it allows for a new, larger, and more trustworthy role for compassion in the pursuit of justice than could ever be attained within the adversarial and adjudicative paradigm. In Part 1, "The Paradoxical Place of Compassion in Adjudication," I begin by examining some of the problems inherent in attempting to give compassion a prominent role in adjudicating between adversaries. I take up Martha Nussbaum's attempt in an article entitled "Compassion: The Basic Social Emotion" to use Aristotle's description of the psychological conditions for spontaneous compassion as a foundation for justice in adjudication. I also engage with Robin West's book *Caring for Justice*. She too argues that compassion should have a direct and central role in judicial decision making. I criticize the idea that spontaneous compassion can act as a substantive guide for the judge. Referring back to Aristotle's descriptive account of compassion, I argue that compassion has both an inherent conservatism and a self-referential aspect to it that inhibit the extension of compassion across lines of race, gender, class, and so forth. Because compassion is buffeted about on the waves of our irrational identifications, because it is ever dependent on the complex politics of compassionate alliance, it is too capricious a force ever to be capable of steering the judge reliably toward the just. The first part of the chapter, therefore, claims that efforts to legitimate a central role for spontaneous compassion in adjudication (not just for empathy or imaginative awareness) fail.

In Part II of this chapter, "A Normative Vision of Restorative Compassion and Justice-as-Repair," I go on to examine the restorative justice vision of the relation between compassion and justice. Restorative justice is able to concede that the relation between compassion and adjudication is prohibitively problematic while at the same time commending restorative justice as offering new possibilities for an interconnected understanding of the two. Restorative justice can also claim that it seeks to educate participants in a theory and practice of compassion that have more moral content than do Aristotle's purely descriptive conditions for compassion. Restorative justice does not attempt to rely on a descriptive account of compassion as an emotional reflex. Rather, it seeks to encourage a discipline of compassion as an ethical achievement characterized by an acknowledgment of: (a) the complexity and concreteness of the inner life of the other; (b) the paradigmatic mutuality of compassion; and (c) the necessity that compassion be grounded in an ethic of humility such that one sees both oneself and others as shared participants in a human condition of vulnerability to loss and a human capacity for renewal and repair. Here, I attempt to explain how this understanding of compassion hopes to dovetail into both the procedural elements of restorative encounter and the conceptual understanding of justice as right-relation.

In Part III of this chapter, I examine "The Practice of Compassion in the Restorative Encounter." Here I delve into the affective dynamics of compassion when victim meets offender. I concede that the procedural and conceptual framework of restorative justice does, at the theoretical level, allow for a much tidier and more natural relationship between compassion and justice than there ever could be in the context of adjudication. However, in this section I attempt to show how a number of the same barriers to compassion that we identified in adjudication resurface in the spontaneous affective momentum of the restorative encounter. Thus the influence of compassion in the search for restorative justice remains deeply problematic, potentially arbitrary, and, as often as not, a force that steers us more toward unfairness than toward justice.

Let's begin this exploration of the relation between compassion and justice by looking at some of the age-old problems that arise when we encourage the judge to rely on compassion.

I. The Paradoxical Place of Compassion in Adjudication

A judge who allows compassion to influence his decision making will be as effective as a carpenter who uses a warped ruler. So says Aristotle in *The Rhetoric*.[1] For Aristotle the aim of justice in adjudication is the impartial and objective application of rules. The judge properly imposes a fiction of antecedent sameness on the parties and looks narrowly to that distinctive form of difference produced by legally recognized wrongs. It should make no difference to the judge "whether a good man has defrauded a bad man or a bad man a good one."[2] Thus the ends of justice are best served by rationality and objectivity – tools that narrow the judge's focus and help him to resist illicit seduction by the emotions.

Yet, while Aristotle was firmly of the view that compassion can only hijack the judicial mind and cannot sensibly direct it, his discussion of pity in *The Rhetoric* reveals that he knew the advocate was best armed with a refined understanding of how to elicit compassion in a judge or jury.[3] The advocate who is trying to persuade must play the odds that a skilful shift into the currency of compassion may successfully entice the judge off the straight and narrow and into a more passionate state of fellow-feeling for his client.

Of course, there's an incongruity here. We cast the relation between compassion and justice as both essential and illicit. The masterful lawyer is able to seduce the judge into a compassionate alliance with his client. The upright judge resists the temptations of compassion and remains staunchly faithful to emotionally neutral decision making. Our favourite stories of the triumph of justice validate both these visions. Compassion tries hard but fails. Yet, at the end of the day, formal justice lines up with the dictates of compassion, and we rejoice in the fulfilment of our longings for a confluence of the two.

Consider, for example, Shakespeare's *Merchant of Venice*. Portia, who is both advocate and judge, pressures Shylock to be compassionate toward Antonio by her very insistence that compassion cannot be coerced.[4] Her argument that "the quality of mercy is not strained" is, ironically, an attempt to force Shylock to be merciful toward Antonio. Yet, in the end, all her verbal and psychological skill in the service of compassion fails. And even though the audience is rooting for her, they secretly celebrate her failure here because it sets the scene for the triumph of her more heroic formalism. Her true victory – and her more thorough humiliation of the Jew – comes when she proves that objective, rational, neutral application of the strict letter of the bond without recourse to any of the perverting influences of emotion, pity, or anger, compel the conclusion that a pound of flesh does not include a drop of blood. Thus Portia delivers the most gratifying of possible legal worlds: one in which the detached application of neutral rules brings victory to those with whom we are in compassionate cahoots. Of course, the audience's gratification is intensified by its experience of *schadenfreude* in relation to the Jew. Portia's legal genius is meant to be seen as enhanced by the total devastation she wreaks on the opponent, who is seen as undeserving of any compassionate concern.[5]

Both Aristotle and Shakespeare depict compassion as having a simultaneously central and yet unlawful relation to justice. Today's theorists of the relationship between compassion and justice, by contrast, are reluctant to embrace this paradox. On the one hand, we have legal formalism, which views compassion as a polluting influence in adjudication.[6] Recourse to extrinsic considerations such as compassion spur a judge to use judicial power to settle moral and material scores not properly before her. The compassionate judge will care where she has no business caring and will enlist the power of her office in the service of her personal feelings. And this caring will erode the authority of law and ultimately its ability to protect us from chaos. Compassion will likewise lure the judge into an illicit alliance with the pain of the poor and the victimized. Such formalists argue that compassion is the duty of institutions other than the courts. Though compassion may properly inspire *legislatures* to Robinhoodlike redistribution, the brand of honour befitting the office of the judge is rightly bound up with stalwart protection of the purity and neutrality of the law.[7]

Law and economics nay-sayers such as Richard Epstein also reprimand the influence of compassion in adjudication.[8] However, since Epstein does see the courts as properly pursuing the extrinsic social goal of efficiency, he cannot go along with the formalist concern to keep law pure of social influence. Thus Epstein grounds his objection to compassion in adjudication in a concern about the purity of compassion itself.[9] It is not the law that will be sullied by the intrusion of compassion; rather, compassion will be sullied – or utterly destroyed – if it is thrust into the coercive arena of the courtroom.

For Epstein, the only thing that counts as compassion is philanthropic beneficence. His core case of compassion is grand-scale charity by the fabulously wealthy.[10] Thus true compassion in the Epsteinian sense is not even an intelligible option for a judge wielding the coercive power of the state.[11] A judge never hands over resources at her own disposal (her car keys, chequebook, and so forth) to alleviate the suffering of a party. Instead, compassion for the plaintiff leads her to compel the defendant to pay. Likewise, compassion for the victim may lead her to compel the convict to do time. Either way, it's compulsion not compassion.

On the other side of this debate, we have those who want openly to legitimate the influence of compassion in judicial decision making.[12] Martha Nussbaum has argued that compassion is an "essential bridge to justice" not just as an empathic skill that gives the judge a keener, more sophisticated perception of what is at stake, but as a substantive guide toward right decision.[13] Nussbaum claims that Aristotle's discussion of pity or *eleos* in *The Rhetoric* provides the foundation for a rational conception of compassion that has vital ties to justice in both politics and adjudication.[14]

Aristotle defines pity as follows: "A feeling of pain caused by the sight of some evil, destructive or painful, which befalls one who does not deserve it, and which we might expect to befall ourselves or some friend of ours, and moreover to befall us soon." Nussbaum extrapolates from this definition three conditions, each necessary, and together sufficient, to inspire compassion: "(1) The belief that suffering is serious rather than trivial; (2) the belief that the suffering was not caused primarily by the person's own culpable actions; and (3) the belief that the pitier's own possibilities are similar to those of the sufferer."[15] Both of the cases Nussbaum highlights here as triumphs of judicial compassion involved compassion toward children. First, following Lynne Henderson,[16] Nussbaum points to the US Supreme Court's decision in *Brown v. Board of Education*.[17] She argues that the court looked to evidence of the emotional suffering and damage to black children's self-esteem caused by segregation. The judges' rational but compassionate attentiveness to black children's suffering led them directly to a just decision: the overruling of the doctrine of separate but equal.[18] The second case that Nussbaum points to as illustrating the legitimate role of compassion in judging is the decision of Judge Richard Posner in *Nelson v. Farrey*.[19] There Posner admitted psychiatric evidence of a child's statements regarding sexual abuse by her father. Nussbaum writes: "We see in his opinion all the materials of compassion: the judgment that the little girl has suffered serious harm through no fault of her own; the judgment that this is a very bad thing and must not be renewed by a courtroom confrontation."[20]

If we look closely at Nussbaum, we see that she does not actually accept the whole of Aristotle's account of pity. First, though she identifies the "belief that the pitier's own possibilities are similar to those of the sufferer" as a necessary condition for compassion, she does not discuss how that condition is met in either *Brown v. Board of Education* or *Nelson v. Farrey*.[21] Yet, as we shall see, the condition that the pitier believe his or her own possibilities to be similar to those of the sufferer is essential to Aristotles's account.[22] Aristotle thought that, as a result of this condition, we feel compassion only for our equals: "We pity those who are like us in age, character, disposition, social standing, or birth; for in all these cases it appears more likely that the same misfortune may befall us also. Here too we have to remember the general principle that what we fear for ourselves excites our pity when it happens to others."[23] Thus Aristotle stresses that this third condition naturally narrows the range of people we are spontaneously inspired to pity. It also fundamentally ties the impulse to feel compassion for others to the impulse to fear for ourselves.

The major difference between Aristotle's discussion of pity in *The Rhetoric* and Nussbaum's use of it, however, is that Aristotle's observations about pity are purely descriptive. They are in aid of rhetorical strategy. He is advising the speaker seeking to elicit compassion in an audience. Aristotle treats compassion as a spontaneous and amoral, yet powerful, emotional response, the stimuli for which are fixed by the contours of our psyche. Aristotle's account is, on its own terms, purely strategic. He does not commend compassion as a virtue. Indeed, his account does not contradict Hannah Arendt's conclusion that "the ancients regarded the most compassionate person as no more entitled to be called the best than the most fearful."[24] Yet Nussbaum sees Aristotle's descriptive account of compassion as capable of carrying considerable normative freight and ultimately of delivering a substantive guide toward justice.

In what follows I will try to show that, contrary to Nussbaum (though not contrary to Aristotle), the three conditions for compassion Nussbaum draws from Aristotle are neither grounded in rationality nor a reliable compass pointing us, or a judge, toward the just. For the most part, I want to defend Aristotle's account of pity as an accurate account of the conditions under which we do spontaneously experience pity or compassion. However, I will try to show that we ought not to pin our hopes on such spontaneous compassion as a redemptive, natural human impulse capable of leading us or the court to justice. As shall become clear, my objections to judicial compassion differ from those of either Epstein or the formalists. Ironically, therefore, I depart from all these other thinkers on compassion, who (though they disagree about whether it is good) all think that compassion, if given free rein, is a force that will lead the judge to use his or her office to promote social equality. The assumption of all is that concern for suffering will lead consistently toward greater concern for those on the downside of social advantage and hence will promote equality. I will try to point out, however, some of the ways in which compassion can be an irrationally conservative force just as likely to be hostile as friendly to the dispossessed.

Serious Suffering

We do not feel compassion for those whose suffering is insignificant. As Nussbaum puts it, "we do not go around pitying someone who has lost a trivial item such as a toothbrush or a paperclip." Indeed, we might even feel wronged by someone who tried to lay claim to our compassion when they had endured only minor suffering.[25] This conclusion sounds true enough. Yet, as even the most committed utilitarian will concede, there are enormous epistemological problems when it comes to measuring the seriousness of the sufferings of others. Because we can't get into their shoes, we simply don't know how serious their suffering is. Moreover, our estimation of the seriousness of others' suffering varies with our (potentially totally irrational) estimation of their sensitivity.

Rousseau, in his discussion of pity in *Emile*, raises some of these difficulties: "The pity one has for another's misfortune is measured not by the quantity of that misfortune but by the sentiment which one attributes to those who suffer it."[26] Rousseau, whose discussion of pity (unlike

Aristotle's) is vitally concerned with the possible role of compassion in motivating actions toward social justice, realizes that this variable creates a serious unreliability in compassion as a normative guide. It means that the rich have no pity for the poor, whom they assume to be too stupid and insensible to be meaningfully miserable.[27]

This problem – that our assessment of the seriousness of the suffering of others varies according to the degree of sensitivity we attribute to them – has its grosser and more subtle variants. In its crudest of forms, this trick of attributing want of feeling to devalued others has long been readily identified as morally suspect.[28] We see this kind of reasoning being condemned, for example, in Charles Dickens's *David Copperfield*. There the character James Steerforth (Nussbaum's heartthrob, whom we met in the previous chapter on eros) says of the working classes: "They are not to be expected to be as sensitive as we are. Their delicacy is not to be shocked, or hurt very easily. They are wonderfully virtuous, I dare say – some people contend for that, at least; and I am sure I don't want to contradict them – but they have not very fine natures, and they may be thankful that, like their coarse rough skins, they are not easily wounded."[29]

Dickens asks us to condemn Steerforth for this line of argument. Steerforth is referring here to David Copperfield's working-class friends, the Peggottys – people whose lives Steerforth will later ruin. Dickens spends half of the rest of the novel drawing us into the pathos of the Peggottys' sufferings and the subtlety of their sensibilities. Thus condemnation of such reasoning is no innovation of twentieth-century political correctness. When today we condemn, for example, the judge who claims that the rape of Aboriginal women is less serious than the rape of a white woman because Aboriginal women are acculturated to withstand sexual violence and therefore suffer less, we are not breaking new moral ground.[30] We've long known enough to repudiate such sentiments when they're made flat-out either in conversation or in a judicial opinion. However, the difficulty of purging the influence of irrational judgments about the relative susceptibility of others to suffering – judgments that either allow us to amplify that suffering or to turn away from its immediacy – is enormous.

Let's consider Robin West's discussion of the role of compassion in adjudication. West, arguing in the same vein as Nussbaum, also sees a strong substantive role for compassion in adjudication.[31] To explain how compassion ought to assist the judge in decision making, West asks us to consider a surrogacy case where the biological mother changes her mind after the birth of the child and does not want to give up custody of the baby to the contracting parents. West argues that the judge ought empathically to identify with and comparatively weigh the seriousness of the anguish of the competing parties: "If she is to correctly apply the law – and hence do justice – she must undertake the comparative empathic work of deciding which party will be most hurt by losing the winner-take-all decision regarding the child's custody."[32]

West seems to assume that if the judge earnestly attends to the suffering of each of the parties, she will be likely to view the suffering of the biological mother – who has carried the child for nine months – as more serious than the combined suffering of the contracting parents, whose relationship to the child is, so far, primarily abstract. However, think again of Rousseau's insistence that our measurement of the quantity of others' sufferings is imperceptibly and irrationally affected by the degree of sensitivity we attribute to them.[33] This tendency introduces a wildcard into the process of compassionate judging. If, as West seems to be anticipating, the judge is predisposed to attribute to the biological mother a sublime feeling of connectedness to the child she has carried and given birth to, the judge's estimation of the seriousness of the suffering of the mother will go up. If, however, she imagines that a woman capable of contracting out her reproductive capacity is likely to be relatively callous – if she imagines the contract itself to be evidence of the mother's insensibility – then the judge's estimate of the seriousness of the mother's suffering will go down. Thus giving a greater role to compassion in adjudication may likewise give correspondingly greater play to judges' arbitrary assumptions about the degree of the parties' sensitivity.

West appears to assume that giving a greater role to compassion in adjudication will be beneficial for feminist causes. However, it is not at all clear that this would be the case. Much of the feminist critique of the criminal justice system's treatment of women in sexual assault cases, for example, denounces this very kind of compassionate reasoning running in the other direction. The judge reasons that the seriousness of the suffering of an innocent-rapist-imprisoned will always exceed that of the truthful-victim-never-vindicated and, therefore, that we should always err on the side of acquittal – *and* that such a comparative compassionate analysis (which asks "which party will be most hurt by losing?") is a legitimate method of deciding sexual assault cases.

Moreover, casting the judge's task as one of weighing the seriousness of the suffering of the parties necessarily, in turn, casts the task of the parties as convincing the judge of the greater seriousness of one's suffering as compared with the other's. Advocacy and the giving of testimony become primarily matters of competitive posturing and performance of pain. The process of seeking justice becomes a potentially humiliating endeavour, wherein one is expected to parade and exploit the seriousness of her suffering. One hesitates even to imagine the levels of bad taste and manipulation lawyers would sink to in "pimping the pain"[34] of their clients if the question "who suffers more from losing?" were openly legitimated as the central question for the judge.

I have here identified a few of the difficulties with the requirement of serious suffering at the core of our understanding of justice in adjudication. However, as will become clear in the next sections, a judge's assessment of the seriousness of a party's suffering will also be directly affected by her judgments about the parties' blamelessness and her intuitions about whether she herself need fear the particular sort of suffering in question.

Blamelessness

We do not feel pity for those who bring about their own demise.[35] Again Nussbaum takes this as a necessary – and rationally grounded – condition for a practice of compassion that would appropriately direct judicial decisions.[36] Yet this condition of blamelessness also gives rise to many a troubling glitch in the relation between compassion and justice. The first obvious difficulty is that judgments about blameworthiness of suffering are judgments about justice. Thus conclusions about facts, wrongdoing, causation, and responsibility must be prior to the impulse to compassion. Yet, if compassion waits on these rational judgments about justice, it is difficult to see how compassion can contribute substantively to the process of judging. The condition of blamelessness puts the cart before the horse. As Nussbaum points out, "the appeal for pity comes closely linked with assertion of one's innocence."[37] Thus, if judgments about the sufferer's blamelessness are arrived at through the application of legal rules, it is difficult to see what compassion adds to judicial decision making other than a dollop of gratuitous *post facto* fellow-feeling for the winner. If, on the other hand, these preliminary determinations of blameworthiness take place prior to the findings of facts and the application of generally binding rules, then we must ask what psychological forces are driving such pre-legal judgments about blameworthiness.

One of the arbitrary psychological factors that can be at play here is the judge's assessment of whether he or she would ever do the sort of thing alleged to have caused the sufferer's own suffering.[38] A judge's examination of his or her own character can sometimes help to dispel hypocrisy and to lead the judge toward more munificent compassion for others. However, judicial self-examination can just as easily cut the other way. Consider the judge who is convinced that her own relative freedom from suffering is the direct consequence of her strict adherence to conventional moral codes. For example, imagine a judge who is certain that she would never have worn the sort of revealing clothes the victim was wearing on the night of an alleged sexual assault, would never have gotten drunk, and would never have gone to her alleged assailant's apartment. This judge might further believe that if she herself *were* ever to behave in such a manner, she would be deserving of serious reproach. She would not then see *herself* as being in a moral position to make allegations of assault. It may be very difficult to get this judge to interpret the victim's suffering as innocent. This judge, however, is not a hypocrite. She does not hold the victim to a standard she does not herself meet. However, her own severe moral code leads her to judge the conduct of other women with severity as well.

Consider now whose suffering is more likely to be judged blameless in West's surrogacy case. It is easy enough to view the biological mother as the author of her own predicament. To make a convincing plea for compassion, she must persuade the judge that she has not caused her own suffering – that she is innocent in her anguish. Yet she signed the contract. She took the money and agreed to hand over the baby. In trying to get the judge to interpret her suffering as blameless, the mother must come up with ways of repackaging that suffering so as to minimize the culpability of her own causal role in it. Again, the judge's intuitions about the blameworthiness of the mother's actions will be influenced by the extent to which the judge can identify morally with the mother's conduct. If the judge can imagine herself doing the same in similar circumstances, she might see the suffering as innocent. If, however, she believes that even the most bitter poverty could not induce her to sell her reproductive capacity, she is significantly less likely to see the mother's suffering as blameless. Likewise, if she sees herself as potentially engaging the services of a surrogate, she may be predisposed to identify with the moral circumstances of the contracting parents; she may see their suffering as more innocent and, therefore, more deserving of compassion.

Thus, where normative conclusions are reached about the blamelessness of the parties' suffering prior to the application of legal rules, these conclusions are driven by the judge's personal and potentially pre-rational identification with one of the parties. The moral contours of the judge's character and self-understanding come, in this way, to be the normative guide by which the relative innocence of the competing claims of suffering are determined. Everything rests on the character of the judge.

The Belief That I Am Not (and Nor Are My Friends) Exempt from Similar Suffering

Nussbaum concedes that we feel compassion primarily when we fear ending up in the same boat as the sufferer. In the preceding discussion, we saw how the condition of blamelessness is intimately bound up with the degree of the pitier's moral identification with the plight of the sufferer. Here we will look at how the third condition ties compassion to the degree of practical identification with the plight of the sufferer. As we have seen, Aristotle saw this condition as linking compassion to fear and confining it within social circles of kinship, friendship, or equality of social and economic position.[39] Applied to adjudication, this condition tells us that judges will feel greater compassion for those parties whose vulnerability to suffering most closely resembles their own. The conservatism here is self-evident.

Rousseau, in his discussion of pity in *Emile*, says that "one pities in others only those ills from which one does not feel exempt."[40] Thus we come to understand: "Why are kings without pity for their subjects? Because they count on never being mere men."[41] Aristotle accepted this uncritically as a condition for pity. Rousseau recognized it as a serious impediment to the hoped-for relationship between compassion and social justice. Rousseau thought that to encourage compassion across lines of inequality and difference, you would have to educate those on the upside of advantage to worry more about the possibility of downfall. He even came close to commending unstable forms of government as a means of educating individuals toward greater compassion. He argued that citizens of volatile regimes are more compassionate because they are less secure. Each understands destitution as a serious possible future: "Why are the Turks generally more humane and more hospitable than we are? It is because, with their totally arbitrary government, which renders the greatness and the fortune of individuals always precarious and unsteady, they do not regard abasement and poverty as a condition alien to them.[42]

Stopping just short of advocating arbitrary government as a means of inculcating compassion, Rousseau goes on to suggest other tactics for instilling the requisite fear. We should show the pupil graphic details of the sufferings of others and remind him of his own vulnerability: "Show him all the vicissitudes of fortune. Seek out for him examples, always too frequent, of people who, from a station higher than his, have fallen beneath these unhappy men."[43]

These strategies attempt to get compassion to do what Aristotle says it doesn't do – to cross over lines of difference and inequality. And, indeed, we are still quite drawn to Rousseau's thinking. We continue to attempt to instill compassion in the middle and upper classes for homeless people through the warning that "it could happen to you" – that it is merely a matter of "falling through the cracks." We try to instill compassion in men for victims of sexual assault not by arguing that it could happen to them, but by instilling fear that it could happen to their wives, mothers, or daughters. Applying this strategy to the judge, we would say that judicial education ought to include not only a curriculum of intense exposure to human suffering, which no judge can avoid in the normal course of things, but also, and most crucially, instructional reminders that (but for the grace of God) judges themselves or those they care about might well end up in the same unfortunate position as the parties before them.

Yet there are serious problems with reliance on the energy of anxiety here. Forcing people to look at graphic details of others' suffering and reminding them of their own vulnerability may inculcate compassion in some.[44] However, such fear-based strategies for inspiring fellow-feeling can just as easily backfire.[45] As conservative politics suggests, fear, when felt by those with power, instead of motivating compassion, often motivates further entrenchment of hierarchies of race, class, and culture in order to "make sure it doesn't happen to us." A judge's fear of destitution for herself or her friends can, therefore, just as easily inspire disgust and contempt for the destitute.

Yet perhaps there is some greater hope in Aristotle's proviso that we feel compassion when we have fear that it could happen not just to ourselves but also *to one of our friends*. If we can identify someone we care about who is vulnerable to the particular sort of suffering in question, this second-order self-concern may also inspire compassion.[46] This proviso could be cause for more optimism about how compassion might extend across lines of difference from the privileged to the dispossessed.[47] We can care about others who are different from us even if we do not anticipate or fear falling prey to the same kinds of suffering they have to endure.

Yet, while reference to the "or someone you care about" proviso is potentially successful as a strategy for eliciting compassion across lines of difference, it is an element of compassion that does as much to shut down compassionate connections across lines of difference as it does to create them. This is partly because, regrettably, friendship and concern rarely extend across lines of class, race, and social difference. Circles of concern tend to be drawn on lines of class, race, nationality, geography, culture, and ethnicity. Thus the proviso "or someone you care about" is just as likely to reinforce those barriers. Moreover, even where compassion is extended by those higher up to those lower down, such compassion can be more like condescension – importing all the negative connotations of the notion of pity – which does more to reinforce social inequality than it does to combat it.[48]

Nussbaum, promoting her view that compassion is importantly related to justice, claims that "Alexis de Tocqueville argued that there was an unusually great potential for compassion in the American democracy, because the Constitution had situated citizens as equal to a degree unknown in Europe."[49] This statement needs considerable qualification. First of all, de Tocqueville saw equality of social position as a force that naturally promoted greater compassion. He did not, however, see compassion as a force that naturally promoted greater equality. Further, de Tocqueville's complimentary statements about the abundance of compassion in America must be read against his condemnation of slavery. I am compelled to quote de Tocqueville at length to illustrate the dangers of reading him as an unqualified admirer of the American capacity for compassion:

> Although the Americans have, in a manner, reduced egotism to a social and philosophical theory, they are nevertheless extremely open to compassion. In no country is criminal justice administered with more mildness than in the United States. Whilst the English seem disposed carefully to retain the bloody traces of the dark ages in their penal legislation, the Americans have almost expunged capital punishment from their codes ... The circumstance which conclusively shows that this singular mildness of the Americans *arises chiefly from their social condition*, is the manner in which they treat their slaves. Perhaps there is not, upon the whole, a single European colony in the New World in which the physical condition of the blacks is less severe than in the United States; yet the slaves still endure horrid sufferings there, and are constantly exposed to barbarous punishments. It is easy to perceive that the lot of these unhappy beings inspires their masters with but little compassion, and that they look upon slavery, not only as an institution which is profitable to them, but as an evil which does not affect them. Thus the same man who is full of humanity towards his fellow creatures *when they are at the same time his equals*, becomes insensible to their afflictions as soon as that equality ceases. *His mildness should therefore be attributed to the equality of conditions, rather than to civilization and education.*[50] (emphasis added)

Leaving aside the woeful inaccuracy of de Tocqueville's impression of the American sensibility about capital punishment, the thrust of de Tocqueville's conclusion here is that compassion comes easiest when it is least needed as a matter of social justice – that is, when people are already substantively equal.[51] In reading de Tocqueville today, one is struck by his staggering prescience and its strange juxtaposition with his now-mystifying conviction that equality of social conditions was the basic fact of American life. *Democracy in America* opens with the words: "Amongst the novel objects that attracted my attention during my stay in the United States, nothing struck me more forcibly than the general equality of conditions." De Tocqueville's conclusions about compassion in America are completely enmeshed with his assumptions about a lived reality of social and economic equality of white Americans. White Americans are compassionate to each other insofar as, and because, they are social equals. It must be stressed here that de Tocqueville's discussion of compassion in America is absolutely devoid of any suggestion that compassion is a force that has succeeded in bridging lines of difference and acting as an impetus toward greater social equality.

Moreover, it also needs to be underlined that de Tocqueville's sense of equality *of conditions* in America is not primarily abstract, formal, or constitutional as Nussbaum suggests.[52] It is equality of social conditions, rather than constitutional equality, that de Tocqueville sees as the cause of compassion. But, even if he were making the claim that equality under the Constitution fosters compassion, we should not be too quick to accept this observation. The countless failures of compassion across lines of race, class, and gender – and certainly not only in the US, but in many constitutional democracies as well where political equality is guaranteed – should make us skeptical about whether formal political equality is really a reliable inspiration to compassion. It may be true (though it is not obviously so) that absence of formal equality assists with the mental processes by which we discount the sufferings of others; it may have been easier, for example, for whites to discount the suffering of blacks in South Africa under apartheid than it is for them to do so under democracy. But what is more obviously true is that an absence of equality of status under a constitution is not needed – that is, we don't rely on it – to dismiss the suffering of devalued others. Indeed, formal equality under a democratic constitution can actually serve as a ready means of deflecting claims to compassion that carry with them demands for greater substantive equality. The "what more could you possibly want now?" response as a means of dismissing the inequality-caused suffering of the dispossessed is far more readily available and more plausible under a constitution where formal equality exists. Democracy is valuable for countless other reasons. But we should be careful about assuming that one of its virtues is its inculcation of a more spontaneous compassion.[53]

We should even be skeptical about too much readiness to go along with de Tocqueville's conclusion that equality of social and economic conditions fosters compassion. A more squarely Aristotelian view might be more plausible: While one feels compassion only for one's equals, one does not *necessarily* feel compassion for one's equals. The mere fact of equality of conditions seems insufficient as a spontaneous motivation toward compassion. Furthermore, it is not at all obvious that the expansion of the number of people who share sameness of situation really fosters the sort of ever-larger web of reciprocally compassionate connection that de Tocqueville envisions. The homogeneous and ever-expanding middle-class North American suburbs – though they are sites of monotonous social and economic equality – are not necessarily also, and by virtue of the equality of conditions, hotbeds of compassion. Much more than equality of social conditions is needed for compassion to flourish.

Again we can readily see how these problems in the relation between compassion, equality, practical identification, and fear will play themselves out in adjudication. Let's briefly revisit West's case once more.

When the judge sits down to weigh the comparative suffering of the surrogate mother and the contracting parents, she will necessarily, if imperceptibly, be affected by her personal anxieties; she will be drawn to feel compassion for those whose vulnerability to suffering is most similar to her own or to that of her friends. Does she fear that she (or one of her friends) might end up in the same boat as one of the parties? Obviously the gender of the judge plays an enormous role. If, as I have been assuming, our compassionate judge is a woman, she is more likely to have a lively fear of being separated from a child she has carried and born. A judge's visceral fear of separation from her biological child, and the compassion it inspires for other women faced with such a risk, may overwhelm all other emotional pulls in the case. However, this fear might be counterbalanced if our judge is well off financially and in no way fears the poverty that might induce her to enter into such a contract. Further, if she is infertile or approaching the end of her fertile years, she might also fear being in the position of the mother who engaged the services of the surrogate. The "or someone you care about" proviso probably doesn't add much here. Social and economic stratifications suggest that the judge's friends and those she cares about are just as likely to be vulnerable to the suffering of the contracting parents as to the suffering of the surrogate mother.

A male judge may be less likely to feel a vivid identification with the fear of losing a child one has carried and given birth to. He may, however, be more likely to experience anxiety around the threat of losing control of his genetic legacy. This fear will lead him into a compassionate connection with the contracting father. The "or someone you care about" proviso is equivocal again. While the proviso can sometimes assist compassionate connection across lines of gender difference, the class difference overlay is an obstacle here. An upper-middle-class male judge is not likely to be inspired to compassion for the surrogate mother by fantasies that his wife or mother might find herself in a similar predicament. His masculine pride may prohibit his entertaining any such fear. The idea of his own wife, mother, or daughter as a surrogate is likely to inspire horror rather than protectiveness. He may have friends, moreover, who might be on the other end of the bargain, that of the contracting parents who now face the loss of the child they hoped to raise. Here again judicial compassion is potentially led by the judge's personal anxieties and is most easily extended when the judge's circumstances and vulnerabilities are on a par with those of one of the parties.

II. A Normative Vision of Restorative Compassion and Justice-as-Repair

We have seen in Part I that Nussbaum fails in her attempt to extract a normative foundation for a compassionate theory of adjudication from

Aristotle's purely descriptive account of spontaneous compassion. This attempt fails not for the reasons that either the formalists or Epstein suggest: that compassion in judging involves the courts in illicit equality-seeking or that combining compassion with judicial coercion would sully the purity of compassion itself. Rather, it fails because spontaneous compassion, as Aristotle sets it out, is a force too much at the whim of the irrational and self-centred impulses of the judge. The judge will side with the party with whom she is most readily able to identify. This identification, in turn, as we have seen, is potentially influenced by the shape of the judge's anxieties and by the extent to which the judge sees each party's predicament as something the judge need fear as a possible risk for herself or those she cares about. This latter factor is influenced by the degree of sameness between the judge's social and economic position and that of the competing parties. It is clear, therefore, that to have any interconnection with justice, compassion will have to become something other than the capricious creature it spontaneously is – something more just than the fickle emotion Aristotle so astutely described it to be.

Restorative justice claims to hold out new hope for compassion in its relation to justice. Indeed, simply going along with the restorative equation of justice with the creation of right-relation, rather than with the consistent application of general rules, makes some of the problems in the relation between compassion and justice disappear immediately. For starters, we no longer have the problem that the judge has two competing parties before her and that extending compassion to one of them is inevitably going to mean withholding it from (and probably inflicting pain upon) the other. The procedural and conceptual structure of restorative justice makes space for a different understanding of the relationship between compassion and justice and potentially gives us reason to be more optimistic about interconnections between the two. The role of compassion within restorative justice is not tied to the vagaries of a judge's preference when presented with the compassion-seeking performances of the parties before her. Restorative justice seeks to elicit compassion from all participants for one another. It does not hope to make any connection between the extension of compassion and the fair application of rules. Restorative justice emerges from the particular context and compassionate impulses of the participants. Restorative compassion is the guide toward right-relation. Beyond this kind of immediate procedural improvement, restorative compassion imposes normative conditions on compassion that are necessary to qualify compassion as capable of being importantly connected to right-relation.

Thus restorative justice acknowledges that the sort of compassion that will potentially contribute to justice-as-repair is an ethical achievement and a normative challenge facing both parties to the conflict as well as members of their supporting communities. In this respect, restorative justice recognizes at the outset that, in order to have normative content, compassion must be something more than a spontaneous impulse of fellow-feeling. While the procedural structure of restorative justice maximizes opportunities for spontaneous compassion, it also recognizes the need morally to educate, direct, and encourage the compassionate impulse. It realizes that we must overcome the moral limitations of compassion as an emotional reflex in order for compassion to have any significant relation to justice.

Here, of course, we come up against the core objection to restorative justice urged by this book: Compulsory compassion is an oxymoron. Restorative justice, rather than relying on spontaneous compassion (which, as we have seen, has little relation to justice), relies on the possibility of inculcating in its participants a more morally elevated practice of compassion. But can institutions of justice demand compassion from the parties to a conflict? Clifford Orwin puts the problem of compelling compassion this way: "Compassion resembles love: to demand it is a good way to kill it. This is no less true when the one of whom I demand it is myself."[54]

In one sense, it is indisputable that respect, love, and compassion are emotional states that cannot be coerced. But, to be fair to restorative justice, we must avoid overstating the force of this objection. Inasmuch as it is obvious that compassion cannot be coerced, it is equally evident that one *can* encourage, nurture, cultivate, and even discipline oneself in a more compassionate sensibility.[55] This possibility exists even though compassion, like respect and love, is a state that – to be what it purports to be – must have some measure of authenticity. One can have optimism about the potential of nurturing and cultivating practices of compassion without believing that it is possible to compel compassion. One can reasonably hold the view that compassion, if left to its own devices, is an irrational and arbitrary force but that it is capable of becoming, when instructed with intelligence and sensitivity, a powerful and refined moral instrument. None of this argument entails the view that compassion can be forcibly demanded to appear on cue. Both as individuals and as a culture, we can work at habituating ourselves and our institutions toward a right-headed understanding of compassion as a moral practice. Moreover, since justice itself is clearly a kind of discipline and achievement, we should not be surprised if a conception of compassion strongly connected to justice were also a discipline and an achievement rather than a spontaneous impulse.

Let us then, momentarily at least, ease up a little on restorative justice. And, in that vein, let us try to piece together a sense of the restorative understanding of a robust notion of compassion capable of sustaining a strong theoretical and practical relationship to justice-as-repair.

Compassion as an Ethical Achievement
In what follows I propose to construct a version of what I take to be the restorative understanding of the normative conditions for compassion. These conditions take spontaneous compassion as important raw material but see it as standing in need of moral refinement. Restorative compassion, as I will call it, refined by these normative conditions, becomes the foundation for practices of justice-as-repair. As we shall see, these normative conditions for restorative compassion track the difficulties with spontaneous compassion we saw in Part I. Further, the normative conditions for restorative compassion dovetail into the procedural structure of the restorative encounter and the conceptual understanding of justice as right-relation.

A Vivid Awareness of the Complexity and Concreteness of the Inner Lives of Others
The restorative understanding of compassion must be grounded in a vivid awareness of the concreteness and complexity of the inner lives of others.[56] This normative condition speaks to the deficiency exposed in our examination of Aristotle's condition of serious suffering. As Rousseau explained, this condition allowed for the discounting of the seriousness of the suffering of others by perceiving them as constitutionally less sensitive to pain than oneself. Restorative justice hopes to be, in some measure, an education for participants toward a lively awareness of the capacity of others for suffering. Through the practices of encounter, conversation, self-disclosure, and truth-telling, restorative justice hopes to give each participant a more vivid sense of the inner life of the other.[57] Restorative justice relies on face-to-face encounter as the means of assisting the connection between participants' experience of the complexity and intensity of their own lives and their imaginative understanding of the complexity and intensity of the inner lives of others.

   Different spiritual traditions use different techniques to accomplish similar ends. Some attempt to expand our imaginative sense of the inner life of the other by asking us to imagine the other as a supremely elevated soul. Mother Teresa, for example, famously describes her compassionate work with the poor of Calcutta as a "willingness to see the face of Jesus in all its alarming disguises." Likewise, Buddhism sometimes urges the practitioner to view every encounter as a meeting with the Buddha himself. Similarly, Jesus said: "Inasmuch as ye have done it unto one of the least of these my brethren, ye have done it unto me." These ideas are all imaginative aids toward mindfulness of the richness of the subjectivity of the other. Another means of enlivening our sense of the complexity and concreteness of the inner lives of others is through the reading of literature.[58]

Restorative justice reasons, however, that these essentially abstract conceptual techniques of attempting to enliven our awareness of the inner life of the other are deficient. Thus, within the restorative paradigm, the need for an enriched sense of the other's subjectivity is understood primarily as a call to conversation. It is by mutual and respectful face-to-face truth-telling and dialogue that we make valuable gains in educating each other about our inner lives.[59]

Mutuality

The second and the most radical normative condition for restorative compassion is that it is paradigmatically mutual rather than unilateral.[60] Restorative compassion admits and entails a request for reciprocal compassion from others. The paradigmatic mutuality of restorative compassion seeks to eliminate the negative connotations of "pity": the superiority of the giver of compassion over the receiver. In the ideal restorative encounter, compassion flows between and among all participants in the process; it flows in all directions through the whole web of interpersonal connections implicated in the conflict.[61]

Our discussion of compassion in the context of adjudication assumed a unilateral flow of compassion from a relatively comfortable spectator judge to the suffering parties. In this unilateral and hierarchical structure of compassion, the judge is a detached onlooker to the suffering of the parties. Yet it is she, and she alone, who is being asked to extend compassion. She decides either to give or withhold her compassion from the competing parties. The idea that compassion might flow in both directions equally from the judge to the parties and from the parties to the judge is not only a non sequitur, but also an affront to the dignity of the judicial office.[62] Likewise, when we speak of compassion as an essential part of adjudication, we do not mean to suggest a need for compassion between the parties.

A mutual and nonhierarchical understanding of restorative compassion naturally dovetails into the procedural structure of restorative justice.[63] The offender is in need of the compassion of the victim and community and plays an important role in extending reciprocal compassion to them. Likewise, for compassion to play a role in restorative justice, the victim must become both a recipient and a donor of compassion. All parties ideally enter the process with an understanding that they will be called upon to extend compassion and with an expectation that they will receive it.

This normative condition of mutuality speaks to Aristotle's condition of blamelessness. By presuming that each person is in need of the reciprocal compassion of others, restorative compassion is prior to and independent of judgments about fault. The consequences of wrongdoing, though potentially great, do not include the withdrawal of restorative compassion. The blameworthy offender is in need of the compassion of the victim and community. Mutual compassion as an element of right-relation – the core of the restorative understanding of justice – is the goal of the process no matter how egregious the wrongdoing. Restorative compassion, then, is not something that is appropriate only in those relations that pass a test of mutual innocence. The good, the bad, and the guilty are all seen as standing in shared need of each other's compassion.

This normative element of restorative compassion aspires to effect a number of other potentially helpful shifts in the relation between compassion and justice. We identified earlier the difficulties with seeing adjudication as a judicial weighing of the seriousness of the parties' suffering. Advocacy became a matter of competitive presentation of suffering. While the compassion-seeking endeavour within restorative justice can still degenerate into competitive posturing, the stakes of the competition are lower since restorative justice assumes at the outset that all participants are deserving of and will receive compassion. Since the process does not require that a judge choose between them, the parties are freed up to more authentic and immediate explanations of what they have gone through. Victim and offender are directed to one another in their explications of suffering and their pleas for compassion. Further, restorative justice also speaks to Epstein's point that compassion can't be connected to justice in adjudication since the judge does not give up anything of her own to relieve the suffering of the parties. The different procedural structure of restorative justice, and the different role of compassion within restorative justice, fixes this glitch in the relation between the two. The participants themselves are the sources of compassion, and they must extend it personally to those present. Insofar as they are able to alleviate the sufferings of others, it is because they grant something of their own to the other party: restitution, apology, forgiveness, or forbearance from revenge.

Humility

The third normative condition of restorative compassion is humility understood as an awareness of one's own and others' implicatedness in a dual condition of human suffering and capacity for renewal. Restorative compassion is grounded in an acknowledgment that we, together with others, are stuck in suffering and that each of us, together with others, are sources of rejuvenation.[64] Restorative compassion entails a humble recognition of one's own and others' implicatedness in the dual conditions of human existence: pain and the possibility of flourishing. Humility as a condition of restorative compassion is a reminder that we are never mere spectators of the suffering of others but rather that we are participants in suffering and vulnerability with them. Likewise, we (together with others) are sources of renewal and flourishing.[65] Humility inspires us to acknowledge others – even wrongdoers — also as sources of renewal and vitality. It requires that we recognize others as competent participants in a process of repair.[66]

Though suffering is wildly unequally distributed among people, to be human is to suffer. There is no one for whom suffering is a mere theoretical possibility. We all participate in an ontological condition that produces and reproduces pain. We can, of course, find many accounts of the ubiquity and inescapableness of this suffering. The Buddhist conception of unsatisfactoriness, the Christian idea of the fall of man, Marx's notion of alienation, Heidegger's idea of homelessness, and many others are various and divergent theoretical and spiritual explanations for the deficiency, anxiety, brokenness, and suffering that are basic to human existence. This sense of deficiency entailed in being human is related to our colossal neediness and to our ever-insistent thirst for happiness and fulfilment. We are "needful things" – bundles of emotional, social, physical, sexual, intellectual, and spiritual needs and longings.[67] We are all, then, to some degree victims of the world's inability to satisfy those insatiable needs.

The humility supporting restorative compassion speaks to that shared sense of loss. It is grounded in the awareness that each individual is potentially subject to physical pain, injury, disease, and hunger, to loss of community, loved ones, and friendships, that everyone's perception and understanding of the world are ever subject to correction by others, that everyone is susceptible to doing wrong to others, that for everyone a feeling of power and sense of security in the world may be undermined, that each may stand in need of the assistance and support of others.[68]

This condition of humility speaks to the problems arising out of Aristotle's third condition for compassion: that we must feel that we or our friends are not exempt from similar suffering. Humility recognizes one's vulnerability to loss and injury generally, whereas Aristotle's condition for spontaneous compassion looks in much greater detail at the practical probability of suffering the particular plight of the other. By operating at a much higher level of generality, humility includes many more predicaments in the range of things to which one sees oneself, or those one cares about, as vulnerable. Humility addresses itself to the broad range of vulnerability inherent in human beings. This condition for spontaneous compassion bypasses the requirement of self-concern, that is, the worry that I (or someone I care about) may end up homeless, or starve to death in a famine, or be forcibly separated from my newborn baby, or be sexually assaulted as a child by a trusted adult.[69] Humility requires, instead, that I cultivate a sense of myself as together with those who so suffer in an ontological condition that includes those possibilities. Thus, even though I may reasonably believe that I am, in all rational probability, exempt from those particular sufferings, I teach myself to relate to such suffering from an awareness that I participate in the same set of fundamental vulnerabilities that rendered those people subject to their suffering.

This point also relates to Rousseau's sense that we ought to try to inculcate compassion by stirring up fear that the particular plight of the sufferer is likely to befall the observer. Restorative compassion, by contrast, is inculcated not by stirring up fear, but by educating participants toward mindfulness and equanimity about one's own inevitable inclusion and participation in all the vulnerabilities, limitations, risks, and susceptibilities to loss and failure entailed in the human condition. This recognition of shared vulnerability is paired with a sense of hopefulness about our shared capacity to act as effective agents of repair.[70]

III. The Practice of Compassion in the Restorative Encounter

As we saw in Part II, the ideally compassionate restorative encounter is one where both victim and offender, through face-to-face conversation, come into a vivid awareness of the concreteness of the subjective life of the other, and thereby come to an understanding of the seriousness of the other's suffering. Differences between the situations of victim and offender are bridged through a practice of humility on the part of each, such that both understand themselves and each other as sharing human vulnerability to suffering as well as competency as agents of renewal and repair. This understanding inspires mutual compassion and a mutual effort to move toward right-relation. The compassion that the offender feels for the victim leads him to do what is possible to compensate for the harm he has caused and to assist the victim in regaining a sense of security and wholeness. The compassion the victim feels for the offender leads the victim to want to do what he can to help the offender to change and to be reunited with the community.

With this theoretical sense of the restorative relation between compassion and justice, let us go on now to look at the practical role of compassion in the restorative encounter. We will approach the problem keeping a watchful eye on the difficulties with compassion that we identified in Part I. We will try to see whether these capricious elements of compassion resurface here again to cause trouble in the relation between compassion and justice.

Eliciting Compassion in the Offender
for Those Harmed by the Crime

A crucial element of restorative justice is its commitment to giving the victim the opportunity to make the wrongdoer fully and immediately aware of the seriousness of the suffering he has caused.[71] Restorative justice presumes that, more often than not, the offender has – in his own mind – justified his wrongdoing by gainsaying the damage to others.[72] Restorative justice gives victims the chance to fully disabuse offenders of this self-serving idea.[73] The victim of crime is given space to detail both the tangible and the hidden forms of suffering caused by the crime: the physical loss as well as the emotional and psychological harms. Unlike "scolding or lecturing," which inspire defensiveness in offenders, restorative justice anticipates that the victim's honest self-disclosure of harm will inspire compassion in the offender. "When offenders are exposed to other people's feelings and discover how victims and others have been affected by their behaviour, they feel empathy for others."[74]

Further, restorative justice seeks to include secondary victims of crime. The optimal restorative encounter is one in which everybody who has been harmed by the offence is present and able to explain the full extent of his or her suffering.[75] Thus restorative encounters are set up to reveal both the depth of suffering to primary victims and the breadth of suffering to others incidentally affected by the crime.[76] It is hoped that bringing the offender face to face with the human damage he has caused will serve, in and of itself, as a form of accountability. The possibility that the offender will "get off on" seeing the human damage he has caused and will enjoy perceiving the full extent of his success in getting even with the world is discounted. Restorative institutions trust that compelling the offender to conceive of the suffering of his victims in a "very lively manner" will inspire compassion in him.[77] Being made to feel compassion for the victim is itself a kind of comeuppance. This is particularly true where this compassion in turn inspires shame and remorse. Thus restorative justice claims a more rigorous form of accountability than traditional institutions of justice.[78] Traditional institutions inflict the impersonal pain of imprisonment without ever forcing the offender in any immediate way to direct his empathic attention to the pain he has caused. Thus participants in restorative justice report that "there is very little real accountability in the revolving door of our criminal justice system ... It's harder to face the victim than to get shuffled through the criminal justice system."[79]

In this idea – that there is an especially tormenting kind of pain for the offender in being forced to attend to and endure the narration of the full extent of the suffering he has caused – we see some overlap between restoration and revenge.[80] The restorative justice critique of punishment is most compelling in its observation that our method of punishment – imprisonment – doesn't get the offender where it really hurts. Imprisonment fails as justice in part because it fails as vengeance. And it fails as vengeance because it can be so easily severed from any meaningful relation to the wrong done to the victim. Restorative encounter is potentially more meaningfully painful and hence more satisfying. It causes suffering that cannot be conceptually or emotionally disengaged from the dignity and suffering of the victim. Restorative justice commends itself as requiring the offender to attend to the humanity and dignity of the people he has wronged. Moreover, the victim becomes the in-your-face – active, and possibly dignified, but most of all *direct* – causal agent of the emotional suffering of the offender. The victim is "empowered" by being restored to the status of active participant. She is no longer infantilized in the tattletale role of the witness hoping to influence a parental judge. Susan Sharpe refers to the words of an ex-convict who is now director of the Kingston chapter of Prison Fellowship Canada to make the point: "He says that 'one of the hardest things for an offender is to face the victim who they hurt, because they feel bad.' He believes most 'would rather work on a rock pile and break rocks all day than go and face the victim or the family of the victim.'"[81]

Consider a typical restorative success story: the familiar tale of a restorative encounter between a burglar and burgled family. In the burglar's estimation, the family suffered simply the inconvenience of having to make a claim on their insurance. In his utilitarian calculus, the thief assesses the transaction as one that maximizes happiness since he gains significantly and his victims don't suffer much at all; indeed, maybe the insurance settlement actually left them better off than they were before the burglary. Restorative justice, instead of merely punishing him impersonally for the violation of the rule, forces him to confront his victims and find out exactly how serious their suffering was. The family details the terror they felt when they realized their home had been violated. The father explains that he is now an insomniac and plagued by anxiety about not being able to protect his family.[82] The mother explains how much the stolen heirloom meant to her; how it belonged to her grandmother, who had given it to her before dying; how she is now afraid to walk outside and also afraid to stay at home.[83] The children, too, may explain their feelings of fear and violation. Perhaps the children's teachers give an account of the difficulties they have been experiencing in school as a result of their anxiety. The family explains how their lives were significantly changed for the worse by the crime. The seriousness of the suffering, once made clear to the offender, inspires compassion in him for his victims, which is followed by remorse and shame. The sense that this process is excruciating for the offender underlies the restorative justice claim that it is not the soft option in comparison to traditional means of punishment.

By such methods, then, does restorative justice hope to elicit compassion in the offender for the victim. Through conversation, the offender comes into a vivid awareness of the victim's pain; he extends compassion from a place of acknowledgment of his own need for reciprocal compassion from his victim; and he identifies with the victim's loss by way of a humility that enables him to recognize himself as together with the victim in a condition of suffering. Let's now look at ways in which Aristotle's conditions for spontaneous compassion discussed in Part I of this chapter might foul up this anticipated structure.

Consider, first, the difficulties surrounding seriousness of suffering. A significant problem arises out of the fact that the victim's suffering may actually not be all that serious. Restorative justice requires some dramatic statement of unanticipated suffering as a necessary kick-off. However, with respect to those not tremendously serious crimes where restorative justice is most often employed – say, breaking and entering and theft under $5,000 – the offender may simply be right to assume that he has caused primarily inconvenience and not much suffering at all. Where the loss is covered by insurance and the victim pays only the deductible, his suffering may amount to nothing more than mere annoyance.

However, in restorative justice narratives, the victim is called upon to elaborate the collateral ways in which she has suffered as a result of the crime. Perhaps the victim of vandalism explains to the offender that she was going through cancer treatment at the time of the offence;[84] the victim whose car was stolen may have lost her job because of not having transportation;[85] or the victim of a burglary may have just completed a year of scrimping and saving to replace items stolen in a burglary the year before.[86] Along with the standard declaration of feeling "so violated," there may be these other aspects of loss that the victim can narrate to engage the offender's compassion. However, unless the victim can come up with a credible story about collateral suffering – especially where the victim is insured against the loss – her suffering may, indeed, not be that serious.[87] The absence of serious suffering on the part of the victim stops the momentum of restorative compassion in its tracks.[88] As the restorative process is not merely about the restitution of material loss, the process is dependent on the victim's willingness and ability credibly to disclose previously hidden wounds inflicted by the offender's conduct.

Second, even if the victim has endured serious suffering, there is the question of whether the offender perceives the victim as having the sensitivity needed to engage the offender's compassion. Recall Rousseau's admonition that "the pity one has for another's misfortune is measured not by the quantity of that misfortune but by the sentiment which one attributes to those who suffer it."[89] Of the examples we looked at in Part I above, all involved situations where those higher up in the social strata viewed those lower down as insensible. Thus the rich had no pity for the poor, whites had no pity for blacks, and so forth. In the context of restorative justice, however, because the perpetrators of crime are likely to occupy a lower socio-economic strata than their victims, we may encounter this same sort of reasoning in an inverted form. It may be that the lower-down offender sees his victims as being too pampered in material comfort to be meaningful sufferers. It may be that the offender has experienced far more serious suffering than he has inflicted on the victim and thus that the victim's narration of her pain may leave the offender cold. An offender may feel contempt for the victim's social and economic advantage.[90] Further, if the offender sees the victim as rich, even the victim's most serious suffering may inspire *schadenfreude* – or even mere disgust – rather than compassion. Disclosure of the victim's sleepless nights worrying about his capacity to defend his upper-middle-class family, for example, may well strike the lower-working-class offender as neurotic, self-cosseting, and undeserving of pity. He may see the suffering he inflicts on the victim as an appropriate evening of the score and even as a just move toward greater equality. And he may regard the victim's sleepless anxieties as a step in the right direction toward more mutual respect.

He may also see the victim as exaggerating the extent of the suffering or the loss. Indeed, some offenders accuse victims of fabricating losses. Umbreit reports that one offender claimed: "We didn't take half the stuff she said we did; either she didn't have it or someone else broke in too." Another protested: "The guy was trying to cheat me – he was coming up with all these lists of things he claims I took."[91] The offender bemoans his bad luck at having robbed a crook. He is now the strange bedfellow of the insurance company, challenging the veracity of the victim's statements about the seriousness of his or her loss.

Third, we have the problem of blamelessness. The question of whether the victim is an innocent sufferer may not arise very often. It may be obvious that the suffering is not the victim's own fault. However, in some contexts, even as the offender hears the victim's narration of her suffering and perceives it in vivid detail, he may also feel that the victim was to blame for her own pain. In cases of domestic violence and sexual assault, for example, the offender may have an underlying belief that the victim asked for it and deserved what she got.[92] Likewise, in some of the hearings of the South African Truth and Reconciliation Commission, one has the sense that the perpetrators believed that their victims had it coming. For example, consider South African police officer Jeffrey Benzien's detailed description of the torture he inflicted on numerous people during police interrogation. Though he clearly recognizes that the suffering he caused was serious, it is equally clear that he viewed his victims as having brought their suffering on themselves by engaging in anti-apartheid activities. Apologizing for his murder of one of his torture victims, Benzien says: "I specifically apologise to the families of Ashly Kriel for the death of their son and brother. Although I deny that I killed him unlawfully and wrongfully, he did however die as a result of an action on my part and for that I apologise."[93] Later, he remarks, "I believed bona fide that due to my expeditious and unorthodox conduct, we made a big difference in the combatting of terror."[94] The possibility of him feeling compassion for his victims is precluded by his view of them as guilty of terrorism. He saw himself as justified in doing what had to be done to prevent their activities. Thus we need to be aware that there are many opportunities for an offender to convince himself that his victims were not innocent in the suffering he inflicted on them and therefore to withhold his compassion for them.[95]

The fourth problem is the practical identification with the suffering of the victim. Here again social stratifications between the victim and offender may play a significant role in obstructing compassion for the victim. The offender may see himself as exempt from the kind of suffering he has inflicted on the victim because he may see himself as unlikely ever to be in a position of sufficient privilege to have what it is that the victim has lost. Here the offender may not simply be unable to identify with the disruption of privilege suffered by the victim; he may also feel hostility arising out of envy of the victim's standing, which allowed her to experience this sort of loss in the first place. To feel compassion for another's loss, one must see her as having fallen from a position previously held meritoriously. Yet, if the thief views the victim's position of security and affluence as undeserved, he may not have much compassion for her downfall.

The normative conditions for restorative compassion would urge the offender to see himself and the victim as sharing in vulnerability to suffering generally, shifting the offender's focus from the details of the victim's loss to the victim and offender's mutual experience as vulnerable human beings. In effecting this shift, the disclosure of collateral harm often becomes necessary to bring compassion into play: The victim needs to supplement her story of material loss with some kind of suffering that the offender is more able to identify with; thus the victim may bring up issues of physical illness, anxiety, and the like. However, once again, it may be that the thief – like the king who has no pity for his subjects – has no pity for his victims because he counts on never having a secure middle-class home and family to protect, or that the rapist counts on never being raped, and so forth. Thus the sort of suffering the offender inflicts on others may be suffering from which he feels exempt, and again this feeling may inhibit his compassion. Though restorative justice seeks to inculcate a more normatively rich understanding of compassion as an ethical achievement, the conditions for spontaneous compassion that Aristotle outlines arise again here to cause trouble.

As before there is the other possibility that the offender may indeed enjoy seeing the victim suffer. Consider the following case, described by

Charles Pollard, of two young men: Ahmed, a Lebanese immigrant, and David, the offender. David robbed Ahmed at knife point, demanding all his money. Ahmed handed over the cash immediately. In the subsequent restorative encounter, Ahmed explained "the fear and humiliation he had felt with a knife at his throat."[96] It is hard to believe that this exchange between two young men would be one of simple explanation of serious suffering and consequent compassion and remorse. David is a young man tough enough to commit an armed robbery. David also appears from the story to enjoy race privilege over Ahmed. It is hard to believe that Ahmed's confession of fear and humiliation would not inspire in David at least some hit of self-satisfaction and an enjoyable feeling of power over Ahmed. It is hard to believe that David might not read Ahmed's testimony as a concession of defeat and as an honouring of David's superior courage. When one young man says to the other "You frightened and humiliated me," isn't this confession as likely to inspire an increase in self-esteem in the listener as it is compassion or remorse?

Let's consider one more example. Football player Najeh Davenport was recently charged with burglary and criminal mischief when he was found in a young woman's dormitory. The report of the incident reads: "According to Miami Shores police, a man entered a female student's dorm room on April 1. The victim awoke at 6:00 a.m. to a strange sound coming from her closet. When she looked in her closet she discovered the stranger, squatting and defecating into her laundry basket."[97] Apparently, such behaviour is not uncommon among burglars.[98] Consider the restorative encounter between this intruder and the victim. Is it not in the nature of such an offence that the wrongdoer is intent on, and even delights in, violating and horrifying the victim? Can we not anticipate that the victim's expression of such horror and violation will be more a satisfying confirmation of the wrongdoer's success than a wake-up call to compassion for the victim? Yet restorative justice consistently disregards the possibility that offenders enjoy both violating the victim and hearing the victim's narration of her distress. And it disregards the further possibility that the offender might enjoy the victim's suffering even as he knows that the right response is to perform compassion and contrition.

These difficulties we have enumerated in eliciting compassion from the offender are sometimes sidestepped by invoking the idea that the compassion of the offender, though necessary, can only be elicited by the suffering of those whom the offender already loves and cares about: his grandmother, grandfather, mother, father, children, friends, and so on. Thus a supplementary disclosure of the seriousness of the suffering of *the offender's* loved ones as secondary victims of the crime is often necessary to engage in a compassionate response in the offender. He is forced to listen to his own grandmother's account of her pain at the disgraceful behaviour of her grandson. Perhaps he might even hear his children's expression of the intense pain they feel at the shame of their father's behaviour. The assumption here is that the suffering of the offender's kin – though potentially not nearly as serious as that of the victims – will be taken more seriously by the offender because of the closeness and caring in the relationship between them.

John Braithwaite concedes that compassionate connections in these closer relations of kinship are often necessary to inspire the offender's shame and remorse.[99] This concession, however, severely limits the range of situations in which restorative justice will be effective. It reveals that restorative justice often relies on the possibility that key members of the offender's kinship group will be willing to, in a sense, betray the offender and side with the victim. Of course, the politics of the kinship group's decision to either defend him or sell him out will be highly complex. However, we can anticipate that the offender's kinship group may be least likely to abandon alliance with him where the offense involves interracial or intergroup violence and the offender's kin share the feelings of intergroup hostility.[100] Likewise, in situations of domestic violence, the batterer's "side of the family" may well feel indignant about aspersions being cast on him and skeptical about the seriousness of the suffering of the victim.[101] If the offender's father taught him how to steal cars, this same father is unlikely to be genuinely distressed by his son's offence.[102] Further, if the offender doesn't have family and community connections, this potential lever into his subjective life will be absent.

Thus there are many instances in which the offender's inner circle – those he cares about and whose suffering he doesn't want to cause – will in fact not suffer as a result of his wrongdoing. They will not feel disgraced by his conduct. Nevertheless, as in blood-feuding societies, the conditions for justice-as-repair are most ripe where the offender is regarded as a liability – a berserk – by his own kin and where they are embarrassed and/or threatened by their associations with him.[103] Once the offender is made aware that his own family and community repudiate him, he knows that he is in much more serious trouble and that he needs to make peace with his victims.

But the offender's compassion for his loved ones is potentially very peripheral to the real forces at play here. Fear may be the driving force. The family's expression of suffering because of the offender's conduct may threaten other potentially more serious punishments to come in the private relations of his community. Their expressions of suffering may indicate primarily that he has displeased people who may have much greater power to make his life miserable than either the victim or the authorities. Thus the emotional hold that the offender's kin have on him may have more to do with his fear that they will inflict extra-legal punishment from within the community than it has to do with his caring about the harm or disgrace he has caused them.

Compassion for the Offender

Even as restorative justice gives more immediate play to the victim's long-ings for satisfying revenge, it also insists that true justice must include a robust reaffirmation of the worth of the offender. The Jewish idea of *tushuvah* – the offender's return to the loving embrace of community – is a necessary condition for justice as repair.[104] Thus the process must somehow engage the victim and community's reciprocal compassion for the offender as the catalyst for the reaffirmation of his moral value. If we look again to Aristotle's conditions for spontaneous compassion, we would presume that generating compassion for the offender was going to be very difficult indeed. First, we have the problems around recogniz-ing the offender's suffering as genuinely serious. His suffering is primar-ily the second-order emotional suffering resulting from his compassion for the victim and his consequent shame and contrition. Yet we know that the offender has self-serving motivations for entering into the pro-cess. One offender speaks about his (voluntary) participation in the process this way: "It wasn't a choice – I didn't want a record."[105] Since he has a self-interested motive for participating, he also has a self-interested motive for delivering a performance of the compassion and remorse required of him. Thus, because we know that his stance of pity and contrition can be feigned, the seriousness of the offender's suffering seems to be pre-sumptively suspect. Second, we might assume that meeting the condition of blamelessness will be an absolute barrier to compassion for the offender. The offender is not innocent in his suffering; he has brought it on him-self by committing the crime. Third, the victim can easily see herself as exempt from the suffering of the offender. It is within her own moral control never to violate others as she has been violated by the offender and, therefore, never to fall prey to the suffering the offender now expe-riences. Thus, as she does not see the offender's suffering as something likely to befall her, she will not have compassion for him.[106]

From these obstacles, we might conclude that no amount of cultiva-tion of a more normatively grounded notion of compassion would be sufficient to outweigh the forces that spontaneously inhibit compassion for the offender. However, oddly enough, once the restorative encounter gets underway, such is not the case. Curiously, as soon as the restorative momentum is in play, spontaneous compassion for the offender becomes the dominant energetic force in the encounter. Further, the compassion we feel for the offender – in its moral and emotional complexity – often upstages the compassion we feel for the victim. Moreover, the victim's compassion for the offender overshadows her desire to receive compassion for her own loss.

A rich mix of stimuli lends a unique element of euphoria to our compassion for offenders. When we behold the hard-hearted wrongdoer racked with compassion for his victims, miserable with remorse for his wrongdoing, chastened in his present humiliation, and disclosing to us the sad past that lead him to a life of crime, we are, in a word, thrilled. Hence the verse in Luke: "Joy shall be in heaven over one sinner that repenteth, more than over ninety and nine just persons, which need no repentance."[107] The suffering of the offender is somehow more interesting – more compelling to our attention than is the suffering of the victim. It irrationally, yet powerfully, registers as more serious, more cathartic, certainly more conducive to joy, and, in some unfathomable sense, more deserving of compassion. This euphoria is at the core of the affective momentum of the restorative encounter.

Let's take a closer look at this idea. At least part of this joy must be *schadenfreude*; there is an enjoyment in seeing the offender miserable. Though this *schadenfreude* may have an element of mean-spiritedness to it, it is primarily righteous. We are happy that the offender is unhappy because his unhappiness is an affirmation of a shared normative order. The offender's pain reassures us that we do live in a moral universe after all.[108] We are also genuinely happy for the sinner inasmuch we want to believe he has truly seen the error of his ways.

George Eliot commends this verse in Luke as an apt rejection of utilitarian willingness to aggregate human suffering and take a statistical approach to morality:

> It was probably a hard saying to the Pharisees, that "there is more joy in heaven over one sinner that repenteth, than over ninety and nine just persons that need no repentance." And certain ingenious philosophers of our own day must surely take offence at a joy so entirely out of correspondence with arithmetical proportion. But a heart that has been taught by its own sore struggles to bleed for the woes of another – that has "learned pity through suffering" – is likely to find very imperfect satisfaction in the "balance of happiness," "doctrine of compensations," and other short and easy methods of obtaining thorough complacency in the presence of pain.[109]

Thus these angels whose joy erupts over the sinner's repentance and who are left cold by the blandness of the just are, for Eliot, insisting on the singularity and incommensurability of human suffering. For Eliot the adage points to the need to view each individual as having untrumpable moral significance: "For angels too there is a transcendent value in human pain, which refuses to be settled by equations."[110]

Yet surely Eliot misses the mark here. The adage is troubling precisely because it does not reject calculations or measurements of suffering and moral worth; rather, it *is* a calculation. It states that the joy over the repentant wrongdoer is rightly *greater than* the joy over the consistent virtue of the ninety-nine just people, that the repentant suffering of one offender is deserving of more moral attention than all suffering and sacrifice hidden in the justness of the ninety-nine boring do-gooders. The verse is pure utilitarianism. The boring just are not the problem; their goodness is discounted because it can be taken for granted. The real gains are all at the margin, and that is where the reclaimed wrongdoer operates.

Certainly the verse owns up to its own unfairness. Yet we can also notice here that it contradicts Socrates' famous admonition that it is better to be a just man who suffers the wrongdoings of others than to be an unjust man who does wrong.[111] Or, at the very least, the verse suggests that it is better to start off as a wrongdoer and to become just later on than it is to be consistently just from the beginning.

Though we balk at the hardness here, the verse describes the restorative justice dynamic to a tee. The guilty suffering of a repentant offender often draws more moral accolade and compassion than the innocent suffering of the victim. Let us try to investigate further, then, why this is so often true, why the euphoric surge of compassion we feel for the contrite offender overshadows the compassion we feel for the victim.

Our compassion for the offender has four primary bases. First, we feel sorry for him insofar as he experiences the pain of compassion for the victim and recognizes himself as the causal agent of her suffering. Second, we feel sorry for the offender in his (closely related) suffering of remorse. We see the offender going through the pain of contrition and extend our compassion to that suffering. Third, we pity the offender in his present humiliation; he is the one who, in the moment of restorative encounter, is being shamed and humiliated. And, finally, we may feel compassion for the offender's life circumstances; we pity the privations, bad influences, and emotional wounds that lead him to crime in the first place.

Let's now look at each of these in turn. Aristotle called pity a kind of pain. Our first ground of pity for the offender is directed to the pain of his compassion, of his having to look in detail at the harmful consequences of what he has done and having to take on board the seriousness of the suffering of his victims. Moreover, his compassion for his victims is not disinterested; it is laced with guilt. He knows that he alone has brought about their suffering. One offender puts it this way: "After meeting the victims, I now realize that I hurt them a lot ... Through mediation,

I was able to understand a lot about what I did. I realized that the victim really got hurt, and that made me feel really bad."[112] We may view the offender's compassion for his victims primarily cynically, yet it is the jumping off point of our fellow-feeling for him.[113]

We feel greater pity, however, in response to the second cause of the offender's suffering: his contrition. We feel sorry for him insofar as he recognizes himself as a wrongdoer. Here our pity for the offender ironically rejoins Socrates' argument that it is worse to be an unjust man who has inflicted harm than a just man who has suffered it. We attribute to the repentant offender a despairing recognition that he has, by his own action, placed himself in the worst possible position. The truly repentant offender perhaps experiences agonies of self-loathing unfathomable to the just person. Thus, if we accept Socrates' idea that it is worse to be unjust than to suffer injustice, the suffering of the critically self-reflective unjust man aware of his injustice *must be* worse than the suffering he has inflicted on his victim. So we have some sense that it may just be true that the second-order pain of the offender is actually more intense than the first-order pain of the victim.

Third, we pity the offender in his humiliation. He is having to place himself in a one-down position. His prostration embarrasses us, and we want to put an end to it. We want, for our own sakes, to end the discomfort we feel at seeing his self-lowering. Watch this dynamic at play in the narration of a pacification ritual in Montenegro, and observe the similarities to the momentum of restorative justice:

And they decreed ... that I should hang the gun which fired the fatal shot around my neck and go on all fours for forty or fifty paces to the brother of the deceased Nikola Perova. I hung the gun to my neck and began to crawl towards him, crying: "Take it, O Kum, in the name of God and St. John." I had not gone ten paces when all the people jumped up and took off their caps and cried out as I did. And by God, though I had killed his brother, my humiliation horrified him, and his face flamed when so many people held their caps in their hands. He ran up and took the gun from my neck. He took me by my pigtail ... and raised me to my feet, and as he kissed me the tears ran down his face, and he said "Happy be our Kumstvo."[114]

Here again we see how the suffering of the offender springs from, yet ultimately outshines, the suffering of the victim. The offender has acknowledged his wrongdoing and connected in sympathy with his victims. He offers himself to them in piteous self-prostration, and the victim and the community feel for the offender in his humiliation. The sources of the spectators' discomfort are many. There is the embarrassment they feel in seeing the wrongdoer in an undignified state. There is the further anxiety they may feel in wondering whether they are becoming wrong-doers through their participation in his humiliation. There is the anxiety of being the object of impassioned supplication along with the sense of success in having broken the offender's will. Further, there is the fact that the offender's suffering is here, now, and of the moment. The urgency and immediacy of the offender's present suffering outdoes the stale suf-fering of the victim.

This discomfort felt by the victim and community is what John McDon-ald and David Moore refer to as a "collective experience of shame." Speak-ing of the emotional momentum of the restorative encounter, they write:

> The crucial dynamic is not that *one* conference participant expresses shame and thereby clears the hurdle beyond which reintegration can occur. Rather, the crucial dynamic is that *all participants* experience a sense of shame, and this experience marks the transition from a gener-ally negative emotional climate to a generally positive emotional climate. The collective experience of shame marks the transition from conflict to cooperation.[115]

This shame on the part of the other participants is a kind of vicarious experience of the offenders' shame and a feeling of compassion for it. All the participants end up feeling shame in a ritual that is, admittedly, designed to embarrass everyone. The reason the emotional climate shifts once the victim and community also feel shame is that they then have a desire to put an end to the offender's humiliation as a means of end-ing their own feelings of shame and social discomfort.

The offender's misery offers the only opportunity for immediate ame-liorating action. In the context of restorative justice, this opportunity to put an end to the offender's suffering becomes irresistible given both the victim's shame and embarrassment and the stated goal of restorative jus-tice to make things better again. While we have no immediate power to undo the pain of the victim, we do have the power to end the offend-er's shame and remorse. Thus, even as the victim's compassion for the offender is, in a sense, parasitic on the offender's compassion for the vic-tim (the victim feels sorry for the offender feeling sorry), so too does restorative justice seek an end to the victim's suffering that is parasitic on the end of the suffering of the offender: Closure for the suffering of the offender is meant to effect a reciprocal release of the victim from the stigma and pain of the wrongdoing.

This dynamic dovetails into the fourth ground of compassion for the offender: We pity the offender's narrative of the hardships and deprivations that lead him to crime. Consider another of Mark Umbreit's case studies.

Josh was a young car thief who had admitted "to stealing forty-one vehicles over the course of about three years."[116] One of the cars he stole was Tammy's – whose losses as a result of the theft included having no way to get to work for an entire month. When she finally got her car back, it had been "trashed." She had to clean up the car herself, yet, as much as she scrubbed and vacuumed, it still felt dirty to her. She did not have enough money to get the starter fixed, so she had to use a screwdriver to start the car.

Going into a restorative encounter with Josh, Tammy was angry. Like most victims, she wanted the offender, Josh, to understand how violated she felt.[117] She was determined that Josh should have to pay the $700.00 it would cost to have the starter repaired. She apparently was not making any further claim for loss of earnings suffered as a result of the theft.[118] Once the restorative encounter was underway, however, Tammy's manner became more subdued. She "shared [her] feelings and the impact of the crime in an honest and heartfelt but gentle manner." Josh then responded by giving some background of his life. He narrated some details of his childhood. At an early age, "'a close adult male family member,' he said, had 'taught me how to steal cars and sell dope.'" Josh explained that he was from a broken home and that he rarely saw his father. At a very early age, he had been "initiated into a gang" for which criminal behaviour was the norm. Josh further revealed that his best friend had recently been "killed in a high-speed chase with police while attempting to evade arrest in the stolen vehicle he was driving." Josh shared his grief at his friend's death and explained that he saw the fact of his being caught in the theft of Tammy's car as the *sine qua non* of his not having died along with his friend. "I would have been with Allen that night if I wasn't in detention ... That would have been *me*."[119] As he spoke, Josh "hung his head" with remorse.[120]

By the end of the restorative encounter, the primary focus of all became concern for Josh and "how much support Josh would have once he got home."[121] After hearing Josh's story, Tammy dropped her claim for monetary restitutions. Reflecting on the experience, Tammy says: "I expected myself to be meaner to him, but I guess my human compassion just kicked in."[122] Tammy begins with the desire to focus the process on *her* suffering. Yet, by the end of the encounter, she sees his suffering as the more pressing concern. Her own suffering in a once-off incident of car theft pales in comparison to Josh's lifetime of hardship, neglect, and loss. Thus Tammy moves into the role of primary giver of compassion and comes to see Josh's needs as more significant than her own. Her compassion for him erases her vigilance about keeping her suffering in the foreground and overshadows her justice-based desire to make Josh pay for her loss.

The case study of Josh and Tammy demonstrates perfectly how the suffering of the offender outdoes the suffering of the victim and how the focus of the restorative process becomes the extension of understanding and support to the offender. It also demonstrates one of the core difficulties of the logic of restorative justice. Restorative justice seeks to elicit the pain of compassionate contrition in the offender. However, it also holds that it is unjust to meet wrongdoing by inflicting more suffering. This conviction, combined as we have seen with the sense that the only way to make things better is to release the offender from the suffering of his contrition, leads inexorably toward a surge of fellow-feeling for the offender. Yet the mark of a truly contrite offender surely must be authentic willingness to endure further serious suffering as penance. People who are genuinely contrite make rigorous demands upon themselves and do not wish to be exempt from the pain of having to make restitution and of having to remain in the misery of their remorse. If Josh *really* were sorry, *he* would make the demand upon *himself* that he pay to fix Tammy's starter. He would not allow the focus of the proceedings to shift from her suffering to his. Thus the only person truly deserving of the benefit of justice-as-repair is the same person who would insist on self-punishment.

Think again of the quotation from George Eliot at the beginning of the chapter. Fred Vincy has just defaulted on a loan guaranteed by Mary Garth's father, Caleb Garth. Both Fred's need of the money and his inability to pay it back were occasioned by his self-indulgent extravagance. The Garths are hardworking, plain-speaking, sensible, and intelligent people of exceptional integrity. Fred Vincy, in comparison to the Garths, is an insubstantial dandy. As a result of Fred's failure to pay, Mrs. Garth, Mary's mother, must now give up her plan of sending their eldest son to school. The money she had been saving for four years is now needed to make up for Fred's debt. Mary's savings too will now be consumed by the same purpose. Yet, in confessing to Mary, Fred focuses on his own pain and misery at having caused the loss and not the pain of those he has harmed. He reproaches Mary, the victim, for her lack of pity for him in the pain of his contrition. Fred's statement embodies the gist of every wrongdoer's speech in the restorative encounter: *"I am so miserable ... if you knew how miserable I am, you would be sorry for me."* And Mary's reply seems to me to be worth careful consideration in this context: *"There are other things to be more sorry for than that. But selfish people always think their own discomfort of more importance than anything else in the world."* Mary sees clearly the spurious strategy of the wrongdoer who tries to make his pain of contrition the centre of attention in the aftermath of his wrongdoing. Fred's counter-argument, too, is not alien to the terrain of restorative justice: the claim that though he has done wrong, he is not a criminal in any significant sense. Note here again how the wrongdoer is placed in the position of accuser of the victim who withholds sympathy. *"It is hardly fair to call me selfish. If you knew what things other young men do, you would think me a good way off the worst."* But there is a right-headedness in Mary's stance, and we are grateful for her attempts to point out to Fred that compassion in the situation should not so readily be transferred from the victim of the wrongdoing to its perpetrator.

Consider now another case Braithwaite sites as supporting the virtues of restorative justice.[123] Fifteen-year-old Danny set a fire in his school library that destroyed the building. Realizing the terrible damage he had caused, Danny gave himself up to the police and confessed. Danny explained to the police that he felt remorseful. Danny was sentenced to two years in a juvenile institution. His response to his sentence was: "Well, if I've learnt anything from all this, then it's not to tell anyone if I do something wrong!" Later, the headmaster of the school made it clear that he did not want to see Danny in prison. A restorative conference was convened in which Danny was able to express contrition and receive forgiveness. The headmaster told Danny, "Now we all have to make sure that you can heal from this experience." "Danny's father, walking behind them, said, 'isn't it wonderful to see those two chatting away ... like the best of friends.'" Braithwaite suggests that there is instruction to be found in Danny's statement "Well, if I've learnt anything from all this, then it's not to tell anyone if I do something wrong!" We do not want to teach offenders that it is not in their best interests to confess or to feel remorse. But the assumption behind Danny's bitterness is that if one is remorseful, one is entitled to mercy – that one ought to be entitled to trade truth and remorse for absolution. But again would genuine remorse not preclude Danny's sense of entitlement to be excused from punishment because he confessed and feels sorry?

A true sign of penitence is if the wrongdoer believes that he will ultimately be, as Socrates says, "less miserable if he be punished and meets with retribution at the hands of gods and men."[124] The repentant offender seeks an indefinite future of suffering. George Eliot puts it this way: "The true penitent, hating his self-besotted error, asks from all coming life duty instead of joy, and service instead of ease."[125] Even the prodigal son, returning from a binge of sin, seeks the humiliation of a life of toil and asks his father to "make me as one of thy hired servants."[126] But, like the compassionate father who responds to the self-humiliation of his son by giving him the finest robe and the biggest party, the compassionate stance of restorative justice can't brook the offender's pain. We want immediately to put the offender and ourselves out of the misery of his remorse and humiliation. We end his suffering by rushing to return him to pride of place within the community.[127]

The offender's suffering ends up counting for more, first, because of the possibility of its actually being that most despairing suffering produced by the recognition of one's unjustness; second, because it marks a break-through, a conversion, an epiphany; third, because, as such, it holds out optimistic promise for positive change; fourth, because it appears to be more immediate than the past suffering of the victim; and, finally, because it is the only suffering to which we have the power to put an end. It is suffering that holds within it the possibility of a collective experience of release from discomfort and despair.

Conclusion

We have covered a lot of ground in this chapter. We began by looking at some of the difficulties in the relationship between compassion and justice-as-adjudication, and I concluded that arbitrary and irrational elements in compassion make it an unreliable guide for the judge. We then went on to try to understand how it is that restorative justice seeks to forge a new and more immediate relationship between compassion and justice. We saw that restorative justice commends conversation and face-to-face encounter as the basic pedagogical tools for inculcating compassion. It strives to offer a procedural framework for, and conceptual understanding of, justice that promotes and makes legitimate space for compassion as an ethical achievement. The egalitarian procedures of restorative justice dovetail into this sense of compassion as the humble recognition of oneself and others as vulnerable to suffering and as competent agents of repair. Restorative justice likewise promotes an understanding of compassion as paradigmatically mutual, which supports the restorative understanding of justice as right-relation understood in terms of mutual equality and respect.

I then went on to critique this understanding of compassion within restorative justice, arguing that with respect to the attempt to elicit compassion for the victim in the offender, restorative justice papers over the fact that the offender has self-serving motivations to perform compassion for the victims. Likewise, there are many potential barriers arising out of Aristotle's conditions for spontaneous compassion that inhibit the offender's feeling genuine compassion for the victim. We then went on to look at how restorative justice seeks to elicit compassion in the victim for the offender, and here we found that Aristotle's conditions for spontaneous compassion, surprisingly, did not intervene to inhibit compassion for the offender. Instead, we saw that the restorative encounter encouraged an outpouring of compassion for the contrite offender. The offender's suffering and humiliation was seen to upstage the suffering of the victim. Further, the dynamics of the encounter created an irresistible magnetic pull toward the release of the offender from the pain of his shame, compassion, and contrition.

Restorative justice, then, is a ritual that we purposefully create with a view to eliciting a performance of the offender's compassion and remorse. We know that his remorse will make us uncomfortable and embarrassed, that we will want to put a stop to this – *our own vicarious discomfort* – and that the only way to do so will be by restoring the offender to pride of place. As Braitwaite puts it, "When someone who has wronged us says they are sorry and walks over to us to shake our hand, not many of us are so determinedly unforgiving as to refuse to extend our hand in response."[128] Thus the ritual is one designed to induce the victim and community "sharply [to] terminate disapproval with forgiveness."[129] The momentum of the restorative encounter thus takes advantage of the good nature of the victim and community, riding on the strange but compelling power of that combined discomfort and euphoria we feel over the sinner who repents.

Epilogue:
Restorative Utopias – "The Fire with Which We Must Play"?

> These conservatives want young people to know that this tawdry old world cannot respond to their demands for perfection ... But ... idealism as it is commonly conceived should have primacy in an education, for man is a being who must take his orientation by his possible perfection ... Utopianism is, as Plato taught us at the outset, the fire with which we must play because it is the only way we can find out what we are. We need to criticize false understandings of Utopia, but the easy way out provided by realism is deadly.
>
> – Allan Bloom, *The Closing of the American Mind*

I hope that in these pages I have been productively criticizing a false understanding of utopia and have not been simply trying to put the kybosh on the worthwhile utopian aspirations of restorative justice by warning that "this tawdry old world cannot respond to [its] demands for perfection." Bloom is right (this time). We should eschew the kind of wet blanket conservatism that will not take any risks in envisioning and aspiring to better worlds and better selves. We ought to support the pursuit of better things. And we ought to lament the crushing power of those nay-saying voices that squelch the optimistic and creative impulse to try our potential for good. But I have come to the conclusion that the vision restorative justice offers us is not a vision of perfection or even of anything genuinely desirable. The sensibility of restorative justice is drawn from a whitewashing culture informed by new-age thinking ("I love and affirm everything in the universe"), self-help ("what I hear you saying is ..."), pop psychology's mantra that "revealing is healing,"[1] and a soft religion that, instead of seeing punishment as an integral part of processes of repentance and forgiveness, sees repentance and forgiveness as a substitute for punishment. Its sensibility is drawn from a culture that not only tells us that everything, including justice, is a matter of expressing and validating our own and other's feelings, but also feeds us canned, synthetic lines for doing both.[2] The so-called magic of the restorative ritual requires us to buy into these ersatz pieties.

Restorative justice tells us the same predictable story over and over again: After the crime is committed, the victim and offender meet. The victim tells the offender about the harm she has suffered, and the offender confesses, is remorseful and apologetic, and may make some, usually nominal, reparation. The victim in turn shows concern for the offender and does something intended to help the offender turn over a new leaf. Victim and offender are now in harmony, and justice is seen to have been done.

My aversion to the reductionism and sentimentality of this vision, my conclusion that it's not utopian in any appealing sense, has driven my attempt to try to draw on counter-stories from good novelists. I am convinced that we need them here because they have the ability to show us more facets of human personality and interaction than the professionalized and hence bowdlerized "I hear your anger" that restorative justice culture is capable of perceiving or relating. It has been my intention to try to show that many of these stories that contradict the premises of restorative justice resonate far more profoundly with our honest perception of ourselves and each other than do the stories that restorative justice asks us to buy as the foundation for a new conception of justice.

Let me conclude by sketching an alternative utopia. In this utopia, victims of crime are validated and protected. And they aren't expected to spend their time and energy sitting down with the people who have raped, assaulted, tortured, or stolen from them, or murdered their loved ones, trying to work toward an amicable agreement. There are strong institutions of criminal justice that are "as little disposed to endure as to offer an injury" to any member of the community.[3] In this utopia the bad guy getting painfully skewered can still potentially be a very good thing.

Moreover, in this utopia, prisons are not crime schools. Nor are they environments where prisoners are routinely subjected to brutal sexual and other assaults and humiliations.[4] Prisons are meaningfully rehabilitative as well as seriously punitive. They inflict suffering on offenders as a matter of justice, restrain the liberty of offenders as a matter of protection, and extend assistance to help offenders make better lives for themselves as a matter of common sense and humanity.[5] In this utopia, prosecutors have enough time to talk to victims at length, and there are people to help victims through the criminal justice system so that they understand and are not intimidated by its complexity.[6] Courtrooms are not threatening arenas for harassing witnesses. Witnesses are reliably protected from violent or other repercussions for giving evidence against wrongdoers. Victims and others are given patient and open space in which to tell their stories with dignity and in a way that makes them feel that they have had their say. When offenders get out of prison, victims are notified and are protected from further violence.

This utopian vision may sound impossible. And the difficulty of achieving it surely has been one of the forces propelling the popularity of the restorative justice movement: Because implementing all these things is too costly and too time-consuming for the government, we turn instead to the dewy-eyed alternative of restorative justice, which tells us that all the benefits of this utopia can be had in a new world of apology, forgiveness, and reconciliation. In the restorative utopia, the duty and costs of administering criminal justice (perhaps the chief responsibility and raison d'être of the state) are, for the most part, offloaded onto victims and communities.[7]

The desirability of a utopian vision is a more important ground for evaluating it than the possibility of its achievement. Even impossible utopian visions can still enliven us and point us in the right direction though we never attain what we imagine. But the utopian vision *must* be worthwhile. And I am skeptical that a vision of justice in which wrongdoing is resolved by reconciliation and making-up between victim and wrongdoer *is* worthwhile. The utopia of restorative justice is one where every story of violation and loss ends happily in right-relation. But think of the amount of authentic human experience that would have to be bulldozed in order to build this utopia. The destruction of honest, spontaneous human response that would be wrought by a system that sought and achieved right-relation between every offender and victim would be staggering. This utopian vision isn't one that challenges us to a greater, more creative, more rigorous life. It is one in which everybody behaves according to a predictable set of expectations, and the rest of us credit them with doing so authentically. This vision is far more Panglossian than it is utopian.

In his book *Punishment and Restorative Crime-Handling: A Social Theory of Trust,* restorative justice advocate Aleksandar Fatić sees restorative justice as a movement directed toward bringing about a culture that is both trusting and pacifist. (I am reminded here of the Muslim proverb: Trust in Allah and tie up your camel.) Institutions of restorative justice are what Fatić calls "trust encouraging." Fatić, who believes we should aim to eliminate punishment completely,[8] argues that restorative justice is not utopian.[9] By this he means that its vision is not unattainable: "I hope to show that the assumption that the existing culture of aggression can in fact be transformed into a pacifist one is not incoherent, nor utopian."[10] He argues that just as our culture has shifted from one where equal opportunity was not a value to one where it is seen as morally required, so can our culture shift from one where coercion is seen as necessary to one where restoration is seen as "morally required."[11] Thus, by a process of "moral enlightenment" spurred on by lobbying and pressure of various kinds, society would eventually come to see a pacifist, healing response to crime as mandatory in a morally defensible world.

But, as we have seen, a morality and practice of pacifism, though it presents a worthwhile ideal, must recognize and embrace martyrdom as its likely end. Certainly Gandhi himself clearly understood facing death to be the practice of his theory. And when he preached pacifism to his followers, he was urging them to accept a death that he also was resolutely willing to, and did, face.

But a pacifism that anticipates and counts on its own success in subduing the violence of others is culpably naive. Reinhold Niebuhr, perhaps the greatest Christian thinker of the twentieth century, puts it this way:

> This kind of pacifism is not content with martyrdom and with political irresponsibility. It is always fashioning political alternatives to the tragic business of resisting tyranny and establishing justice by coercion. However it twists and turns, this alternative is revealed upon close inspection to be nothing more than a capitulation to tyranny. Now capitulation to tyranny in the name of nonresistant perfection may be very noble for the individual. But it becomes rather ignoble when the idealist suggests that others besides himself shall be sold into slavery and shall groan under the tyrant's heel.[12]

Niebuhr is speaking of pacifism in the international context, but the point can equally be made about the pacifism of restorative justice. It is possibly (though not necessarily) very noble for a victim of crime as an individual to follow a self-imposed ethic of pacifism in relation to one who has wronged him and to seek repair of relations instead of punishment.[13] (Our present system, however, has good reasons for not always allowing a victim's pacifism to carry the day.) But for restorative justice advocates to urge this pacifism on others besides themselves with promises of healing is to give over to professional enthusiasm and lofty ideals while at the same time being reckless with the interests of others. Restorative justice is yet another trendy alternative to getting down to "the tragic business of ... establishing justice by coercion." Moreover, the power that restorative justice capitulates to is not even primarily that of criminals cunning enough to know how to play restorative justice's expectations to their advantage. Its more significant capitulation is to the benumbing power of a synthetic sensibility. Restorative justice perhaps rightly assumes that crime is a function of the offender's alienation from society. But it refuses to acknowledge the possibility that participation in staged rituals of reconciliation might intensify this alienation rather than relieve it.

Let me conclude with an argument in favour of restorative justice made by Chief Justice Bayda of Saskatchewan. It is perhaps the most persuasive one I've heard. As John Braithwaite reports: "Bayda invited his audience to imagine they were alone late at night in the dark streets of a metropolis. There are two routes home. On one street live 1,000 criminals who have been through the Canadian prisons system. On the other street are 1,000 criminals who have been through a restorative justice process.

Which street do you choose?"[14] I'm inclined, at first blush, to choose the restorative justice road. But why? Perhaps it is because I suspect that the criminals who live there will be less angry and less hardened, less likely to want to get back at the world.[15] But this expectation only demonstrates that the best thing restorative justice has going for it is our awareness of the terrible failure of the prison system.[16] Moreover, it also demonstrates that restorative justice is, to some degree, emotionally grounded in fear of criminals and a craven hope that they will be nicer to us if we don't offend them with punishment. Ultimately, however, it looks to me as though, whichever road I take here, I am going to get mugged, beaten, and maybe even murdered. The thing for me to keep in mind is that, if I take the restorative justice road, after the violence is over, I am (or, if I'm dead, my family is) going to have to sit down with the criminals and try to repair that broken relation in a restorative, healing encounter. Perhaps I'll take the other road after all.

Notes

Chapter 1: The Seductive Vision of Restorative Justice

1 Van Ness and Strong, *Restoring Justice*, 2nd ed., 49.
2 Sharpe, *Restorative Justice*, 3.
3 Christie, "Conflict as Property."
4 Pollard, "Victims and the Criminal Justice System," 11-12.
5 Zehr, *Changing Lenses*, 34.
6 Bianchi, *Justice as Sanctuary*, 35; Braithwaite, *Crime, Shame, and Reintegration*, Ch. 2, "The Dominant Theoretical Traditions: Labelling, Subculture, Control, Opportunities and Learning Theories"; Van Ness and Strong, *Restoring Justice*, 2nd ed., 7; Zehr, *Changing Lenses*, Ch. 3, "The Offender."
7 Llewellyn and Howse, "Institutions for Restorative Justice," 357, and *Restorative Justice*, 37-41.
8 Llewellyn and Howse, "Institutions for Restorative Justice," 376, emphasis in the original.
9 Heyward, *Staying Power*, 16-17. Heyward uses the phrase "right-relation" to explain Martin Buber's concept of I and Thou. See also, for example, Buber's discussion of relationality in *I and Thou*, 69-72; Umbreit, *Handbook of Victim Offender Mediation*, xxxi, Item 5.
10 Van Ness and Strong, *Restoring Justice*, 2nd ed., 55.
11 For a persuasive account of the benefits of restorative justice on this score – especially with respect to victim inclusion in the process – see Pollard, "Victims and the Criminal Justice System."
12 See Christie, "Between Civility and State."
13 We can turn to Michael L. Hadley's introduction to *The Spiritual Roots of Restorative Justice* for a classic statement of restorative justice: "Restorative justice, with its principles of repentance, forgiveness, and reconciliation, is instead [of a quick fix] a deeply spiritual process. It is never the easy way out; neither for the offender, the victim, or the community. It requires all of us to come to grips with who we are, what we have done, and what we can become in the fulness of our humanity. It is about doing justice as if people really mattered; it addresses the need for a vision of the good life, and the Common Good. To borrow the title of a recent study the restorative approach is concerned with restoring the moral bond of community" (9).
14 As Pollard notes, the present system usually requires victims and perpetrators to deal with their respective difficulties in isolation ("Victims and the Criminal Justice System," 7).
15 Llewellyn and Howse, "Institutions for Restorative Justice," 375; Llewellyn, *Restorative Justice*, 2.
16 Braithwaite, "Restorative Justice and Social Justice."
17 Mary Daly, *Gyn/Ecology*; Dworkin, *Intercourse*; MacKinnon, *Toward a Feminist Theory of the State*.
18 Robert Solomon argues that these negative emotions have been given too short shrift in our understanding of justice, that we have been too quick to disown the energy of

their affective force toward justice, and that we have privileged the relationship between justice and those kinder gentler emotions like compassion and empathy. But this analysis appears unaware that certain struggles for justice – particularly gender justice – are powerfully and inextricably identified with anger and vitriol. See Solomon, *A Passion for Justice*, Ch. 6, "The Cultivation of Justice and the Negative Emotions."

19 On feminism and the politics of resentment, see Elshtain, "Politics and Forgiveness," 44. See also Martin, "Retribution Revisited."

20 On the question of whether love is threatened by an increase in justice in an intimate relationship, see Okin, *Justice Gender and The Family,* 28 et seq. Okin rejects Michael Sandel's idea that love is a higher virtue than justice and his claim that moves toward greater love can sometimes threaten love, shared purpose, and spontaneous affection (*Liberalism and the Limits of Justice,* 31 et seq.).

21 For a feminist discussion of restorative justice as an alternative to retributive justice for violence against women, see Martin, "Retribution Revisited."

22 Braithwaite, *Crime, Shame, and Reintegration.*

23 Jurevic, for example, notes: "When I practiced law, the legal remedies I was able to offer and procure for my clients often did not bring significant or meaningful change to their lives. The abused wife who received custody of her children would return with an illegal eviction notice or a problem with receiving public benefits or a dispute concerning access visits. Training students to enter the legal profession seemed like adding to the problem, and my attempts at introducing alternative perspectives on dispute resolution were often met with questions such as 'What does this have to do with The Law,' or 'How will this help me get Articles?' Researching issues such as the Stolen Generations or Domestic Violence was becoming unsatisfying given the constraints imposed by legal thought, theory, and language. I, like many other lawyers, felt little joy when contemplating anything legal" (*"What's Love Got to Do With It?"* prologue).

24 Buber, *I and Thou,* 62.

25 Braithwaite, *Restorative Justice and Responsive Regulation,* 10.

26 Van Ness and Strong, *Restoring Justice,* 1st ed., 152; Zehr, *Changing Lenses,* 28; Umbreit, "Crime Victims Seeking Fairness Not Revenge."

27 Kerruish, *Jurisprudence as Ideology,* 17, 172. In many ways, Valerie Kerruish's critique of rights provides a sophisticated foundation for restorative justice. Kerruish argues that like the fetishist who replaces the lover with a shoe, our legal system puts rights in place of the experience of respect in relationship. See herein Chapter 3, "Three Precarious Pillars of Restorative Justice," Section 1, "Malleability of the Meaning of Justice."

28 Llewellyn and Howse, "Institutions for Restorative Justice," 376. See also Nietzsche, *On the Genealogy of Morals,* 14.

29 Zehr, *Changing Lenses,* 42.

30 See, for example, Fatić's discussion of restorative justice as a "trust encouraging" institution and the possibility of creating a pacifist culture through institutions of restorative justice (*Punishment and Restorative Crime-Handling,* 222-23).

31 *ABC Nightline,* 1 January 1999; *All Things Considered,* 13 December 1996; *All Things Considered,* 15 April 1996. See, generally, *Truth and Reconciliation Commission of South Africa Report* and "Truth, the Road to Reconciliation: Official Truth and Reconciliation Commission Website," <http://www.truth.org.za/index.htm> (6 June 2002).

32 Evers, "A Healing Approach to Crime." This understanding of the role of restorative justice as a means of conclusively putting an end to relations between victims and perpetrators of sexual assault goes against Heyward's discussion of right-relation as paradigmatically erotic. It essentially adopts the idea that sometimes right-relation can and should mean no relation. See herein Chapter 5, "'Lovemaking is Justice-Making': The Idealization of Eros and the Eroticization of Justice."

33 *Ideas,* "Justice as Sanctuary," with Herman Bianchi, Part 1, Canadian Broadcasting Corporation Radio Program; Umbreit, *Handbook of Victim Offender Mediation:* "One of the most powerful and perhaps most powerful expressions of the transformative qualities of empowerment and recognition has been consistently observed in the small but

growing application of mediation and dialogue between parents of murdered children and the murderer" (8-9).

34 Evers, "A Healing Approach to Crime," 46. It is sometimes only the perpetrator who has the information necessary to assist the victim with healing; that is, the perpetrator is the only source of information about the details of the abuse in cases where the victim has repressed memories of it. Likewise the perpetrator is the only one in a position to give an unqualified acknowledgment of reality of the abuse and an absolute assurance that it was not the fault of the victim. This is not to say that others cannot assist the victim with understanding that the abuse was not her fault. However, victims report being particularly affected by the statements of wrongdoers to that effect.

35 For a discussion of the shared stigma of victims and offenders, see Van Ness and Strong, *Restoring Justice,* 2nd ed., 101. See also La Prairie, "Developments in Criminal Law and Criminal Justice," 581.

36 For a discussion of the requirement of the lack of consistency in restorative justice, see Delgado, "Goodbye to Hammurabi," 759.

37 See Ashworth, "Some Reservations about Restorative Justice," and "Responsibilities, Rights and Restorative Justice."

38 Allen, "Balancing Justice and Social Utility," 317.

39 It is interesting to note that Voltaire's *Candide* can be retrospectively read as a critique of the present new-age movement. So many ideological staples of the new-age movement (by which restorative justice is tremendously influenced, not to mention fuelled), in particular the idea that everything that happens is rightly construed as being somehow for the good, are fully formulated in the character of Dr. Pangloss and subsequently ridiculed. But the Western intellectual history of new-age hyperoptimism is far older than the movement itself seems to be aware.

40 Van Ness and Strong, *Restoring Justice,* 2nd ed., 249.

41 Hadley, *The Spiritual Roots of Restorative Justice,* 9.

42 Braithwaite, *Restorative Justice and Responsive Regulation,* 3. Braithwaite attributes the insight to Aug San Suu Kyi and the Dalai Lama.

43 See, for example, Biggar: "The ultimate of fulfilment of justice is reconciliation ... and ... reconciliation requires forgiveness." He uses this formulation, however, to conclude that in this world, "full justice in the case of murder is impossible, since the victim, being dead, cannot forgive" (ed., *Burying the Past,* 18).

44 Derrida, *On Cosmopolitanism and Forgiveness,* 32-3.

45 See Arendt, *The Human Condition.* Both Arendt and Derrida stress that punishment and forgiveness are not in opposition to one another. Arendt writes: "The alternative to forgiveness, but by no means its opposite, is punishment, and both have in common that they attempt to put an end to something that without interference could go on endlessly. It is therefore quite significant, a structural element in the realm of human affairs, that men are unable to forgive what they cannot punish and that they are unable to punish what has turned out to be unforgivable" (241).

46 Again here *Arendt* would disagree with Derrida to say that the impossibility of proportionate punishment entails the impossibility of forgiveness (*The Human Condition,* 241).

47 Derrida, *On Cosmopolitanism and Forgiveness,* 39.

48 Ibid., 42. See *Truth and Reconciliation Commission of South Africa Report,* vol. 1. The commission's mandate with respect to amnesty is to facilitate "the granting of amnesty to persons who make full disclosure of all the relevant facts relating to acts associated with a political objective" (55). So the criteria for amnesty are disclosure and political purpose. Neither apology nor remorse were conditions of amnesty under the terms of the Truth and Reconciliation Commission.

49 Derrida, *On Cosmopolitanism and Forgiveness,* 35-6.

50 For example, Umbreit writes: "Although forgiveness may be an outcome of the dialogue for some, it is not the goal of the program. To recognize the humanity of the person who took the life of your child is not easy but can be done. To want that person as well as yourself to heal and therefore to become better at living nonviolently is understandable

and attainable. But to forgive the individual for what she or he has done requires almost superhuman effort" (*Handbook of Victim Offender Mediation,* 286).

51 In *Justice as Sanctuary,* Bianchi acknowledges the huge difficulties of adopting time-consuming restorative practices in our time-is-money culture (117).

52 Llewellyn and Howse, "Institutions for Restorative Justice," 378-79. Restoration must take place in the relationship between victim, offender, and the community.

53 *Ideas,* "Justice as Sanctuary," with Herman Bianchi, Part 2, Canadian Broadcasting Corporation Radio Program.

54 See Bianchi, *Justice as Sanctuary,* Ch. 5, "Sanctuary," in which he reviews historical precedents for restorative justice drawn from ancient, medieval, and early-modern practices.

55 Boehm, *Blood Revenge,* 136; Miller, *Bloodtaking and Peacemaking,* 122-24, 171-74; Hasluck, *The Unwritten Law in Albania;* marriage was another means of pacification (257). Interestingly, we also see this idea being put forward in the epic film *Gandhi,* where Gandhi's advise to a penitent Hindu wishing to make amends for violence done to Muslims was that the man should take an orphan Muslim child and bring it up as though it were his own.

56 Miller, *Bloodtaking and Peacemaking,* 172.

57 Ibid.

58 Ibid.

59 For a discussion of debt-slavery, see Miller, *Bloodtaking and Peacemaking,* 29, 75, 129, 148-49.

60 It's interesting that the persuasiveness of stories advocating restorative justice often rests on the wrong-headed rejection of imagined restorative solutions whereas the persuasiveness of stories critiquing revenge often rests on the presence of botched and unsatisfying revenge.

61 While restorative justice advocates will often say that the victim and offender need not be friends, most restorative case studies or vignettes end up with some sense of friendship and affection between the victim and offender. Take, for example, Braithwaite's description of the relation between a teenager who burned down the school library and the school's headmaster after a restorative conference. The boy's father remarks: "To be honest with you I couldn't see that this would do any good, and have wondered if it might make things worse ... but isn't it wonderful to see those two chatting away like the best of friends" (*Restorative Justice and Responsive Regulation,* 9). All three of Umbreit's case studies in *The Handbook of Victim Offender Mediation* end with affirmations of friendship between victim and offender. The first ends with the robber, Jim, inviting the victims, Bob and Anne, over for dinner: "The meeting was scheduled two months later at Jim's home, with a mediator present. Jim offered to cook lasagna. Bob and Anne quickly indicated their interest" (90). The second case study ends with the victim of car theft, Tom, offering unconditional support to the offender, Josh. "Tom gave Josh his home telephone number and told Josh he would be available any time of the day or night if Josh needed to talk, needed support, or for any reason at all. Josh's eyes filled with tears as he thanked each one of them. He said he couldn't believe that they could care so much for him after what he had done to them" (97). The final case study ends with the offenders hugging the victim. "As the mediators closed the session, most of the parents and young people [the offenders] came over to hug Barbara [the victim] and offer words of encouragement" (104).

62 Of course, it is also true that retributive justice is grounded in fantasies of the satisfaction of vengeance. See Miller, "In Defence of Revenge" and "Clint Eastwood and Equity." Interestingly, however, restorative critiques of vengeance are often built upon a combination of concrete examples of botched revenge and fantasized examples of restorative healing.

63 Allen, "Balancing Justice and Social Utility," 317.

64 Dinnen, "Restorative Justice in Papua New Guinea"; Kwochka, "Aboriginal Injustice"; La Prairie, "Developments in Criminal Law and Criminal Justice" and "Some Reflections on New Criminal Justice in Canada"; Ross, "Restorative Justice"; Yazzie, "'Hozho Nahasdlii.'"

65 Umbreit, *Handbook of Victim Offender Mediation,* 5.

66 Umbreit, "Holding Juvenile Offenders Accountable" and "Restorative Family Group Conferences"; Umbreit and Coates, "Multicultural Implications of Restorative Juvenile Justice."

67 Umbreit and Bradshaw, however, report that victims are about as satisfied with victim-offender mediation when the offender is an adult as they are when the offender is a juvenile. The authors use the study to argue that restorative justice should be expanded into the area of adult crime ("Victim Experience of Meeting Adult vs. Juvenile Offenders").

68 It is interesting to note that Braithwaite's initial theories about reintegrative shaming were fleshed out in the context of corporate crime, where the loss and the means to repair tended to be primarily financial and where offenders would be more likely to have financial means of making amends. See Braithwaite, *Crime, Shame, and Reintegration,* Ch. 9, "Reintegrative Shaming and White Collar Crime," 124.

69 A more thorough-going retributivist would say that even the bona fides of the contrition of the offender and his capacity to change for the better would still be insufficient and that a righting of the balance through intentional infliction of suffering on the offender is absolutely necessary to justice. On the idea that restorative justice sees offenders as good people who do bad things, see Sharpe, *Restorative Justice,* 12.

70 Allen, "Balancing Justice and Social Utility," 317.

71 This is true for the most part, but there are also highly sophisticated and progressive theologians whose sensibilities are very hard-nosed about what justice entails in terms of violence and punishment. Reinhold Niebuhr, for example, while viewing Christian love as relevant to all aspects of life, also contends that practices of justice necessarily have to be very tough-minded about the persistence and depth of sin and the need for violence that sin entails (*The Nature and Destiny of Man,* 254). See also, generally, Nieburh, *Love and Justice.*

72 Fatić, for example, sees restorative justice as a pacifist method of "crime-handling" (*Punishment and Restorative Crime-Handling,* 222-23).

73 For an interesting discussion and critique of the "nirvana stories" of restorative justice, see Kathleen Daly, "Restorative Justice: The Real Story," 67-8.

74 Kathleen Daly is one advocate of restorative justice who is not as keen to try to keep these categories distinct. She convincingly argues that restorative justice contains elements of retributive justice and that it need not eschew punishment or infliction of suffering on offenders as categorically nonrestorative. Likewise, she sees rehabilitative justice as a potential aspect of restorative justice. She argues that these spaces of overlap do and should exist at both the practical and theoretical levels and holds the view that restorative justice can and should include the aim of punishment ("Restorative Justice in Diverse and Unequal Societies," "Diversionary Conferencing in Australia," "Restorative Justice: Moving Past the Caricatures," "Revisiting the Relationship between Retributive and Restorative Justice"). See also Kathleen Daly, "Restorative Justice: The Real Story."

75 Some proponents of restorative justice stress the justice element more than others. Bianchi, Howse, and Llewellyn are probably the most justice focused – as are most writers defending restorative justice in the political context of civil conflict. See, for example, Elshtain, "Politics and Forgiveness." Writing about restorative justice in the context of the South African Truth and Reconciliation Commission, Elshtain says:

> Never the less, many ... will continue to ask: What about Justice? Here the South Africans believe they are making a contribution in challenging the most prevalent models of justice that reign among us. What they are aiming for, they insist, is *politically restorative* justice, a form of political forgiveness concerned with justice. This means it is neither cheap forgiveness nor the dominant Western mode of retributive justice. Restorative justice aims for a future that generates no new victims of the sorts of systemic misdeeds and criminality that blighted the past. Politically restorative justice, they argue, addresses the legitimate concerns of victims and survivors while seeking to reintegrate perpetrators into the community. (53, emphasis in the original)

See also Teitel, *Transitional Justice*, and Nigel Biggar's argument that the primary elements of justice have to do with vindication of the victim rather than with punishment of the offender ("Making Peace or Doing Justice," 6). Braithwaite, by contrast, especially in his most recent book, *Restorative Justice and Responsive Regulation*, treats restorative justice primarily as a pragmatic tactic of social control rather than as a theory of justice. Fatić goes so far as to say that we should reject justice itself and calls his theory, therefore, a theory of "crime-handling" rather than a theory of justice (*Punishment and Restorative Crime-Handling*, 195). In this book, however, I am focusing on restorative justice as a theory of justice rather than merely as a potentially effective means of getting people to behave differently.

76 As John Braithwaite puts it: "One reason that restorative justice ought to do better at rehabilitation than rehabilitative justice is that it does not have rehabilitation as its aim. Rehabilitation is like spontaneity as an objective; when you try to be spontaneous, you are not very spontaneous" (*Restorative Justice and Responsive Regulation*, 96).

77 Llewellyn and Howse, "Institutions for Restorative Justice," 376. But, for a defence of restorative justice as making legitimate accommodation for justice-as-revenge, see Barton, *Getting Even*. See also Anthony Duff's argument for the compatibility of hard treatment and reconciliation as core elements of punishment (*Punishment, Communication, and Community*). Further, see Duff, "Restoration and Retribution."

78 Braithwaite, *Restorative Justice and Responsive Regulation*, 11.

79 Aristotle, *Nicomachean Ethics*.

80 It is also interesting to note here that Umbreit, for example, claims that the courts will not allow any payment for pain and suffering to be made to the victim in an agreement arising out of victim-offender mediation. He does not give any authority for the proposition, and it is unclear why this would be the case (*The Handbook of Victim Offender Mediation*, 63).

81 Pollard, "Victims and the Criminal Justice System," 6. But note that restorative justice often defines community in a narrow way and, more generally, struggles with the concept of community. See Johnstone, *Restorative Justice*, Ch. 7, "Mediation, Participation, and the Role of Community."

82 Delgado, critiquing restorative justice, claims that it is about going back to the status quo ("Goodbye to Hammurabi," 764) and, therefore, that it does not address inequalities and problems existing *ex ante*. However, Llewellyn and Howse describe restorative justice more accurately as having greater aspirations than simply restoration of the status quo. The South African Truth and Reconciliation Commission, for example, clearly aspired to something better than the status quo; restorative justice was about building a new community of equality and respect. See also Elshtain, "Politics and Forgiveness," 49.

83 Pollard writes that "the significance of the offence – to them [the parties involved] – lay in its social context, not its legal one" ("Victims and the Criminal Justice System," 7).

84 Robert Howse was part of the legal team advising the South African government on the legislative framework for the commission and Jennifer Llewellyn worked with the research department of the commission.

85 For an interesting play on the difference between matters of justice and matters of taste, see Charles Dickens, *Little Dorrit*, Bk. 2, Chs. 26 and 27, particularly the advice of Mr. Rugg to Mr. Clennam.

86 Heyward, *Touching our Strength*.

87 Nussbaum, "Compassion."

Chapter 2: "Essentially and Only a Matter of Love"

1 Note 50 in Charles Jarvis's translation of *Don Quixote de la Mancha* reads: "'A Tologue.' In Spanish 'tologo'; a blunder of Sancho's for 'teologo,' *a divine*."

2 Chiba, "Hannah Arendt on Love and the Political," 534.

3 See Dr. Martin Luther King, Jr., who also offers this idea that brotherly love is a commitment to community: "*Agape* is the willingness to go to any length to restore community" (*Stride Toward Freedom*, 71; reprinted in *A Testament of Hope*, 20).

4 Zehr, *Changing Lenses*, 139.

5 Ibid., 151.
6 Zehr, *Restoring Justice*, 21.
7 Van Ness and Strong, *Restoring Justice*, 2nd ed., 249. Biblical references are to the Old Testament (Jer. 31:3-4 and Amos 5:24). But the scriptural quotations are in the context of Van Ness and Strong's explanation of how the Christian faith community and church have supported their work and faith in restorative justice.
8 Ibid., 116. Van Ness and Strong write: "The commandments to love one's neighbor and (even more) to love one's enemy are a compelling reason for churches to rise to the responsibility for assisting with reintegration."
9 Allard and Northey, "Christianity," 120-21.
10 See "Forgiveness and Reconciliation."
11 Zehr, *Changing Lenses*, 51.
12 Bianchi, *Justice as Sanctuary*; Colson, "Truth, Justice, Peace." Articulating restorative justice in terms of shalom, Colson writes: "Shalom ... means the presence of right-relationships between people, relationships which are harmonious, whole, wholesome and complete. It is a term which describes the ideal state of relationships between individuals, communities, nature and God" (5). The writing of Christian proponents of restorative justice evidences an anxiety around the familiarity and long-standing ethical failure of the Christian injunction to love one's enemy. Big institutional Christianity has for too long been the accomplice of other big and oppressive institutions of power in the Western world for us to be sanguine about its potential contribution to radically transformative practices of justice. See Allard and Northey, "Christianity," 126. Chris-tian rhetoric often registers as exclusionary and hegemonic and so provides but precarious inspiration for a radical and inclusive vision of justice-as-repair. Even obviously Christian advocates for restorative justice tend to be anxious to find non-Christian, fresher-sounding, and often either Jewish or Aboriginal spiritual authorities for restorative justice. See also Van Ness and Strong, *Restoring Justice*, 2nd ed., 42; and Zehr, *Changing Lenses*, 130-37.
13 Marshall, *Beyond Retribution*, 28. On justice and love as merged in a concept of right-relation, see also Heyward, *Touching our Strength*.
14 Marshall, *Beyond Retribution*, 92.
15 Pashaura Singh, "Sikhism and Restorative Justice," 201, quoting Avatar Singh, *The Ethics of Sikhs*, 187.
16 Edwin C. Hui and Kaijun Geng, "The Spirit and Practice of Restorative Justice in Chinese Culture," 108.
17 David M. Loy, "Healing Justice," 95.
18 Burnside, "Tension and Tradition in the Pursuit of Justice," 43. Van Ness and Strong also take up this sentiment, adding that "under such a 'passionate construal' of justice, the goddess might throw off her blindfold and draw her sword in righteous anger or open her arms in a merciful embrace" (*Restoring Justice*, 2nd ed., 244).
19 Griffiths, "Ideology in Criminal Procedure or A Third Model of the Criminal Process," 371.
20 Ibid.
21 Braithwaite, *Restorative Justice and Responsive Regulation*, 218.
22 Ibid., 53.
23 Ibid., 218.
24 Van Ness and Strong, *Restoring Justice*, 2nd ed., 243, quoting Lila Rucker's account of workshops for nonviolent conflict resolution in "Peacemaking in Prisons," 243.
25 Niebuhr, *Love and Justice*, 28; see also 32.
26 Quoted in Teays and Purdy, *Bioethics, Justice, and Healthcare*, xi.
27 Outka, *Agape*, 1.
28 Ibid., 7.
29 Ricoeur, "Love and Justice," 24.
30 Prov. 25:15, King James Bible.
31 Lewis, *Babbitt*, 278.
32 Tweedie, *In the Name of Love*; Sandel, *Liberalism and the Limits of Justice*; Okin, *Justice Gender and the Family*.

33 Bell, "Review of Daniel C. Maguire, *A New American Justice."*
34 La Rochefoucauld, *Maxims,* 330.
35 Nietzsche, *On the Genealogy of Morals,* 179.
36 de Tocqueville, *Democracy in America,* 772.
37 Braithwaite, *Restorative Justice and Responsive Regulation,* 4.
38 Gandhi, *The Story of My Experiments with Truth,* 312-13.
39 King, "Non-Violence and Racial Justice," 8.
40 Prov. 25:21-22: "If thine enemy be hungry, give him bread to eat; and if he be thirsty, give him water to drink. For thou shalt heap coals of fire upon his head, and the LORD shall reward thee" (King James Bible, capitals in the original.) I am grateful to Lisa Statt for pointing out that the verse first appears in Proverbs.
41 Rom. 12:19-21, King James Bible.
42 An exception to this tendency is found in Kathleen Daly and Immarigeon: "Although many contemporary histories of restorative justice in North America begin in 1974 with a victim-offender reconciliation program in Kitchener, Ontario, our history does not. Rather, we view the civil rights and women's movements of the 1960s as crucial starting points" ("The Past, Present, and Future of Restorative Justice," 23).
43 Note that the language of violence is often used in conjunction with the language of nonviolence for dramatic effect. For example, see King, "Showdown for Non-Violence," 64.
44 Miller, *Humiliation,* 137. Miller talks about humiliation in terms of the "deflation of pretensions." Gandhian strategies worked in part because they deflated the white rulers' pretensions to morally legitimate political authority.
45 See, however, Braithwaite's discussion of reintegrative shaming and the power of the offender's shame at having disappointed and hurt his own loved ones with his criminal behaviour (herein, Chapter 6, "Compulsory Compassion: Justice, Fellow-Feeling, and the Restorative Encounter").
46 Of course, in the context of the South African Truth and Reconciliation Commission, one powerful motivating force behind the decision to adopt a restorative model of justice was that the new democratic state simply didn't have the resources necessary to punish the offenders of apartheid.
47 Some African-American critics of King's method and of the focus on Christian love in the context of race struggle in the United States do see even this sort of extension of love to the enemy as indulgent and as letting him off the hook too easily. See Bell, "Review of Daniel C. Maguire, *A New American Justice,"* 862.
48 The valour we attribute to these moral heroes is in large measure bound up with our recognition of them also as physically courageous. For a discussion of the need for physical courage as a precondition for finding moral courage, see Miller, *The Mystery of Courage,* 256.
49 Ricoeur, "Love and Justice," 33-4.
50 Ibid., 35.
51 Fatić, *Punishment and Restorative Crime-Handling,* 230.
52 Both Gandhi and King were at pains to distinguish the sort of universal love they were advocating from romantic love. At the same time as they distanced themselves from the romantic, they also insisted that nonviolence was an active, rather than a passive, method. Both these moves were interestingly bound up with the need for these racialized leaders to avoid effeminacy of image. Both the practice of "taking it" and the rhetoric of love needed to be given a convincingly masculine face, and the disparaging of both romantic feeling and passivity were, I think, in aid of that more macho image. See King: "This method is passive physically but strongly active spiritually; it is not aggressive physically but dynamically aggressive spiritually" (*A Testament of Hope,* 7).
53 Zehr, *Changing Lenses,* 139.
54 Of course, Zehr would probably respond that what is on offer for the victim is healing, which is facilitated by restorative justice inasmuch as it fulfills the victim's need for answers to questions like: "1. What happened? 2. Why did it happen to me?" (*Changing Lenses,* 26). Zehr also suggests that healing is promoted by restorative justice's superior

ability to give the victim a sense of "closure" (*Changing Lenses,* 32). See also Johnstone, *Restorative Justice,* Ch. 4, "Healing the Victim." These claims about the ability of restorative justice to offer healing to the victim will be addressed in Chapter 3, Section 3, "Transcendability of the Victim's Loss."

55 de Rougemont treats the story of Tristan and Iseult extensively. See *Love in the Western World,* Bk. 1, "The Tristan Myth," 18.

56 de Rougemont's argument in *Love in the Western World* is basically that, given the arbitrariness of whom we love and why, we ought simply to pick one person relatively arbitrarily. Since it is impossible to predict who will bring us true happiness, and since our desires are socially constructed anyway, we ought to discipline ourselves to love simply some other person much in the same way as we have to use discipline in learning to love ourselves.

57 Ibid., 312.

58 Many of de Rougemont's themes are echoed in C.S. Lewis's *The Four Loves.* On the matter of erotic love and fashion, see also the example of de Montaigne, who, on the "sole authority of the ancient and widespread ... saying" that lame women make the best lovers, "once got [him]self to believe that [he] had derived greater pleasure from a woman because she was deformed, even counting her deformity among her charms" (*The Complete Essays,* 1171).

59 Matt. 6:3, King James Bible.

60 Austen, *Northanger Abbey,* 112.

61 Although affinities sometimes take a while to emerge (as in *Emma,* where the growth of the protagonist's love for Mr. Knightly is parallelled by her own moral growth), generally speaking love is the unfolding of a preordained affinity. In *Sense and Sensibility* Marianne's coming to love Colonel Brandon after her terrible disappointment with Willoughby is perhaps a (not tremendously convincing) exception to this general rule of love in Austen's novels.

62 During my attendance of the Law Commission of Canada Roundtable on Restorative Justice, I was deeply troubled that the overwhelming majority of examples of restorative success stories involved women victims and male offenders. See also Hudson, "Restorative Justice." On restorative conferences as "gendered events," see Kathleen Daly, "Restorative Justice in Diverse and Unequal Societies," 178.

Chapter 3: Three Precarious Pillars of Restorative Optimism

1 See Chapter 6, "Compulsory Compassion: Justice, Fellow-Feeling, and the Restorative Encounter."

2 Llewellyn and Howse, "Institutions for Restorative Justice," 376.

3 Ibid.

4 Ibid.

5 Ibid.

6 Bianchi, *Justice as Sanctuary,* 48.

7 Eliot, *Romola,* 649.

8 Again, see Braithwaite: "One answer to the 'What is to be restored?' question is whatever dimensions of restoration matter to the victims, offenders, and communities affected by the crime. Stakeholder deliberation determines what restoration means in a specific context" (*Restorative Justice and Responsive Regulation,* 11).

9 Brunk, "Restorative Justice and the Philosophical Theories of Criminal Punishment," 45.

10 Ibid., 44. However, it is interesting to note that Carriere, Malsch, and Vermunt in their study "Victim Offender Negotiations: An Exploratory Study on Different Damage Types and Compensation" found that victims who suffered only material damage had a higher degree of satisfaction with restorative justice than did those who suffered serious psychological damage from the offence. The study does not involve real victims, however, but is based on a survey of people who have gone through computer simulation of crime and have been asked to imagine themselves as victims of particular crimes.

11 Hadley, *The Spiritual Roots of Restorative Justice,* 10.

12 Brunk, "Restorative Justice and the Philosophical Theories of Criminal Punishment," 51.

13　Kerruish, *Jurisprudence as Ideology*, 18.

14　Ibid., 17.

15　See also Nedelsky, "Reconceiving Rights as Relation" and "Reconceiving Autonomy."

16　Kerruish, *Jurisprudence as Ideology*, 172.

17　Llewellyn and Howse, "Institutions for Restorative Justice," 378.

18　Kerruish, *Jurisprudence as Ideology*, 173.

19　William Ian Miller convincingly argues that revenge itself is not vulnerable to the familiar critique that it is *inherently* without limit. He notes that in revenge cultures such as that of Saga Iceland, people who didn't know how to apportion their vengeance judiciously were seen as troublesome berzerkers. Thus revenge, for Miller, has the same elements of control and proportionality as retribution. See "Clint Eastwood and Equity."

20　Nozick, *Philosophical Explanations*, 366-70.

21　Nietzsche, *On the Genealogy of Morals*, 81.

22　Braithwaite: "All of us have caring and uncaring selves, wise and foolish selves, self-seeking and other-regarding selves. Part of the genius of restorative justice institutions is that they induce expectations that we will all try to put our best self forward. Put another way, we all know we are there as an obligation of caring citizenship, so we do our best to play the responsible citizen" ("Repentance Rituals and Restorative Justice," 125).

23　Umbreit, *The Handbook of Victim Offender Mediation*, 89. Here Umbreit seems to suggest that while the expression of anger is a legitimate part of the victim-offender encounter, it should not be allowed to escalate to the level of "direct verbal attack" on the offender by the victim.

24　Ibid., 88.

25　Umbreit, 89.

26　Note also that Sharpe stresses the importance of ensuring the offender feels that the restorative outcome is fair: "It is ... important not to pressure (or knowingly allow) an offender to accept terms that feel unfair to him or her. To do so is to betray the premise of restorative justice. And that is no small betrayal" (*Restorative Justice*, 24).

27　Braithwaite, *Restorative Justice and Responsive Regulation*, 47. See also Strang, *Victim Participation in a Restorative Justice Process*.

28　Fatić, *Punishment and Restorative Crime-Handling*.

29　Llewellyn and Howse, "Institutions for Restorative Justice," 363-64.

30　Markel, "Are Shaming Punishments Beautifully Retributive?" 2190.

31　Braithwaite, *Restorative Justice and Responsive Regulation*, 5; Llewellyn and Howse, "Institutions for Restorative Justice," 372; Braithwaite, *Crime, Shame, and Reintegration*, 117-18; Bianchi, *Justice as Sanctuary*, 138-45. Zehr does note that, historically, community justice could be "summary and brutal" (*Changing Lenses*, 106).

32　Miller, *Bloodtaking and Peacemaking*; Boehm, *Blood Revenge*; Durham, *High Albania*; Hasluck, *The Unwritten Law in Albania*.

33　Braithwaite, *Crime, Shame, and Reintegration*, 12, 101.

34　Hadley, *The Spiritual Roots of Restorative Justice*, 259.

35　Some traditions actually see love as incompatible with respect. Some robust understandings of love admit of a kind of good-hearted mockery and affectionate affront to the dignity of the other that are incompatible with the sober notions of respect that we are considering here. See Cuddihy, *The Ordeal of Civility*, 22.

36　In "Disciplinary Tolerance," Brown argues that we have posited toleration as a value even in the face of the clear truth that nobody wants to be merely tolerated. We want some richer form of regard than mere toleration offers.

37　Miller, *Anatomy of Disgust*, 239.

38　Ibid., 236-37.

39　Delgado, "Goodbye to Hammurabi," 766.

40　Kerruish, *Jurisprudence as Ideology*, 17.

41　Miller, *Faking It*.

42　Ibid.

43　Miller, *Faking It*, Ch. 8, "In Divine Services and Other Ritualized Performances."

44 Acorn, "Making Sense." There are of course exceptions to the rule against the admission of both similar fact evidence and evidence of bad character.
45 For an excellent and extremely sensible critique of the idea that restorative justice transforms the character of the offender, see Kathleen Daly, "Restorative Justice: The Real Story," 66-71. In this article, Daly debunks four myths about restorative justice. The fourth myth is that "restorative justice can be expected to produce major changes in people."
46 Braithwaite, *Restorative Justice and Responsive Regulation,* 36.
47 Sherman, Strang, and Woods, *Recidivism Patterns in the Canberra Reintegrative Shaming Experiments (RISE).*
48 Braithwaite, *Restorative Justice and Responsive Regulation,* 36.
49 Foucault, *History of Sexuality,* vol. 1, 67.
50 Zehr, *Changing Lenses,* 33
51 Sharpe: "The third criterion is that the offender must admit *taking the action in question* and must accept responsibility for the harm that is caused" (*Restorative Justice,* 21, emphasis added). Note Sharpe's hesitance to use the language of wrongdoing. She says that the reason for not wanting to use "admit the crime" is that the offender may take responsibility for the action and its consequences – for example, damage caused during a fist fight – while still viewing himself as not guilty of assault because he has a defence (say, self-defence) under criminal law.
52 Zehr notes that there are two kinds of criminologists: those who think of criminals as different from themselves and those who acknowledge them as fundamentally similar (*Changing Lenses*).
53 Law Commission of Canada, "Community Participation in the Justice System."
54 Ibid.
55 Ibid.
56 See also Church Council on Justice and Corrections, *Collaborative Justice Project.*
57 See generally Miller, *Bloodtaking and Peacemaking.*
58 Lazlo also continues to lie to his daughter about his guilt, which compounds his betrayal of her.
59 Plato, *Euthyphro, Apology, Crito, and Symposium.* See also Becker, "Impartiality and Ethical Theory."
60 Plato, *Euthyphro, Apology, Crito, and Symposium,* 4.
61 The question of whether one should treat one's loved ones with strict impartiality has, of course, received a tremendous amount of philosophical attention. See Adams, "Love and Impartiality"; Becker, "Impartiality and Ethical Theory"; Baron, "Impartiality and Friendship"; Cornell, "Loyalty and the Limits of Kantian Impartiality."
62 Socrates sees the prosecution of a relative as justifiable only when the father has murdered some other relative to whom a duty of loyalty is also owed.
63 For a number of essays discussing the tension between allegiance to one's kin or country and allegiance to the broader community of the world, see Nussbaum, *For Love of Country.*
64 *R. v. Henry Hugh Rawlinson,* 2 S.C.R. 393, 1989.
65 Delgado, "Goodbye to Hammurabi," 765.
66 Twain, *The Adventures of Huckleberry Finn,* 16-17.
67 Ibid., 17.
68 Brunk: "But offenders, victims' families, mediators, judges and lawyers who participate all speak of the 'magic,' or 'deeply spiritual' aspects of the events that take place when offenders come to terms with the pain they have inflicted on victims or their families and express repentance, and when victims or their families experience personal healing from offenders' acts of repentance and from their own ability to forgive" ("Restorative Justice," 51).
69 Again, for an excellent critique of this idea, see Kathleen Daly's discussion of the myth that "restorative justice can be expected to produce major changes in people" ("Restorative Justice: The Real Story," 66-71).
70 For example, Umbreit, endorsing Lois Gold's paradigm of healing, writes: "Understanding

and practising humanistic mediation in the context of the paradigm of healing offered by Gold is ultimately grounded in a profound recognition of the precious gift of human existence, relationships, community, and the deeper spiritual connectedness among all of us in our collective journey through this life regardless of religious, cultural, political, and lifestyle differences. Gold notes that the language of healing is not the language of problem solving but rather the language of the soul" (*Handbook of Victim Offender Mediation*, 8).

71 There is a certain amount of double talk around these promises. While the rhetoric of healing and reconciliation are ubiquitous in the theory of restorative justice, and while Umbreit in *The Handbook of Victim Offender Mediation* endorses the language of healing as a "language of the soul" that is more helpful in the struggle toward justice than "the language of problem solving" (8), he also warns not to use this language around victims lest they get their hopes up too high: "Using such words as *healing, restoration,* or being *made whole* to describe possible outcomes for mediation may elevate victims' hopes unrealistically" (25, emphasis in the original). See also the discussion of not using such language with victims under Umbreit's list of "Don'ts" for mediators (63-4).

72 Palk, Hayes, and Prenzler, "Restorative Justice and Community Conferencing."

73 Miers, Maguire, and Goldie, *An Exploratory Evaluation of Restorative Justice Schemes.*

74 Umbreit, *Handbook of Victim Offender Mediation,* 397.

75 Umbreit doesn't even think you should use the word "restoration" with victims for fear of raising hopes too high (*Handbook of Victim Offender Mediation,* 25).

76 See Miller's discussion of Lazarus (*The Mystery of Courage*).

77 See Bertrand's discussion of the gendering aspects of the rhetoric of healing in corrections for women offenders ("Incarceration as a Gendering Strategy").

78 *Truth and Reconciliation Commission of South Africa Report,* vol. 5, Ch. 9.9, 352. See also Shriver's discussion of Sikwepere's statement before the commission ("Where and When in Political Life Is Justice Served by Forgiveness?" 27-8).

79 As Brandon Hamber notes: "The long-term ability of a once-off statement or public testimony to address the full psychological impact of the past is questionable" ("Does the Truth Heal?" 135).

80 Zehr, *Changing Lenses,* 45 et seq.

81 For a discussion of the "Christianizing" aspects of Tutu's interpretation of the work of the Truth and Reconciliation Commission, see Derrida, *On Cosmopolitanism and Forgiveness,* 42.

82 *Truth and Reconciliation Commission of South Africa Report,* vol 1, "Chairperson's Forward," 18-19.

83 Luke 15:7, Kings James Bible "I say unto you, that likewise joy shall be in heaven over one sinner that repenteth, more than over ninety and nine just persons, which need no repentance."

84 Kathleen Daly asks "How often, then, does the exceptional or 'nirvana' story of repair and goodwill occur? ... I suspect ... it may happen 10 percent of the time, if that" ("Restorative Justice: The Real Story," 70).

85 I'm borrowing the phrase from Patricia Williams, who speaks of "the possibility that simple cantankerous coexistence may be what we should be aiming for in a democracy based on live-and-let-live" (*The Rooster's Egg,* 192).

86 Miller, *Anatomy of Disgust,* Ch. 9, "Mutual Contempt and Democracy."

87 Walker, *The Battered Woman.*

88 For another interesting list of the conditions of a meaningful apology, see Schneider: "[The modern usage of 'apology'] has shifted to mean 'to acknowledge and express regret for a fault without defense.' This modern definition captures the core elements of apology: (1) acknowledgement, (2) affect, and (3) vulnerability" ("What It Means to Be Sorry," 266).

89 One legitimate qualification for a good apology with which batterers' apologies rarely comply is that they should not be veiled attempts to coerce forgiveness (see Augsburger, "The F Word"). Nevertheless, in the context of restorative justice, most apologies are attempts to put victims in a position where they feel compelled to forgive.

90 Pollard claims that "apology reaffirms trust that the 'appropriate moral standards are shared by the offender'" ("Victims and the Criminal Justice System," 10).

91 For another example of how apology and forgiveness can sustain inequality and in-justice, consider the relationship between the US Marines and the civilian population (particularly the women) of Okinawa, Japan. This relationship is reported to be charac-terized by multiple acts of exploitation against, and disrespect on the part of US ser-vicemen for, the Japanese residents of Okinawa. The conduct in question ranges from cases of sexual assault of Japanese women and girls by US servicemen to problems of drunk driving and disorderliness by US Marines in Okinawa and the failure of US mil-itary personnel to take responsibility for children they have fathered in Okinawa with Japanese women. The relationship, however, appears to be managed and maintained at least in part by periodic apologies made by US military officials. In 1995 Defense Sec-retary William J. Perry apologized on behalf of the United States for the conduct of three servicemen later convicted of the rape of a twelve-year-old Okinawa girl. In July 2000 another US apology was issued by the top military official in the United States for the sexual assault of a fourteen-year-old Japanese girl by a US marine. Japanese anger and resentment, and the desire to get rid of the marines' base in Okinawa, is handled and defused by way of periodic statements of contrition and promises to change (Feifer, "The Rape of Okinawa"; Bandow, "Cycle of Unease in Okinawa"; "Marine General Bows in Apology to Okinawa"; see also "Fired Admiral Gives Public Apology").

92 Augsburger argues that forgiveness can never mean going back to the way things were – that it always has to mean the creation of some other relationships in which levels of intimacy are readjusted to ensure that they are appropriate to the level of trust after the wrongdoing. This is a very significant modification to the usual understanding of for-giveness, which entails a wiping clean of the slate and a release from the consequences of wrongdoing ("The F Word").

93 Eliot, *Romola*, 479.

94 Sharpe says that victim participation should be encouraged without exerting pressure (*Restorative Justice*, 22). Umbreit uses the same language in *Handbook of Victim Offender Mediation* (22).

95 Braithwaite, *Crime, Shame, and Reintegration.*

96 Eliot, *Romola*, 499.

Chapter 4: Sentimental Justice

1 Schiller, "On Naive and Sentimental Poetry," 240.

2 See Douglas's discussion of the sentimentality of the death of Little Eva (*The Feminiza-tion of American Culture*, 3-5).

3 Van Ness and Strong do draw on the high culture of Homer's *The Iliad*, which will be discussed at length later in this chapter.

4 Orwell masterfully describes the sentimentality of good bad poetry as follows: "A good bad poem is a graceful monument to the obvious. It records in memorable form – for verse is a mnemonic device, among other things – some emotion which very nearly every human being can share" ("Rudyard Kipling," 214).

5 Callan discusses the failings of a sentimental civic education and identifies the senti-mental as "the inculcation of strong and abiding beliefs in certain fictions of moral purity" (*Creating Citizens*, 100). This brand of sentimentality is divided into two sub-categories. First, there is the image of innocence that grossly oversimplifies the nature of persons or relations in order to highlight qualities of "sweetness, dearness, littleness, blamelessness, and vulnerability" (106). Second, there is the complementary marker of mastery, by which persons or relationships are grossly oversimplified in order to high-light qualities of greatness, glory, and invulnerability (108). I would add that the incul-cation of these beliefs in moral purity is often accomplished through the depiction of the death of moral purity. This stands to reason since death preserves both larger-than-life greatness and sweeter-than-life innocence.

6 Orwell, "Rudyard Kipling," 213. Orwell describes Kipling as a good bad poet and Har-riet Beecher Stowe as a good bad novelist. See also Orwell, "Good Bad Books," 318.

7 Tanner, "Sentimentality," 130.

8 Orwell, "Charles Dickens," 35.

9 Niebuhr, *Love and Justice*, 20.
10 On restorative justice and the decrease in recidivism, see Van Ness and Strong, *Restoring Justice*, 2nd ed., 68; Sharpe, *Restorative Justice*, 15. But see also Llewellyn and Howse, who argue that we should not view restorative justice in terms of these instrumental or utilitarian goals, which are essentially abstracted out of concerns about *justice* itself. In their view restorative justice also commends itself better as an understanding of *justice* than does retributivism ("Institutions for Restorative Justice," 373-74). The question of whether restorative justice does decrease recidivism is a difficult one. Sherman, Strang, and Woods, in their study *Recidivism Patterns in the Canberra Reintegrative Shaming Experiments (RISE)*, found that there was a significant decrease in recidivism in violent offenders, no difference in repeat offending for property offences, and an increase in reoffending for drunk driving. See also Braithwaite's discussion of Sherman, Strang, and Woods (*Restorative Justice and Responsive Regulation*, 57). Thus the evidence about whether restorative justice is effective in limiting repeat offending is equivocal. See also Delgado, "Goodbye to Hammurabi." On the point about whether restorative justice is more satisfying for victims, a study by Palk, Hayes, and Prenzler, "Restorative Justice and Community Conferencing," indicates that while all participants in the restorative justice experiments studied showed high levels of satisfaction with the fairness of the process, victims reported lower levels of satisfaction than did others.
11 Solomon, *A Passion for Justice*, 235.
12 Ibid., 239.
13 Ibid., 238. For an extremely interesting discussion of the contribution of sentimental fiction to humanitarianism, see Laqueur, "Bodies, Details, and Humanitarian Narrative."
14 Solomon, *A Passion for Justice*, 237.
15 Ibid.
16 Wilde, *The Importance of Being Earnest*, 11.
17 Solomon, *A Passion for Justice*, 238. Solomon cites Mark Twain for the proposition that "the most profound insights invariably lie on the surface."
18 Midgley, "Brutality and Sentimentality," 386.
19 Ibid.
20 Solomon, *A Passion for Justice*, 238.
21 Orwin, "Compassion."
22 Aristotle, *The Rhetoric and the Poetics*; Nussbaum, "Compassion."
23 Miller, *Anatomy of Disgust*, 245.
24 Miller, *Faking It*.
25 Indeed, for example, Orwell's critique of Dickens as sentimental is essentially a critique of Dickens's failure as a political influence. Orwell argues that though Dickens critiqued all English institutions, the critique never had any real political bite. See also Ann Douglas's provocative comment that "sentimentalism might be defined as the political sense obfuscated or gone rancid. Sentimentalism, unlike the modes of genuine sensibility, never exists except in tandem with failed political consciousness" (*The Feminization of American Culture*, 254).
26 Emerson, *Compensation and Self-Reliance*, 32.
27 Orwell, "Charles Dickens."
28 Douglas, *The Feminization of American Culture*, 254.
29 Sedgwick, *Epistemology of the Closet*, 114.
30 Pollard discusses the "emotionally stunted trial system" and how restorative justice makes more appropriate space for the emotional realities of victims' experience of crime ("Victims and the Criminal Justice System," 7-8). For a number of essays exploring the complexities of these issues, see Bandes, ed., *The Passions of Law*. See also Morris: "The rituals, procedures and language [of the courtroom] seem designed to be emotionally cool: there is no legitimate place for strong emotions ... For them [defendants, victims, and families] a court appearance *is* an emotional experience, but this remains unacknowledged, even an inconvenience. An adjournment for a tearful witness to recover his or her composure, for example, is mainly viewed as wasting the judge's time rather than

as bringing home to the offender the consequences of his or her actions" ("Shame, Guilt and Remorse," 159).

31 Bellow, *Herzog,* 237.
32 Adam Smith, *The Theory of Moral Sentiments,* 11.
33 Tanner, "Sentimentality," 139.
34 Bellow, *Herzog,* 240.
35 Miller convincingly refutes Nozick's claim that retribution qualifies as justice because it is stripped of any emotional quality ("Clint Eastwood and Equity").
36 See, for example, Lerman, who argues that restorative justice remedies the "just the facts ma'am" influence ("Forgiveness in the Criminal Justice System," 1671).
37 Adam Smith, *The Theory of Moral Sentiments,* 30.
38 The comic strip, which originated in 1924, was actually significantly less sentimental than the 1977 Broadway version or the 1987 film of Annie's story. The original comic strip version, which ran from 1924 to the death of its creator, Harold Gray, in 1968, was focussed on Annie's adventures, which followed the events of the day and included even outsmarting the Nazis. The Broadway musical and film versions focus instead on the hardships of Annie's life in the orphanage and on the joy of her meeting and forming a relationship with Daddy Warbucks. See Gray, *Arf! The Life and Hard Times of Little Orphan Annie, 1935-1945;* Bruce Smith, *The History of Little Orphan Annie.*
39 Bianchi, *Justice as Sanctuary,* 42.
40 Ibid.
41 *Ideas,* "Justice as Sanctuary," with Herman Bianchi, Part 1, Canadian Broadcasting Corporation Radio Program.
42 It should be noted that in the same interview Bianchi also tells the story of a criminal who does not accept responsibility for his wrongdoing, for whom Bianchi has no sympathy and in the case of whom Bianchi believes restorative justice would not work. Bianchi clearly believes in two categories of offenders: those who are capable of owning up to their wrongdoing and embarking on processes of healing and those who are not and for whom severe punishment by imprisonment is the appropriate response. The division line appears to be dependent upon the character of the offender.
43 McFall, "What's Wrong with Bitterness?"
44 There is, of course, a whole religious tradition of praying for assistance in vengeance. See, for example, Psalm 137:9, King James Bible: "Happy shall he be, that taketh and dasheth thy little ones against the stones." Or see Queen Margaret's speech in Shakespeare's *Richard III:* "Dear God I pray that I may live and say the dog is dead" (Act IV, Scene 4).
45 Van Ness and Strong, *Restoring Justice,* 2nd ed., 55.
46 Ibid., 56.
47 Ibid., 69, emphasis in the original.
48 Homer, *The Iliad,* 450.
49 Ibid., 452.
50 Ibid.
51 Van Ness and Strong, *Restoring Justice,* 2nd ed., 55.
52 Homer, *The Iliad,* 453.
53 Ibid.
54 Ibid., 451-52.
55 Van Ness and Strong, *Restoring Justice,* 2nd ed., 56.

Chapter 5: "Lovemaking Is Justice-Making"

1 Heyward, *Touching Our Strength.*
2 Nussbaum, "Steerforth's Arm," 335.
3 Ibid., 361.
4 Ibid., 360.
5 Nussbaum speaks exclusively in terms of the relation between desire and morality. My extension of this discussion to the relation between desire and justice may seem a bit

of a stretch. Obviously, a discussion of the difference between morality and justice is far beyond the scope of this book. I would note only that the restorative conception of justice contracts the space between the two.

6 Nussbaum, "Steerforth's Arm," 345, emphasis in the original.

7 David's second wife, Agnes, is for Nussbaum the epitome of this alternative of dreary prudence. She sees the novel as being framed so as to contrast Agnes's bourgeois conventionality and Steerforth's ethic of pleasure and erotic presence ("Steerforth's Arm," 348). Dickens, *David Copperfield,* 348-52.

8 Adam Smith, *The Theory of Moral Sentiments,* 28.

9 Miller, *Anatomy of Disgust,* 189-90.

10 Adam Smith, *The Theory of Moral Sentiments,* 29.

11 Even Aristotle, though he saw the impetuses to fear as being found in the imagination, recognized fear to be a bodily state (*Nicomachean Ethics,* 105).

12 Miller, *Anatomy of Disgust,* 190. Note that Nussbaum appears to be of the view that pornography is a counter-example to Smith's point ("Steerforth's Arm," 341).

13 Adam Smith, *The Theory of Moral Sentiments,* 29.

14 Ibid.

15 Interestingly, as we saw in the previous chapter, Braithwaite also claims that when victims understate their losses, they are more likely to engage the sympathy of the offender ("Repentance Rituals and Restorative Justice," 120).

16 Adam Smith, *The Theory of Moral Sentiments,* 24.

17 Nussbaum, "Steerforth's Arm," 345.

18 Adam Smith, *The Theory of Moral Sentiments,* 31.

19 Quoted in Fisher, "The Nature and Evolution of Romantic Love," 25.

20 Adam Smith, *The Theory of Moral Sentiments,* 31.

21 Ibid., 29.

22 Ibid., 32.

23 Miller, *Anatomy of Disgust,* 195. Note also how Miller's discussion of the incommunicable nature of love echoes Hannah Arendt's statements about love as unspeakably private: "Love, in distinction from friendship, is killed, or rather extinguished, the moment it is displayed in public. ('Never seek to tell thy love/Love that never told can be.') Because of its inherent World-lessness, love can only become false or perverted when it is used for political purposes such as the change or salvation of the world" (*The Human Condition,* 52).

24 Nussbaum sees us as being so caught up in our passion for Steerforth that we cease to care about Mr. Mell or the Peggottys. She sees Em'ly's ruinous decision to risk everything in order to run away with Steerforth as the right decision and doesn't see Em'ly as deserving of sympathy: "We don't care to attend to the injustice done to poor Mr. Mell; we suspend all general sympathy. We don't even care for Ham Peggotty, since we know, with Em'ly that he is indeed a 'chuckleheaded fellow' and that we too would gladly have followed Steerforth wherever he beckoned" ("Steerforth's Arm," 351).

25 Nussbaum focuses on David's romantic love for Steerforth. Nussbaum doesn't indicate that she is trying to give a queer reading to the book, but, as her discussion reveals, there is certainly sufficient evidence in the novel to suggest a strong erotic and even sexual relationship between David and Steerforth.

26 Nussbaum, "Steerforth's Arm," 335.

27 Ibid., 360.

28 Ibid., 356.

29 As noted in the previous chapter, however, restorative justice (rightly I think) holds that the only way to actually engender sympathy is by facilitating face-to-face conversation. Where restorative justice errs is in assuming that face-to-face conversation can reliably be counted on to generate that sympathy.

30 Note the following conversation between David and his Aunt Betsy Trotwood:

"Someone that I know, Trot," my aunt pursued, after a pause, "though of a very pliant disposition, has an earnestness of affection in him that reminds me of poor

Baby. Earnestness is what that Somebody must look for, to sustain him and improve him, Trot. Deep, downright, faithful earnestness."

"If you only knew the earnestness of Dora, aunt!" I cried.

"Oh, Trot!" she said again; "blind, blind!" and without knowing why, I felt a vague unhappy loss or want of something overshadow me like a cloud. (Dickens, *David Copperfield*, 489-90)

31 The only flicker of a capacity for critical self-reflection we ever see in Steerforth is in his parting words to David:

"Daisy, if anything should ever separate us, you must think of me at my best, old boy. Come! Let us make that bargain. Think of me at my best, if circumstances should ever part us!"

"You have no best to me, Steerforth," said I, "and no worst. You are always equally loved, and cherished in my heart." (Ibid., 424)

32 This again needs qualification because, while romantic love is something that, as spectators, we know ourselves to be prone to enter into on the basis of morally irrelevant characteristics, it is not the case that all love of celebrities is romantic; nor is it the case that our collective judgments about the lovable are never importantly grounded in moral judgments. Moral and political celebrities such as Mohandas K. Gandhi, Martin Luther King, Jr., the Dalai Lama – and perhaps we can include here even John F. Kennedy, Hitler, Socrates, Jesus, and Buddha – inspire the passionate collective of multitudes of spectators to love on largely moral (though there is no small element of charisma in any of these cases) grounds. And fully fledged communities of judgment are founded upon agreement about the worthiness of these persons as objects of love – which suggests that we do enter into love of others as spectators and furthermore that, to some degree, we do so on what we take to be morally motivated grounds. Further, to the extent that we do enter into love of moral celebrities as spectators of their heroism, we sometimes do so in a way that can be said to organize our shared moral aspirations and bind us together as communities of moral judgment.

33 On the connection between mutuality and justice, see also Braithwaite's discussion of Confucius (*Restorative Justice and Responsive Regulation*, 23).

34 Heyward, *Touching Our Strength*, 3.

35 Heyward, *Staying Power*, 17.

36 Marshall, *Beyond Retribution*, 28.

37 Heyward, *Touching Our Strength*, 3.

38 Ibid., 22-3.

39 Lorde, "Uses of the Erotic."

40 Heyward, *Touching Our Strength*, 108-9.

41 Ibid., 39-40.

42 Ibid., 108.

43 Ibid., 4.

44 Ibid.

45 For an excellent discussion of the viability of restorative justice in the context of sexual assault, see Kathleen Daly, "Restorative Justice and Sexual Assault."

46 For a discussion of how restorative justice could be effective in cases of sexual assault if retribution were factored back into restorative justice, see Kathleen Daly, "Restorative Justice and Sexual Assault."

47 *Restorative Justice and Family Violence*, edited by Heather Strang and John Braithwaite, contains a number of essays that grapple with the question of whether restorative justice can honour victim integrity and secure victim safety in the context of sexual and intimate violence.

48 Heyward, *Touching Our Strength*, 21-2.

49 This notion of the fundamental interconnectedness of victim and offender is found in much of the restorative justice literature. For example, Umbreit lists "belief in the

connectedness of all things and our common humanity" as the first value underlying restorative justice (*Handbook of Victim Offender Mediation*, 5).

50 Colson, *Justice that Restores*, 141.

51 Gibbon also notes how Christians who were hostile to the idea of sex tried to purify it by seeing sex within marriage as a replication of the union between Christ and the church: "The sensual connection was refined into a resemblance of the mystic union of Christ with his church, and was pronounced to be indissoluble either by divorce or by death" (*The Decline and Fall of the Roman Empire*, vol. 1, 528).

52 Phelan, *Sexual Strangers*.

53 Heyward, *Touching our Strength*, 3.

54 Ibid., 17, emphasis in the original.

Chapter 6: Compulsory Compassion

1 "It is not right to pervert the judge by moving him to anger or envy or pity – one might as well warp a carpenter's rule before using it" (Aristotle, *The Rhetoric and the Poetics*, 19, Bk. 1, Part 1, 1354a).

2 Aristotle, *Nicomachean Ethics*, 180.

3 Aristotle, *The Rhetoric and the Poetics*, 113, Bk. 2, Part 8, 1385b. This section contains Aristotle's discussion of pity, which will be examined at length in this chapter.

4 Shakespeare, *Merchant of Venice*, Act 4, Scene 1.

5 Though the Duke spares Shylock's life, the grand finale of the court scene in the play is Portia's total devastation of Shylock. Most of his goods are confiscated, he is forced to will what he has to the daughter who has betrayed him and the man who has stolen his daughter from him, and, if he wants to avoid having the remainder of his property confiscated and distributed between the state and Antonio, he must convert to Christianity. The total humiliation and ruin of Shylock are dressed up as Christian mercy (Shakespeare, *Merchant of Venice*, Act 4, Scene 1).

6 We can see this suggestion in Weinrib, *The Idea of Private Law*, 210 et seq., and "Legal Formalism," 339.

7 Weinrib, *The Idea of Private Law*, 219.

8 Epstein, "Compassion and Compulsion."

9 The way that these two objections parallel the late-nineteenth- and early-twentieth-century objections to the admission of women to the legal profession is very interesting. Some saw the influx of women as a threat to the integrity of the law. Others saw the admission of women as a sullying of the beauty of the feminine.

10 "The great robber barons of the nineteenth century, most of them set up universities or museums ... Their major task in life was to find out how to give large sums of money away -- intelligently ... I think the simplest explanation for why this pattern is fine is that the compassion that is exhibited is compassion paid for out of resources owned and otherwise at the complete disposal of the individual who makes the gift. With voluntary transfers, the element of compulsion drops out of the picture, so you have a pure system of compassion" (Epstein, "Compassion and Compulsion," 25).

11 Ibid., 26.

12 There are also those in the middle who think that empathy – that is, imaginative attentiveness to the plight of the parties – should inform judicial decision making. See Nedelsky, "Embodied Diversity and the Challenges to Law" and "Communities of Judgment and Human Rights"; Minow and Spelman, "Passion for Justice"; Shytov, *Conscience and Love in Making Judicial Decisions*.

13 Nussbaum, "Compassion," 37. Nussbaum's new book, *Upheavals of Thought*, contains a lengthy section on compassion that is essentially a reworking and watering-down of this article (see Chapter 6, "Compassion: Tragic Predicaments," 297). Here Nussbaum has backed off her earlier position and has conceded the basic capriciousness of spontaneous compassion. She allows that compassion has to be educated in order for it to serve progressive ends. However, the earlier article is still of significant interest because it provides an opportunity for us to attempt to see whether Aristotle's conditions for compassion can be linked to justice.

14 Nussbaum acknowledges at the outset that she uses the words "empathy," "pity," and "compassion" interchangeably ("Compassion," 29). In so doing, she immediately addresses the potential objection that pity and compassion are not synonymous and that pity has a connotation of condescension, of "feeling sorry for," that is not present in the more humanist notion of compassion. Nussbaum resists this distinction. She acknowledges that the word "pity" has come to have "nuances of condescension and superiority to the sufferer" but argues that this meaning was grafted onto the word "pity" by the Victorians. Nussbaum notes that the Greek word *eleos*, which is generally translated as "pity" in English, had no such connotations for the ancients and thus could equally have been translated into our more egalitarian notion of compassion. The historical nuances of the meanings of the words *eleos*, "compassion," and "pity" are, however, beside the point since it is clear that Nussbaum considers Aristotle's discussion of *eleos* (generally translated as "pity") to be an attractive conception of that fuller, more humanist emotion that we today speak of as "compassion."

15 Nussbaum, "Compassion," 31. See also Nussbaum, "Tragedy and Self-Sufficiency." Nussbaum frequently contrasts Aristotle's discussion of the place of pity in *The Rhetoric and the Poetics*, which she prefers, to Plato's argument that pity ought to be shunned rather than cultivated since it is an impediment to rational deliberation.

16 Henderson, "Legality and Empathy," 1593.

17 *Brown v. Board of Education*, 347 U.S. 483, 1954.

18 For a discussion of why empathy was not necessary for the court to reach its decision in *Brown v. Board of Education*, see Massaro's argument that the court needed only to come to the long-overdue and purely factual conclusion that separate was not equal.

19 *Nelson v. Ferry*, 874 F. 2d 165, 7th Cir., 1989. In her discussion of the cases, Nussbaum is careful to stress the interplay between cognition and emotion. For another discussion of the role of cognition in feelings of compassion and their relation to judgments about justice, see Pillsbury, "Emotional Justice."

20 Nussbaum, "Compassion," 55.

21 In *Upheavals of Thought*, Nussbaum attempts to reframe this condition so as to mask its inherent political conservatism. She has reworked it so that she now sees the third condition for compassion as the making of a "eudaimonistic judgment" that the sufferer is "an end whose good is to be promoted": "The Aristotelian *judgment of similar possibilities* is an epistemological aid to forming the *eudaimonistic judgment* – not necessary, but usually very important" (321, emphasis in the original). The same kinds of problems with a conclusion that I or my friends might be subject to similar suffering resurface in Nussbaum's new notion of eudaimonistic judgment.

22 Adam Smith agrees with Aristotle that we pity only when we do not feel exempt from similar suffering. He adds the nuance, however, that it is only when I am certain that I would experience the same kind of suffering if I were subjected to the same conditions as the person principally concerned that I will be inclined to feel compassion for the sufferer before me (*The Theory of Moral Sentiments*, 16).

23 Aristotle, *The Rhetoric and the Poetics*, 113, Bk. 2, Part 8, 1385b.

24 Arendt, *Men in Dark Times*, 15.

25 Aristotle doesn't exactly identify seriousness as a condition. This emphasis results from Nussbaum's gloss.

26 Rousseau, *Emile*, 225.

27 Ibid. Likewise, Rousseau notes that since we pity according to the amount of feeling we attribute to the other, we pity people more than animals (though Rousseau does not think we should do so since both are capable of feeling pain). It is also interesting to note that the colonizers sometimes justified their lack of compassion for indigenous peoples on the basis that they were not capable of romantic love in the European sense. It was assumed that indigenous people viewed each other as interchangeable sexual partners and their own biological children as interchangeable with the children of others. Thus it was assumed that the emotional existence of indigenous peoples was significantly less intense than that of the colonizers (see Jankowiak, ed., *Romantic Passion*).

28 Harriet Beecher Stowe, for example, in her fascinating novel *Uncle Tom's Cabin*, condemns

the proslavery argument that "we can't reason from our feelings to those of this class of persons" (200). She condemns those who imagine that the suffering a black woman feels when her child is taken away from her and sold is not nearly as serious as the suffering that a white woman would feel in the same situation. One of Stowe's primary tactics in drawing the reader into compassion for blacks is her compelling narration of black women's love for and connection to their children. Glorifying white motherhood along the way, Stowe passionately urges reasoning from the feelings of white women to the feelings of black women:

> And you, mothers of America, you who have learned, by the cradles of your own children, to love and feel for all mankind, by the sacred love you bear your child; by your joy in his beautiful, spotless infancy; by the motherly pity and tenderness with which you guide his growing years; by the anxieties of his education; by the prayers you breathe for his soul's eternal good; I beseech you, pity the mother who has all your affections, and not one legal right to protect, guide, or educate, the child of her bosom! (623)

See also Spelman, who points out that these kinds of comparisons always flatter whites at the same time as they attempt to elicit compassion for blacks (*Fruits of Sorrow*, 127). Stowe also exposes how assumptions about the insensitivity of blacks spuriously served as a springboard for the twisted conclusion that slave owners ought not artificially to sensitize slaves by treating them decently – since to do so would cause only needless additional suffering. We see this idea in the reasoning of the slave trader Haley in the first chapter of the book:

> S'pose not; you Kentucky folks spile your niggers. You mean well by 'em, but 'tan't no real kindness, arter all. Now, a nigger, you see, what's got to be hacked and tumbled round the world, and sold to Tom, and Dick, and the Lord knows who, 'tan't no kindness to be givin' on him notions and expectations, and bringin' on him up too well, for the rough and tumble comes all the harder on him arter. Now, I venture to say, your niggers would be quite chopfallen in a place where some of your plantation niggers would be singing and whooping like all possessed. Every man, you know, Mr. Shelby, naturally thinks well of his own ways; and I think I treat niggers just about as well as it's ever worth while to treat 'em." (49)

Nussbaum says *Uncle Tom's Cabin* "can hardly be read today" (*Upheavals of Thought*, 433). Of course, there are lots of things about the novel that one now sees either as corny (for example, Little Eva and her sentimental death) or as offensive (for example, that Stowe locates black humanity primarily in black Christianity). However, the work remains a masterful exploration of the boundaries of compassion and one that, for the most part, takes Aristotle's conditions for compassion as physiological givens that need somehow to be overcome.

29 Dickens, *David Copperfield*, 286-87. David is alarmed by Steerforth's statement and assumes that Steerforth is joking. Yet we are given to assume that this reasoning is the foundation of Steerforth's justification for seducing Em'ly, disgracing her, taking her away from her family, and refusing to marry her because she is too far beneath him socially.

30 Whitney, "The Seriousness of the Offence."

31 West is less inclined than Nussbaum to argue for the connections between rationality and compassion. West perhaps seems to think of compassion more as a raw empathic and emotional identification with suffering *(Caring for Justice)*.

32 West, *Caring for Justice*, 57. This "who will suffer more by losing" test is troubling on many different levels. West does not explain the link between the legal standard of best interests of the child and her notion that custody should go to the party who will suffer more from losing. Yet it is clear that while there may be some overlap between the two, it is not obvious that the one is a reliable guide to the other.

33 Rousseau, *Emile*, 225.

34 I'm borrowing the phrase from Spelman, *Fruits of Sorrow*.

35 There are several subcategories of people who cause their own suffering. We have those who are reckless in relation to their own best interests – like John F. Kennedy, Jr, for example, who took an irresponsible risk by going up in a small airplane in a storm and paid with his life. We also have intentional infliction of harm upon the self. However, suicidal conduct is not really what is meant by the category. The largest category of people who cause their own suffering and are therefore undeserving of compassion are those who harm others and thereby incur punishment. A final category is those who are simply "bad people" and therefore deserving of whatever ills befall them.

36 See also Spelman, *Fruits of Sorrow*, 41.

37 Nussbaum, "Compassion," 33.

38 *Uncle Tom's Cabin* provides another example of this. Consider the cynical but relatively compassionate slave owner Augustine St. Clare's explanation of his failure as a plantation disciplinarian: "Being myself one of the laziest of mortals, I had altogether too much fellow-feeling for the lazy; and when poor shiftless dogs put stones at the bottom of their cotton-baskets or filled their sacks with dirt, with cotton at the top, it seemed so exactly like what I should do if I were they, I couldn't and wouldn't have them flogged for it" (Stowe, 342). Here, St. Clare's self-understanding, his forthright perception of how he would behave if stuck in similar circumstances – as well as his willingness to place himself imaginatively in that position – becomes the basis for his judgment that the slaves are not blameworthy. His admission that he would have done the same thing works as an argument that the act ought not to be viewed as blameworthy at all. Stowe, through St. Clare, is asking readers to rethink their condemnation and reject their conclusion that slaves are blameworthy and hence undeserving of compassion. Stowe is calling her readers on their hypocrisy and is asking them critically to evaluate whether they, if placed in the position of the slave, would not have committed the same infractions they are so ready to condemn. By inviting the conclusion that "you would do the same thing," she is attempting to get her readers to conclude that the act is innocent.

39 Aristotle also sees sameness or equality as a condition for friendship. See Kahane, "Diversity, Solidarity, and Civic Friendship."

40 Rousseau, *Emile*, 224.

41 Ibid.

42 Ibid.

43 Ibid.

44 Fear-based strategies work best in relation to the fear of illness since we are all relatively equally subject to disease. While demographic variations clearly exist, no one is beyond the possibility of being stricken by cancer, heart disease, or what have you. Thus the "it could happen to you" strategy is fairly persuasive in this context.

45 Of course, as Nussbaum points out, John Rawls's (*A Theory of Justice*) veil of ignorance is an attempt to artificially create fear about the social class one will end up in as a means of manufacturing a kind of synthetic compassion for those lower down in the process of setting up political institutions ("Compassion," 36).

46 In Nussbaum's example of Posner's judicial compassion for the suffering of the victim of child sexual abuse (*Nelson v. Ferry*, 874 F. 2d 165, 7th Cir., 1989), she focuses on the conditions of "seriousness" and "blamelessness" while ignoring Aristotle's further condition that the pitier would have to see the suffering as something that could happen to him or someone he cares about: "We see in his opinion all the materials of compassion: the judgment that the little girl has suffered serious harm through no fault of her own; the judgment that this is a very bad thing and must not be renewed by a courtroom confrontation" ("Compassion," 55). The "or someone he cares about" proviso is obviously necessary here. Nussbaum in *Upheavals of Thought* has now expressly dropped this condition and has replaced it with a need for the pitier to make a "eudaimonistic judgment" that the other is "an end whose good is to be promoted" (321).

47 For example, instead of taking the tack of simply shaming whites by arguing that they did not care at all about blacks, Stowe tried to capitalize on whatever existing concern

there was on the part of nonbrutal slave owners for their slaves. Spelman criticizes this kind of encouraging of compassion through flattery (*Fruits of Sorrow*, 127-28). But we can see how the strategy accepts that Aristotle is right about the conditions under which we feel compassion and the colossal difficulty of getting compassion spontaneously to extend across lines of difference. Stowe tried to address moderate slave owners as though they were people who cared about and shared some, however limited, ground of friendship with their own slaves. Thus the argument against slavery that Stowe repeated over and over was that, so long as the institution of slavery existed, any slave, no matter how well cared for or even loved by his or her beneficent white master, was vulnerable literally to being sold down the river to a brutal master and into a state of absolute destitution. She was trying to create fear in white slave owners who believed their own reasonableness was sufficient protection against ill treatment of those slaves about whom they cared and for whom they felt a bond of friendship. The main plot lines of Stowe's novel are structured to reveal how the kindness of so-called beneficent slave owners could not protect the slaves whom they cared about from the most horrible fates that slavery had to offer. Thus financial ruin (as in the case of Mr. Shelby) or sudden death of an owner (as in the case of Augustine St. Clare) were events that resulted in the total vulnerability of their slaves to the cruelest and most inhumane of abuses. Though the white slave owners knew absolutely that they were exempt from the particular sufferings of slaves, Stowe sought to remind them that while the institution existed, they did not have the power to protect those blacks they cared about from the maximum violence and barbarity of slavery.

48 Spelman, *Fruits of Sorrow*.
49 Nussbaum, "Compassion," 57. Nussbaum reiterates this claim in *Upheavals of Thought*, 421.
50 de Tocqueville, *Democracy in America*, 699, emphasis added.
51 The only other discussion of compassion in *Democracy in America*, to the best of my knowledge, is in the following passage, which claims that southern white Americans are more compassionate toward blacks because they feel confident in their ability to humiliate them back into submission if need be, whereas northern white Americans feel a greater need for cold distance from blacks because they genuinely fear black power:

> In the South, where slavery still exists, the Negroes are less carefully kept apart; they sometimes share the labors and the recreations of the whites; the whites consent to intermix with them to a certain extent, and although legislation treats them more harshly, the habits of the people are more tolerant and compassionate. In the South the master is not afraid to raise his slave to his own standing, because he knows that he can in a moment reduce him to the dust at pleasure. In the North the white no longer distinctly perceives the barrier that separates him from the degraded race, and he shuns the Negro with the more pertinacity since he fears lest they should some day be confounded together. (415)

This sentiment is again reflected by Stowe in *Uncle Tom's Cabin*. Augustine St. Clare, speaking of his father, says: "*Among his equals*, never was a man more just and generous; but he considered the negro, through all possible gradations of color, as an intermediate link between man and animals, and graded all his ideas of justice or generosity on this hypothesis" (355, emphasis in the original).

52 For example, de Tocqueville was absolutely opposed to women's suffrage, yet he would not have thought that the constitutional disenfranchisement of women resulted in any lack of compassion for them. He assumes that men and women share equality of conditions even though they do not share constitutional equality. So it is not the absence of formal legal equality to which de Tocqueville can be referring in using the example of slavery to demonstrate that American compassion does not extend beyond the existing equality.

53 See Weiler: "Democracy is not the end. Democracy, too, is a means, even if an indispensable means. The end is to try, and try again, to live a life of decency, to honour

our creation in the image of God, or the secular equivalent. A democracy, when all is said and done, is as good or bad as the people who belong to it. The problem of Haider's Austria is not an absence of democracy. The problem is that Austria is a democracy; that Haider was elected democratically, and that even the people who did not vote for him are content to see him and his party share in government. A democracy of vile persons will be vile" ("Federalism with Constitutionalism, 65-66).

54 Orwin, "Compassion," 331.

55 Fatić, for example, states that "restorative crime-handling is similar to Christie's conflict-resolution in that it requires a certain kind of moral enlightenment. Yet, this moral enlightenment does not rest on the assumption of the goodness of human nature. Instead, restorative crime-handling concentrates on those mechanisms, arising from the necessity of trust, without which individuals simply cannot do in society, and it proposes to create such conditions, through its minimal institutions, under which individuals will be best off by accepting the moral norms arising from the principle of refraining from punitive infliction of pain as pain of justice and vengeance and from the adoption of reconciliatory and restorative values" (*Punishment and Restorative Crime-Handling,* 220).

56 As usual Eliot puts it better than you can even imagine anyone being able to: "We are all of us born in moral stupidity, taking the world as an udder to feed our supreme selves: Dorothea had early begun to emerge from that stupidity, but yet it had been easier to her to imagine how she would devote herself to Mr. Casaubon, and become wise and strong in his strength and wisdom, than to conceive with that distinctness which is no longer reflection but feeling – an idea wrought back to the directness of sense, like the solidity of objects – that he had an equivalent centre of self, whence the lights and shadows must always fall with a certain difference" (*Middlemarch,* 208).

57 This is also sometimes spoken of in terms of fostering awareness of how the other person has been affected by the crime. See Wachtel and McCold, "Restorative Justice in Everyday Life," 127.

58 Nussbaum makes this argument in her discussion of *David Copperfield,* treated above.

59 For a discussion of the dangers of empathy without conversation, see Spelman, *Fruits of Sorrow,* Ch. 5, "Changing the Subject: On Making Your Suffering Mine."

60 Umbreit, *Handbook of Victim Offender Mediation,* 6.

61 McDonald and Moore, "Community Conferencing as a Special Case of Conflict Transformation." The authors speak of restorative justice as promoting the values of "mutual respect, civility and reciprocity" (133).

62 Consider, for example, the compassion we felt for the plight of Judge Lance Ito in the O.J. Simpson case and how being an object of compassion diminished, in some measure, his judicial dignity.

63 Umbreit, *Handbook of Victim Offender Mediation,* xxxi, Item 9.

64 This sense of all participants as competent sources of renewal is paired with the hopeful philosophy that we should never "give up on" a wrongdoer. And one would assume that this outlook also means that we should never give up on a victim's capacity for rejuvenation. See Braithwaite and Strang, eds., *Restorative Justice and Civil Society,* 12.

65 Shearing, "Transforming Security," 22.

66 Umbreit, for example, puts the need to recognize oneself and others as competent agents of repair in terms of a "belief in the capacity of all people to draw on inner reservoirs of strength to overcome adversity, to grow and to help others in similar circumstances" (*Handbook of Victim Offender Mediation,* 5).

67 Johnson, ed., *Freedom and Interpretation,* 2.

68 This concept of humility is reflected in the egalitarian architecture of the restorative encounter where the "room seats everyone in positions of equal status in a circle" (Sherman, "Two Protestant Ethics and the Spirit of Restoration," 48).

69 Indeed, this shift from the particular to the general actually obviates the need for the troubling proviso "or someone I care about" in the assessment of vulnerability to risk. If compassion is grounded in a more generalized awareness of one's vulnerability to loss, injury, violence, the devastation of abusive tyrannical power, and so forth, rather than in this particular inquiry about one's own prospects for suffering, compassion will be

felt more easily for those who are beyond one's lived circle of concern. Humility as a foundation for compassion, then, allows for compassion even where we do not reasonably fear that either ourselves or those within our immediate and even extended circle of concern will be subject to a similar kind of suffering.

70 Fatić, for example, claims that under a system of restorative justice, "the tribunals would be significantly different from present-day criminal courts, because in them the arrogance of the detached robes symbolising 'blind' justice would be replaced by the humbleness of ordinary people trying to persuade other ordinary people to forgive and to enable others to forgive" (*Punishment and Restorative Crime-Handling*, 263).

71 Umbreit states that dialogue between victim and offender is what generates "victim empathy in the offender," which he claims "can lead to less criminal behavior in the future" (*Handbook of Victim Offender Mediation*, xl).

72 Zehr, *Changing Lenses*, 41

73 There is also the expectation that the offender will be surprised by the extent of the harm caused. See Wachtel and McCold, "Restorative Justice in Everyday Life," 126.

74 Ibid., 128.

75 Van Ness and Strong, *Restoring Justice*, 2nd ed., Ch. 4, "Encounter."

76 Ibid., 38.

77 Adam Smith: "How selfish soever man may be supposed, there are evidently some principles in his nature, which interest him in the fortune of others, and render their happiness necessary to him though he derives nothing from it except the pleasure of seeing it. Of this kind is pity or compassion, the emotion which we feel for the misery of others, when we see it or are made to conceive it in a very lively manner" (*A Theory of Moral Sentiments*, 9).

78 Wachtel and McCold put this in terms of a quadrant containing four paradigms: punitive, restorative, permissive, and neglectful. The punitive system creates limits but gives no support, the restorative sets limits and gives support, the neglectful neither sets limits nor gives support, and the permissive gives support but doesn't set limits ("Restorative Justice in Everyday Life," 124).

79 Umbreit, *Handbook of Victim Offender Mediation*, 231.

80 Sendor, "Restorative Retributivism."

81 Sharpe, *Restorative Justice*, 14.

82 Van Ness and Strong, *Restoring Justice*, 1st ed., 56.

83 Ibid., 55-6.

84 Umbreit, *Handbook of Victim Offender Mediation*, 103.

85 Ibid., 95. Here the victim doesn't lose her job but loses pay for a number of days during the month her car is missing.

86 Ibid., 85.

87 Some studies indicate that victims are happiest with restorative justice where the loss is only monetary. See Carriere, Malsch, and Vermunt, "Victim-Offender Negotiations."

88 Braithwaite says, however, that when victims understate their losses, offenders are actually more likely to experience shame ("Repentance Rituals and Restorative Justice," 120). Note that while Braithwaite is an advocate of shaming offences (as opposed to offenders), other restorative justice advocates see all shaming as counterproductive. See Sharpe, who argues that shame should not be a part of the process but rather that the wrongdoer should be made aware that more was expected of him or her (*Restorative Justice*, 95). See also Morris, "Shame, Guilt and Remorse."

89 Rousseau, *Emile*, 225.

90 Miller, *Anatomy of Disgust*, 210-11.

91 Umbreit, *Handbook of Victim Offender Mediation*, 166.

92 Zehr concedes that offenders often see their victims as deserving what they got, but he argues that it is the prison system that encourages this and allows offenders to insulate themselves from the truth that the victim didn't deserve it. He claims that the restorative encounter makes offenders face up to the reality that their victims did not deserve to be hurt (*Changing Lenses*, 40-1).

93 Brooks, ed., *When Sorry Is Not Enough*, 457.

94 Ibid., 459.

95 Braithwaite claims, however, that victims who blame themselves for the crime during the restorative encounter often elicit more heartfelt repentance from the offender ("Repentance Rituals and Restorative Justice," 123).

96 Pollard, "Victims and the Criminal Justice System," 14.

97 "Packers' Pick Arrested on Burglary Charge," *South Florida Sun Sentinel,* 9 July 2002.

98 Goffman, *Relations in Public.*

99 Braithwaite, "Repentance Rituals and Restorative Justice," 120. See also Braithwaite, *Crime, Shame, and Reintegration,* Ch. 5, "Social Conditions Conducive to Reintegrative Shaming." See also Pollard, who writes that "thus the system singularly fails to confront offenders with the impact of their actions on others – not only in respect of the victim and the community, but also their own family – the single element most likely to make them feel genuine remorse, to want to apologize and to think seriously about their future conduct" ("Victims and the Criminal Justice System," 12). Pollard also cites Braithwaite as authority for this proposition. He maintains further that there are few offenders who do not have some community of care that will be there to support and encourage their remorse. He notes that even homeless people have "street families" that can serve as this kind of community of care for the offender (14). For a persuasive critique of such arguments, see Johnstone, *Restorative Justice,* 53-4.

100 Hudson, "Restorative Justice."

101 Busch and Hooper, "Domestic Violence and the Restorative Justice Initiatives."

102 Umbreit, *Handbook of Victim Offender Mediation,* 93.

103 Miller, *Bloodtaking and Peacemaking,* 177.

104 Bianchi, *Justice as Sanctuary,* 42-5.

105 Umbreit, *Handbook of Victim Offender Mediation,* 182.

106 It should be noted that Sharpe recognizes the significance of the proviso in the context of community compassion for the victim. Here we have not discussed the role of the community as givers of compassion in much detail. But the proviso is obviously a major factor in what the community members' reactions to the crime will be. As Sharpe notes, "the more similar a victim seems to oneself (living in the same neighbourhood, travelling the same routes, living the same lifestyle) the more clear it seems that 'this could happen to me too'" (*Restorative Justice,* 46).

107 Luke 5:15, King James Bible.

108 One of Archbishop Desmond Tutu's commonly used phrases in talking about the South African Truth and Reconciliation Commission is the notion of its affirmation that we are in a moral universe. See Tutu, Interview with Danny Schechter.

109 Eliot, *Scenes of Clerical Life,* 314.

110 Ibid., 315.

111 Plato, *The Republic,* Bks. 1 and 2.

112 Umbreit, *Handbook of Victim Offender Mediation,* 209.

113 Harriet Beecher Stowe plays interestingly with the moral ironies of pity for the pain of pity. She cuts short her own description of the horrors of slavery, saying "but we forbear, out of sympathy to our readers' bones" (*Uncle Tom's Cabin,* 158). She ironically conceives a compassionate duty to refrain from inflicting the pain of compassion on her readers. We see her using this technique again when describing the condition in which the young black slave child Topsy arrived at the St. Clare household: "It is not for polite ears to hear the particulars of the first toilet of a neglected, abused child. In fact, in this world, multitudes must live and die in a state that it would be too great a shock to the nerves of their fellow mortals even to hear described" (354-55). In this conceptual turn, Stowe anticipates (and at the same time ridicules) criticisms that would soon be heaped upon her work that she was exaggerating the suffering of the slaves. Stowe both indulges and mocks this notion that she is causing too much pain to whites by making them conceive of the pain of slaves in a lively manner. If it is too painful to the spectator even to hear about this suffering, she implies, how can he be indifferent to the pain of those who actually have to go through such suffering?

114 Boehm, *Blood Revenge,* 134.

115 McDonald and Moore, "Community Conferencing as a Special Case of Conflict Trans-
     formation," 138.
116 Umbreit, *Handbook of Victim Offender Mediation*, 92.
117 Ibid., 95.
118 Although loss of earnings would presumably be included in what Umbreit calls "out of
     pocket expenses," he cautions mediators that they may not write up an agreement
     between victim and offender that requires the offender to pay compensation for the vic-
     tim's pain and suffering. He claims that the courts do no allow payments to the victim
     for pain and suffering, but he gives no authority for the claim (ibid., 63).
119 Ibid., 93.
120 Ibid., 97.
121 Ibid.
122 Ibid.
123 Braithwaite, *Restorative Justice and Responsive Regulation*, 9.
124 Plato, *Gorgias*, Part 2, 87, sec. 509d.
125 Eliot, *Felix Holt*, 258.
126 Luke 15:19, King James Bible.
127 We see this as well in the aftermath of sexual assault accusations against Catholic priests
     in the United States. When Archbishop Rembert G. Weakland apologized for an "in-
     appropriate relationship" with a man who accused him of rape, Weakland received a
     standing ovation, the crowd applauding him for "more than a minute" (Fountain, "Arch-
     bishop Offers Milwaukee Faithful a Public Apology," *New York Times*, 1 June 2002). See
     also Shriver:

> Desmond Tutu tells of the [Truth and Reconciliation Commission] hearing in the
> Eastern Cape near the site of the Bisho Massacre. Black as well as white police car-
> ried out this atrocity. The three most responsible for ordering the killing appeared
> before the Commission, confessed the details of the crime and expressed great sor-
> row for it. As the details came spilling out, said Tutu, the hostility of the audience
> rose visibly. Anger was in the air. Then, one of the three turned to the audience
> and said, "We are heartily sorry for this terrible act. We hope that you will find it
> possible to forgive us." After a pregnant pause, the audience rose spontaneously to
> their feet and responded in loud applause. ("Where and When in Political Life Is
> Justice Served by Forgiveness?" 33)

     Shriver's note reads: "Tutu's account was part of his sermon at the French Church in
     Berlin on the occasion of the presentation by the Evangelical Church in Germany of its
     Bonhoeffer Peace Award to the Truth and Reconciliation Commission, 25 April 1999"
     (39).
128 Braithwaite, "Repentance Rituals and Restorative Justice," 123.
129 Braithwaite, *Crime, Shame, and Reintegration*, 12.

Epilogue

1 Linfield, "Trading Truth for Justice," <http://bostonreview.mit.edu/BR25.3/linfield.html>
   (15 January 2002).
2 For example, Umbreit counsels that the victim's anger is not counterproductive to the
   process where it is stated in terms of "I" messages and where it is "owned" by the victim. Thus Umbreit adopts the pop-psychology staple that one is meant to use "not blam-
   ing statements" like "I felt hurt and angry when you punched me," as opposed to blam-
   ing statements like "You hurt me" or "You made me angry" (*Handbook of Victim Offender
   Mediation*, 44). On "I" messages in pop psychology, see, for example, Lerner, *The Dance
   of Anger*, 88-90, and *The Dance of Intimacy*, 91; John Gray, *Men Are from Mars, Women
   Are from Venus*, 168-74.
3 Gibbon, *The Decline and Fall of the Roman Empire*, vol. 1, 13.
4 Zehr, *Changing Lenses*, 35.
5 Braithwaite seems to include all caring attempts to help offenders within the rubric of

restorative justice. For example, he cites programs to assist sex offenders getting out of prison with establishing new lives and resisting the impulse to reoffend as a restorative justice initiative (*Restorative Justice and Responsive Regulation,* 75). This type of initiative, however, is completely consistent with a retributive framework. For an extremely helpful conceptual typology of different kinds of reforms in the area of criminal justice, see Dignan and Cavadino, "Towards a Framework for Conceptualising and Evaluating Models of Criminal Justice from a Victim's Perspective."

6 Dignan and Cavadino refer to this type of reform initiative as the "welfare model" ("Towards a Framework for Conceptualising and Evaluating Models of Criminal Justice from a Victim's Perspective," 160).

7 Biggar, ed., *Burying the Past,* 8.

8 Fatić writes: "The supreme moral principle of restorative crime-handling is abolition of punitive reactions to crime" (*Punishment and Restorative Crime-Handling,* 221).

9 It is interesting to note that even Thomas More offers a kind of version of restorative justice (and community service for offenders) in his *Utopia.* The restorative aspects of his vision are more evident when one takes into account that he is writing in opposition to the administration of capital punishment in cases of theft:

> Those that are found guilty of theft among them are bound to make restitution to the owner, and not as it is in other places, to the prince, for they reckon that the prince has no more right to the stolen goods than the thief; but if that which was stolen is no more in being, then the goods of the thieves are estimated, and restitution being made out of them, the remainder is given to their wives and children: and they themselves are condemned to serve in the public works, but are neither imprisoned, nor chained, unless there happened to be some extraordinary circumstances in their crimes. They go about loose and free, working for the public. If they are idle or backward to work, they are whipped; but if they work hard, they are well used and treated without any mark of reproach, only the lists of them are called always at night, and then they are shut up. They suffer no other uneasiness, but this of constant labor; for as they work for the public, so they are well entertained out of the public stock, which is done differently in different places. (23)

10 Fatić, *Punishment and Restorative Crime-Handling,* 222.

11 Ibid., 223.

12 Niebuhr, *Love and Justice,* 277.

13 But it is not even necessarily so. In the context of crime the forbearing victim who seeks reconciliation does not put only herself at risk by protecting the perpetrator from coercion. Society as a whole is put at greater risk by the victim's forbearance. This is why, traditionally, our criminal system has not seen the victim as "owning the conflict." The conflict belongs not just to the victim or to the victim and her immediate community, but to the society as a whole, which has the right to proceed against the wrongdoer.

14 Braithwaite and Strang, "Introduction: Restorative Justice and Civil Society," in *Restorative Justice and Civil Society,* 1-13 at 4.

15 Note again here the empirical evidence on recidivism rates following restorative justice versus those characterizing the ordinary criminal justice system (see Delgado, "Goodbye to Hammurabi," 765 and note 85).

16 Delgado also notes that accepting the failures of the existing criminal justice system as the only alternatives to restorative justice is demoralizing ("Goodbye to Hammurabi," 773). He suggests that a healthy competition between the two systems might be beneficial. However, the idea that restorative justice would be in competition with the usual system for clients raises even more anxiety about the problems of restorative justice promoting itself and touting its successes to the detriment of parties who fall for the sell.

References

ABC Nightline. ABC News, 1 January 1999. ET Transcript # 99010101-jo7.

Acorn, Annalise. "Making Sense: Similar Fact Evidence and the Principles of Inductive Reasoning." *Oxford Journal of Legal Studies* 11 (1991): 63-91.

Adams, Don. "Love and Impartiality." *American Philosophical Quarterly* 30, 3 (1993): 223-34.

All Things Considered. National Public Radio, 15 April 1996. ET Transcript # 2184-13.

–. National Public Radio, 13 December 1996. ET Transcript # 96121306-212.

Allard, Pierre, and Wayne Northey. "Christianity: The Rediscovery of Restorative Justice." In *The Spiritual Roots of Restorative Justice*, edited by Michael L. Hadley, 119-41. Albany: State University of New York Press, 2001.

Allen, Jonathan. "Balancing Justice and Social Utility: Political Theory and the Idea of a Truth and Reconciliation Commission." *University of Toronto Law Journal* 49 (1999): 315-55.

Ammar, Nawal H. "Restorative Justice in Islam: Theory and Practice." In *The Spiritual Roots of Restorative Justice*, edited by Michael L. Hadley, 161-80. Albany: State University of New York Press, 2001.

Andrews, Penny. "Review of David Dyzenhaus, *Judging the Judges, Judging Ourselves: Truth Reconciliation and the Apartheid Legal Order* [Oxford: Hart Publishing, 1998]." *Melbourne University Law Review* 24 April (2000): 236-47.

Archibald, Bruce P. "Fault, Penalty and Proportionality: Connecting Sentencing to Subjective and Objective Standards of Criminal Liability (with Ruminations on Restorative Justice)." *Criminal Law Quarterly* 40 (1998): 263-86.

Arendt, Hannah. *Men in Dark Times.* New York: Harcourt, Brace and World, 1955.

–. *The Human Condition.* Chicago: University of Chicago Press, 1958.

Aristotle. *The Rhetoric and the Poetics.* Translated by W. Rhys Roberts and Ingram Bywater. New York: Random House, 1954.

–. *"Nicomachean" Ethics.* Translated by David Koss. Oxford: Oxford University Press, 1986.

Ashworth, Andrew. "Some Reservations about Restorative Justice." *Criminal Law Forum* 4, 2 (1993): 277-99.

–. "Responsibilities, Rights and Restorative Justice." *British Journal of Criminology* 42 (2002): 578-95.

Augsburger, David. "The F Word: Forgiveness and Its Imitations." <http://www.nacronline.com/dox/library/forgive.shtml> (2 November 2000).

Austen, Jane. *Emma.* New York: Bantam Books, 1981 [1815].

–. *Sense and Sensibility.* Ware: Wordsworth Editions, 1992 [1811].

–. *Northanger Abbey.* Ware: Wordsworth Editions, 1993 [1818].

Bandes, Susan, ed. *The Passions of Law.* New York: New York University Press, 1999.

–. "When Victims Seek Closure: Forgiveness, Vengeance and the Role of the Government." *Fordam Urban Law Journal* 27 (June 2000): 1599-1606.

Bandow, Doug. "Cycle of Unease in Okinawa." <http://www.cato.org/dailys/08-01-00.html> (2 November 2000).

Baron, Marcia. "Impartiality and Friendship." *Ethics* 101, 4 (July 1991): 836-58.

Barton, Charles K.B. *Getting Even: Revenge as a Form of Justice.* Chicago: Open Court, 1999.

Bazemore, Gordon, and Mara Schiff. *Restorative Community Justice: Repairing Harm and Transforming Communities.* Cincinnati: Anderson Publishing, 2001.

Beaches. Directed by Gary Marshall. Film. 1988.

Becker, Lawrence C. "Impartiality and Ethical Theory." *Ethics* 101, 4 (July 1991): 698-700.

Bell, Derrick. "Review of Daniel C. Maguire, *A New American Justice* [New York: Doubleday, 1980]." *Harvard Civil Rights-Civil Liberties Law Review* 16 (1982): 855.

Bellow, Saul. *Herzog.* New York: Penguin, 1996.

Bertrand, Marie-Andrée. "Incarceration as a Gendering Strategy." *Canadian Journal of Law and Society* 14 (Spring 1999): 45-60.

Bianchi, Herman. "Tsedeka-Justice." In Review for *Philosophy and Theology.* London: Blackwell, 1973.

–. *Justice as Sanctuary: Toward a New System of Crime Control.* Bloomington: Indiana University Press, 1994.

Biggar, Nigel. "Making Peace or Doing Justice: Must We Choose?" In *Burying the Past: Making Peace and Doing Justice after Civil Conflict,* edited by Nigel Biggar, 1-14. Washington, DC: Georgetown University Press, 2001.

–, ed. *Burying the Past: Making Peace and Doing Justice after Civil Conflict.* Washington, DC: Georgetown University Press, 2001.

Blagg, Henry. "Restorative Visions and Restorative Justice Practices: Conferencing, Ceremony and Reconciliation in Australia." *Current Issues in Criminal Justice* 10 (July 1998): 5-14.

Bloom, Allan. *The Closing of the American Mind.* New York: Simon and Schuster, 1987.

Blue, Arthur, and Meredith A. Rogers Blue. "The Case for Aboriginal Justice and Healing: The Self Perceived through a Broken Mirror." In *The Spiritual Roots of Restorative Justice,* edited by Michael L. Hadley, 57-79. Albany: State University of New York Press, 2001.

Boehm, Christopher. *Blood Revenge: The Anthropology of Feuding in Montenegro and Other Tribal Societies.* Lawrence: University Press of Kansas, 1984.

Braithwaite, John. *Crime, Shame, and Reintegration.* Cambridge: Cambridge University Press, 1989.

–. "Repentance Rituals and Restorative Justice." *The Journal of Political Philosophy* 8, 1 (2000): 115-31.

–. "Restorative Justice and Social Justice." *University of Saskatchewan Law Review* 63, 1 (2000): 185-94.

–. *Restorative Justice and Responsive Regulation.* Oxford: Oxford University Press, 2002.

Braithwaite, John, and Heather Strang, eds. *Restorative Justice and Civil Society.* Cambridge: Cambridge University Press, 2001.

Brooks, Roy L., ed. *When Sorry Is Not Enough: The Controversy over Apologies and Reparations for Human Injustice.* New York: New York University Press, 1999.

Brown, Wendy. "Reflections on Tolerance in the Age of Identity." In *Democracy and Vision: Sheldon Wolin and the Vicissitudes of the Political,* edited by W. Connolly and A. Botwinick, 99-117. Princeton: Princeton University Press, 2001.

Brunk, Conrad G. "Restorative Justice and the Philosophical Theories of Criminal Punishment." In *The Spiritual Roots of Restorative Justice,* edited by Michael L. Hadley, 31-56. Albany: State University of New York Press, 2001.

Buber, Martin. *I and Thou.* Translated by Walter Kaufmann. New York: Simon and Schuster, 1970.

Burnside, Jonathan. "Tension and Tradition in the Pursuit of Justice." In *Relational Justice: Repairing the Breach,* edited by Jonathan Burnside and Nicola Baker, 42-52. Winchester, UK: Waterside Press, 1994.

Busch, Ruth, and Stephen Hooper. "Domestic Violence and the Restorative Justice Initiatives: The Risks of a New Panacea." *Waikato Law Review* 4 (1996): 101-30.

Callan, Eamonn. *Creating Citizens: Political Education and Liberal Democracy.* Oxford: Oxford University Press, 1997.

Carriere, R.M., M. Malsch, and R. Vermunt. "Victim Offender Negotiations: An Exploratory Study on Different Damage Types and Compensation." *International Review of Victimology* 5 (1998): 221-34.

Chiba, Shin. "Hannah Arendt on Love and the Political: Love, Friendship, and Citizenship." *Review of Politics* 57, 3 (1995): 506-35.

Christie, Nils. "Conflict as Property." *British Journal of Criminology* 17, 1 (1977): 1-15.

–. "Between Civility and State." In *The New European Criminology: Crime and Social Order in Europe,* edited by Vincenzo Ruggiero, Nigel South, and Ian Taylor, 119-24. London: Routledge, 1998.

Church Council on Justice and Corrections. *Collaborative Justice Project.* <http://www.ccjc.ca/news/collaberative.cfm> (8 January 2002).

A Clockwork Orange. Directed by Stanley Kubrick. Film. 1971.

Colson, Charles W. "Truth, Justice, Peace: The Foundations of Restorative Justice." *Regent University Law Review* 10 (1998): 1-9.

–. *Justice That Restores.* Wheaton Illinois: Tyndale House Publishers, 2001.

Cornell, Drucilla. "Loyalty and the Limits of Kantian Impartiality." *Harvard Law Review* 107 (June 1994): 2081-94.

Cragg, Wesley. *The Practice of Punishment: Towards a Theory of Restorative Justice.* London: Routledge, 1992.

Cuddihy, John Murray. *The Ordeal of Civility: Freud, Marx, Lévi-Strauss, and the Jewish Struggle with Modernity.* 2nd ed. Boston: Beacon Press, 1987.

Daly, Kathleen. "Diversionary Conferencing in Australia: A Reply to the Optimists and Skeptics." Paper presented to the American Society of Criminology Annual Meeting, Chicago, November 1996. <http://www.gu.edu.au/school/ccj/kdaly.html> (15 May 2002).

–. "Restorative Justice: Moving Past the Caricatures." Paper presented to the Seminar on Restorative Justice, Institute of Criminology, University of Sydney Law School, April 1998. <http://www.gu.edu.au/school/ccj/kdaly.html> (22 August 2000).

–. "Restorative Justice in Diverse and Unequal Societies." *Law in Context* 17, 1 (1999): 167-90.

–. "Revisiting the Relationship between Retributive and Restorative Justice." In *Restorative Justice: From Philosophy to Practice,* edited by John Braithwaite and Heather Strang, 33-54. Aldershot: Dartmouth, 2001. <http://www.gu.edu.au/school/ccj/kdaly.html> (5 February 2002).

–. "Restorative Justice: The Real Story." *Punishment and Society* 4, 1 (2002): 55-79.

–. "Sexual Assault and Restorative Justice." In *Restorative Justice and Family Violence,* edited by Heather Strang and John Braithwaite, 62-88. Cambridge: Cambridge University Press, 2002. <http://www.gu.edu.au/school/ccj/kdaly.html> (24 December 2002).

Daly, Kathleen, and Russ Immarigeon. "The Past, Present, and Future of Restorative Justice: Some Critical Reflections." *Contemporary Justice Review* 1 (1998): 21-45.

Daly, Mary. *Gyn/Ecology: The Metaethics of Radical Feminism.* Boston: Beacon Press, 1990.

de Cervantes, Miguel. *Don Quixote de la Mancha.* Translated by Charles Jarvis. London: S.A. and H. Oddy, 1809.

Delgado, Richard. "Goodbye to Hammurabi: Analysing the Atavistic Appeal of Restorative Justice." *Stanford Law Review* 52 (2000): 751-75.

de Montaigne, Michel. *The Complete Essays.* Translated by M.A. Screech. London: Penguin, 1987.

de Rougemont, Denis. *Love in the Western World.* Translated by Montgomery Belgion. Princeton: Princeton University Press, 1983 [1940].

Derrida, Jacques. *On Cosmopolitanism and Forgiveness.* Translated by Mark Dodey and Michael Hughes. Thinking in Action series. London: Routledge, 2001.

de Tocqueville, Alexis. *Democracy in America.* Translated by Henry Reeve. New York: Bantam, 2000 [1835].

Dickens, Charles. *Little Dorrit.* Oxford: Oxford University Press, 1982 [1857].

–. *Our Mutual Friend*. Ware: Wordsworth Editions, 1997 [1864-65].

–. *A Tale of Two Cities*. New York: Penguin Books, 1997 [1859].

–. *David Copperfield*. Oxford: Oxford University Press, 1999 [1849-50].

Dignan, James, and Michael Cavadino. "Towards a Framework for Conceptualising and Evaluating Models of Criminal Justice from a Victim's Perspective." *International Review of Victimology* 4 (1996): 153-82.

Dinnen, Sinclair. "Restorative Justice in Papua New Guinea." *International Journal of the Sociology of Law* 25 (1997): 245-62.

Dostoyevsky, Fyodor. *The Idiot*. 1868. Ware: Wordsworth Editions, 1996.

Douglas, Ann. *The Feminization of American Culture*. New York: Alfred A. Knopf, 1977.

Drumbl, Mark A. "Punishment, Postgenocide: From Guilt to Shame to *Civis* in Rwanda." *New York University Law Review* 75, 5 (2000): 1221-1326.

Duff, Anthony. *Punishment, Communication, and Community*. Oxford: Oxford University Press, 2001.

–. "Restoration and Retribution." In *Restorative Justice and Criminal Justice: Competing or Reconcilable Paradigms?* edited by A. Von Irsch et al., 43-60. Oxford: Hart Publishing, 2003.

Durham, Edith. *High Albania: A Victorian Traveller's Balkan Odyssey*. 1909. London: Phoenix Press, 2000.

Dworkin, Andrea. *Intercourse*. New York: The Free Press, 1987.

Dyzenhaus, David. "Debating South Africa's Truth and Reconciliation Commission." *University of Toronto Law Journal* 49 (1999): 311-53.

Eliot, George. *Adam Bede*. New York: Penguin, 1981 [1859].

–. *Felix Holt: The Radical*. Ware: Wordsworth Editions, 1997 [1866].

–. *Middlemarch*. Oxford: Oxford University Press, 1997 [1872].

–. *Scenes of Clerical Life*. London: Penguin, 1998 [1857].

–. *Romola*. Koln: Konemann, 2000 [1862-63].

Elshtain, Jean Bethke. "Politics and Forgiveness." In *Burying the Past: Making Peace and Doing Justice after Civil Conflict,* edited by Nigel Biggar, 40-56. Washington, DC: Georgetown University Press, 2001.

Emerson, Ralph Waldo. *Compensation and Self-Reliance*. Westwood: Fleming H. Revell Company, 1962.

Epstein, Richard. "Compassion and Compulsion." *Arizona State Law Journal* 22 (1990): 25-30.

Evers, Tag. "A Healing Approach to Crime." *The Progressive* 62, 9 (1998): 30.

Fatić, Aleksandar. *Punishment and Restorative Crime-Handling: A Social Theory of Trust*. Aldershot: Avenbury, 1995.

Feifer, George. "The Rape of Okinawa." *World Policy Journal* 17, 3 (Fall 2000). <http://www.worldpolicy.org/journal/feifer.html> (31 October 2000).

Fenwick, Helen. "Procedural Rights of Victims of Crime: Public or Private Ordering of the Criminal Justice Process." *Modern Law Review* 60, 3 (May 1997) 317-33.

"Fired Admiral Gives Public Apology." CNN World News, 20 November 1995. <http://www.cnn.com/WORLD/9511/macke_speaks/index.html> (31 October 2000).

Fisher, Helen. "The Nature and Evolution of Romantic Love." In *Romantic Passion: A Universal Experience?* edited by William Jankowiak, 23-41. New York: Columbia University Press, 1995.

"Forgiveness and Reconciliation: Religious Contributions to Conflict Resolution." <http://www.forgiveandreconcile.org/docs/tutu.html> (31 October 2000).

Foucault, Michel. *History of Sexuality*. Vol. 1. 1976. Translated by Robert Hurley. London: Penguin, 1990.

Fountain, John W. "Archbishop Offers Milwaukee Faithful a Public Apology." *New York Times*, 1 June 2002.

From Restorative Justice to Transformative Justice: Discussion Paper. Ottawa: Law Commission of Canada, 1999. Catalogue No. JL2-6/1999.

Gandhi. Directed by Richard Attenborough. Film. 1982.

Gandhi, Mohandas K. *The Story of My Experiments with Truth*. Translated by Mahadev Desai. New York: Dover Publications, 1983 [1948].

Gibbon, Edward. *The Decline and Fall of the Roman Empire.* Vol. 1. New York: Alfred A. Knopf, 1993.

Goffman, Erving. *Relations in Public.* New York: Basic Books, 1971.

Gold, Lois. "Influencing Unconscious Influences: The Healing Dimension of Mediation." *Mediation Quarterly* 11 (1993): 55-66.

Geula, Marianne. "South Africa's Truth and Reconciliation Commission as an Alternate Means of Addressing Transitional Government Conflicts in a Divided Society." *Boston University International Law Journal* 18 (Spring 2000): 57-84.

Gray, Harold. *Arf! The Life and Hard Times of Little Orphan Annie, 1935-1945.* New York: Arlington House, 1970.

Gray, John. *Men Are from Mars, Women Are from Venus: A Practical Guide to Improving Communication and Getting What You Want in Your Relationships.* New York: Harper Collins, 1992.

Greenblatt, Stephen. *Renaissance Self-Fashioning: From More to Shakespeare.* Chicago: University of Chicago Press, 1980.

Griffiths, John. "Ideology in Criminal Procedure *or* A Third Model of the Criminal Process." *Yale Law Journal* 79 (1970): 359-417.

Hadley, Michael L. "Multifaith Reflections on Criminal Justice." In *The Spiritual Roots of Restorative Justice,* edited by Michael L. Hadley, 1-29. Albany: State University of New York Press, 2001.

–, ed. *The Spiritual Roots of Restorative Justice.* Albany: State University of New York Press, 2001.

Hamber, Brandon. "Does the Truth Heal? A Psychological Perspective on Political Strategies for Dealing with the Legacy of Political Violence." In *Burying the Past: Making Peace and Doing Justice after Civil Conflict,* edited by Nigel Biggar, 131-48. Washington, DC: Georgetown University Press, 2001.

Hampton, Jean, and Jeffrey Murphy. *Forgiveness and Mercy.* Cambridge: Cambridge University Press, 1988.

Hasluck, Margaret Masson Hardie. *The Unwritten Law in Albania.* Cambridge: Cambridge University Press, 1954.

Henderson, Lynne N. "Legality and Empathy." *Michigan Law Review* 85 (1987): 1575-1653.

Heyward, Carter. *Speaking of Christ: A Lesbian Feminist Voice.* Edited by Ellen C. Davis. New York: Pilgrim Press, 1989.

–. *Touching Our Strength: The Erotic as Power and the Love of God.* San Francisco: Harper, 1989.

–. *Staying Power: Reflections on Gender, Justice, and Compassion.* Cleveland: Pilgrim Press, 1995.

Homer, *The Iliad.* Translated by E.V. Rieu. Harmondsworth: Penguin, 1985.

Huculak, Bria. "Justice as Hope." In *The Spiritual Roots of Restorative Justice,* edited by Michael L. Hadley, 217-23. Albany: State University of New York Press, 2001.

Hudson, Barbara. "Restorative Justice: The Challenge of Sexual and Racial Violence." *Journal of Law and Society* 25, 2 (June 1998): 237-56.

Hui, Edwin C., and Kaijun Geng. "The Spirit and Practice of Restorative Justice in Chinese Culture." In *The Spiritual Roots of Restorative Justice,* edited by Michael L. Hadley, 99-117. Albany: State University of New York Press, 2001.

Ideas. "Justice as Sanctuary." With Herman Bianchi. Part 1. Canadian Broadcasting Corporation Radio Program. October 1997.

Jankowiak, William, ed. *Romantic Passion: A Universal Experience?* New York: Columbia University Press, 1995.

Johnson, Barbara, ed. *Freedom and Interpretation.* The Oxford Amnesty Lectures, 1992. New York: Basic Books, 1993.

Johnstone, Gerry. *Restorative Justice: Ideas, Values, Debates.* Cullompton: Willan, 2002.

Jurevic, Linda. *"What's Love Got to Do With It?" Addressing Spirituality within the Context of Transformative Mediation.* LL.M. thesis. University of Melbourne. June 2000.

Kahane, David. "Diversity, Solidarity, and Civic Friendship." *Journal of Political Philosophy* 7, 3 (1999): 243-62.

Kerruish, Valerie. *Jurisprudence as Ideology.* London: Routledge, 1991.

King, Jr., Martin Luther. *Stride Toward Freedom: The Montgomery Circle.* New York: Harper and Row, 1958.

–. "Non-Violence and Racial Justice." In *A Testament of Hope: The Essential Writings and Speeches of Martin Luther King, Jr.,* edited by James M. Washington, 5-9. San Francisco: Harper Collins, 1986.

–. "Showdown for Non-Violence." In *A Testament of Hope: The Essential Writings and Speeches of Martin Luther King, Jr.,* edited by James M. Washington, 64-72. San Francisco: Harper Collins, 1986.

–. *A Testament of Hope: The Essential Writings and Speeches of Martin Luther King, Jr.* Edited by James M. Washington. San Francisco: Harper Collins, 1986.

Kwochka, Daniel. "Aboriginal Injustice: Making Room for a Restorative Paradigm." *Saskatchewan Law Review* 60, 1 (1996): 153-87.

Lansing, Paul, and Julie C. King. "South Africa's Truth and Reconciliation Commission: The Conflict between Individual Justice and National Healing in the Post-Apartheid Era." *Arizona Journal of International and Comparative Law* 15, 3 (Fall 1998): 753-89.

La Prairie, Carol. "Developments in Criminal Law and Criminal Justice: Conferencing in Aboriginal Communities in Canada: Finding Middle Ground in Criminal Justice." *Criminal Law Forum* 6 (1995): 576-99.

–. "Some Reflections on New Criminal Justice in Canada: Restorative Justice, Alternative Measures and Conditional Sentences." *The Australian and New Zealand Journal of Criminology* 32, 2 (1999): 139-52.

Laqueur, Thomas W. "Bodies, Details, and Humanitarian Narrative." In *The New Cultural History,* edited by Lynn Hunt, 176-204. Berkeley: University of California Press, 1989.

La Rochefoucauld. *Maxims.* Ware: Wordsworth Editions, 1997.

Law Commission of Canada. "Community Participation in the Justice System: Restorative Justice Approaches to Conflict." <http://www.lcc.gc.ca/en/ress/audio/index.html> (16 January 2002).

Lerman, David M. "Forgiveness in the Criminal Justice System: If It Belongs, Then Why Is It so Hard to Find?" *Fordham Urban Law Journal* 27 (2000): 1663-75.

Lerner, Harriet. *The Dance of Intimacy: A Woman's Guide to Courageous Acts of Change in Key Relationships.* New York: Harper Perennial, 1990.

–. *The Dance of Anger: A Woman's Guide to Changing the Patterns of Intimate Relationships.* New York: Harper Perennial, 1997.

Lewis, C.S. *The Four Loves.* New York: Harcourt and Brace, 1960.

Lewis, Sinclair. *Babbitt.* New York: Penguin Books, 1996 [1922].

Life Is Beautiful. Directed by Roberto Benigni. Film. 1998.

Linfield, Susie. "Trading Truth for Justice." *Boston Review* 27 (Summer 2000). <http://bostonreview.mit.edu/BR25.3/linfield.html> (15 January 2002).

Llewellyn, Jennifer J., and Robert Howse. *Restorative Justice: A Conceptual Framework.* Discussion paper prepared for the Law Commission of Canada. 1998.

Llewellyn, Jennifer J., and Robert Howse. "Institutions for Restorative Justice: The South African Truth and Reconciliation Commission." *University of Toronto Law Journal* 49 (1999): 355-88.

Lorde, Audre. *Sister Outsider.* Trumansburg, NY: Crossing Press, 1984.

Loy, David M. "Healing Justice: A Buddhist Perspective." In *The Spiritual Roots of Restorative Justice,* edited by Michael L. Hadley, 81-97. Albany: State University of New York Press, 2001.

MacKinnon, Catherine A. *Toward a Feminist Theory of the State.* Cambridge: Harvard University Press, 1989.

"Marine General Bows in Apology to Okinawa." *New York Times,* 7 July 2000. <http://www.sptimes.net/News/070700/Worldandnation/Marine_general_bows_i.shtml>.

Markel, Dan. "The Justice of Amnesty: Toward a Theory of Retributivism in Recovering States." *University of Toronto Law Journal* 49 (1999): 389-445.

–. "Are Shaming Punishments Beautifully Retributive? Retributivism and the Implications for the Alternative Sanctions Debate." *Vanderbilt Law Review* 54 (2002): 2157-2242.

Marshall, Christopher D. *Beyond Retribution: A New Testament Vision for Justice, Crime and Punishment.* Grand Rapids: Wm. B. Eerdmans, 2001.

Martin, Dianne L. "Retribution Revisited: A Reconsideration of Feminist Criminal Law Reform Strategies." *Osgoode Hall Law Journal* 36 (1998): 151-88.

Massaro, Toni M. "Empathy, Legal Storytelling, and the Rule of Law: New Words, Old Wounds?" *Michigan Law Review* 87 (1989): 2099-127.

Masters, Guy, and David Smith. "Portia and Persephone Revisited: Thinking about Feeling in Criminal Justice." *Theoretical Criminology* 2, 1 (1998): 5-27.

McDonald, John, and David Moore. "Community Conferencing as a Special Case of Conflict Transformation." In *Restorative Justice and Civil Society,* edited by John Braithwaite and Heather Strang, 130-48. Cambridge: Cambridge University Press, 2001.

McFall, Lynne. "What's Wrong with Bitterness?" In *Feminist Ethics,* edited by Claudia Card, 146-60. Lawrence: The University Press of Kansas, 1991.

Midgley, Mary. "Brutality and Sentimentality." *Philosophy* 54 (July 1979): 385-89.

Miers, David, Mike Maguire, and Shelagh Goldie. *An Exploratory Evaluation of Restorative Justice Schemes.* London: U.K. Home Office, 2001.

Miller, William Ian. *Bloodtaking and Peacemaking: Feud, Law, and Society in Saga Iceland.* Chicago: University of Chicago Press, 1990.

–. *Humiliation.* Ithaca: Cornell University Press, 1993.

–. *The Anatomy of Disgust.* Cambridge: Harvard University Press, 1997.

–. "Clint Eastwood and Equity: The Virtues of Revenge and the Shortcomings of Law in Popular Culture." In *Law and the Domains of Culture,* edited by Austin Sarat and Thomas Kearns, 161-202. Ann Arbor: University of Michigan Press, 1998.

–. "In Defense of Revenge." In *Medieval Crime and Social Control,* edited by Barbara A. Hanawalt and David Wallace, 70-89. Minneapolis: University of Minnesota Press, 1999.

–. *The Mystery of Courage.* Cambridge: Harvard University Press, 2000.

–. *Faking It.* Cambridge: Cambridge University Press, 2003.

Minow, Martha L. *Between Vengeance and Forgiveness: Facing History after Genocide and Mass Violence.* Boston: Beacon Press, 1998.

Minow, Martha L., and Elizabeth V. Spelman. "Passion for Justice." *Cardozo Law Review* 10 (1988): 37-76.

More, Thomas. *Utopia.* Edited and with introductions and notes by J. Churton Collins. Oxford: Clarendon Press, 1904.

Morris, Allison. "Shame, Guilt and Remorse: Experiences from Family Group Conferences in New Zealand." In *Punishing Juveniles: Principle and Critique,* edited by Ido Weijers and Anthony Duff, 157-78. Oxford: Hart Publishing, 2002.

The Music Box. Directed by Constantin Costa-Gavras. Film. 1989.

Nedelsky, Jennifer. "Reconceiving Autonomy: Sources, Thoughts and Possibilities." In *Law and the Community: The End of Individualism?* edited by A.C. Hutchinson and L.J.M. Green, 219-52. Toronto: Carswell, 1989.

–. "Reconceiving Rights as Relationship." *Review of Constitutional Studies* 1 (1993): 1-26.

–. "Embodied Diversity and the Challenges to Law." *McGill Law Journal* 42 (1997): 91-117.

–. "Communities of Judgment and Human Rights." *Theoretical Inquiries in Law* 1 (2000): 245-82.

Neufeldt, Ron. "Justice in Hinduism." In *The Spiritual Roots of Restorative Justice,* edited by Michael L. Hadley, 143-60. Albany: State University of New York Press, 2001.

Niebuhr, Reinhold. *Moral Man and Immoral Society: A Study in Ethics and Politics.* New York: Charles Scribner's Sons, 1941.

–. *The Nature and Destiny of Man.* New York: Scribner, 1964.

–. *Love and Justice: Selections of the Shorter Writings of Reinhold Niebuhr.* Cleveland: World Publishing, 1967.

Nietzsche, Friedrich. *On the Genealogy of Morals.* Translated by Walter Kaufmann. New York: Random House, 1989.

Nozick, Robert. *Philosophical Explanations.* Cambridge: Harvard University Press, 1981.

Nussbaum, Martha C. *Love's Knowledge: Essays on Philosophy and Literature.* Oxford: Oxford University Press, 1990.

–. "Steerforth's Arm: Love and the Moral Point of View." In *Love's Knowledge: Essays on Philosophy and Literature*, 335-64. Oxford: Oxford University Press, 1990.

–. "Tragedy and Self-Sufficiency: Plato and Aristotle on Fear and Pity." In *Essays on Aristotle's Poetics*, edited by Amélie O. Rorty, 261-90. Princeton: Princeton University Press, 1992.

–. "Compassion: The Basic Social Emotion." *Social Philosophy and Polity* 13, 1 (1996): 27-58.

–. *For Love of Country: Debating the Limits of Patriotism*. Edited by Joshua Cohen. Boston: Beacon Press, 1996.

–. *Upheavals of Thought: The Intelligence of Emotions*. Cambridge: Cambridge University Press, 2001.

Okin, Susan Moller. *Justice, Gender, and the Family*. New York: Basic Books, 1989.

Orwell, George. *The Road to Wigan Pier*. London: Penguin, 1989.

–. "Charles Dickens." In *Essays*. With an introduction by Bernard Crick, 35-78. London: Penguin, 2000.

–. "Good Bad Books." In *Essays*. With an introduction by Bernard Crick, 318-21. London: Penguin, 2000.

–. "Rudyard Kipling." In *Essays*. With an introduction by Bernard Crick, 203-15. London: Penguin, 2000.

Orwin, Clifford. "Compassion." *The American Scholar* 49 (Summer 1980): 309-33.

–. "Rousseau and the Discovery of Political Compassion." In *The Legacy of Rousseau*, edited by Clifford Orwin and Nathan Tarcov, 296-320. Chicago: University of Chicago Press, 1997.

–. "Compassion and the Softening of Mores." *Journal of Democracy* 11, 1 (2000): 142-48.

Outka, Gene. *Agape: An Ethical Analysis*. New Haven: Yale University Press, 1972.

"Packers' Pick Arrested on Burglary Charge." *South Florida Sun Sentinel,* 9 July 2002.

Palk, Gerard, Hennessey Hayes, and Timothy Prenzler. "Restorative Justice and Community Conferencing: Summary of Findings from a Pilot Study." *Current Issues in Criminal Justice* 10 (1998): 138-55.

Phelan, Shane. *Sexual Strangers: Gays, Lesbians, and Dilemmas of Citizenship*. Philadelphia: Temple University Press, 2001.

Pillsbury, Samuel H. "Emotional Justice: Moralizing the Passions of Criminal Punishment." 74 *Cornell Law Review* 655 (1989).

Plato. *Euthyphro, Apology, Crito, and Symposium*. Translated by Benjamin Jowett. Chicago: Regnery, 1953.

–. *Gorgias*. Translated by Terence Irwin. Oxford: Clarendon Press, 1979.

–. *The Republic*. Translated by Desmond Lee. 2nd ed., revised. Harmondsworth: Penguin, 1979.

Pollard, Charles. "Victims and the Criminal Justice System: A New Vision." *The Criminal Law Review* [2000]: 5-17.

Rawls, John. *A Theory of Justice*. Oxford: Clarendon Press, 1972.

"Relatives of Guguletu Seven Break Into Song." South African Press Association. <http://www.truth.org.za/media/1997/9702/s970218e.htm>.

"Restorative Injustice." Editorial. *New Zealand Law Journal* 72 (April 1996): 121-22.

Ricoeur, Paul. "Love and Justice." *Philosophy and Social Criticism* 21, 5/6 (1995): 23-39.

Ross, Rupert. "Restorative Justice: Exploring the Aboriginal Paradigm." *Saskatchewan Law Review* 59 (1995): 431-35.

Rousseau, Jean-Jacques. *Emile*. Translated by Allan Bloom. New York: Basic Books, 1976.

Rucker, Lila. "Peacemaking in Prisons." In *Criminology as Peacemaking*, edited by Harold E. Pepinsky and Richard Quinney, 172-80. Bloomington: Indiana University Press, 1991.

Sandel, Michael J. *Liberalism and the Limits of Justice*. 2nd ed. Cambridge: Cambridge University Press, 1982, 1998.

Schiller, Friedrich. "On Naive and Sentimental Poetry." In *Essays*, edited by Walter Hinderer and Daniel O. Dahlstrom, 179-260. New York: Continuum, 1993 [1975].

Schindler's List. Directed by Stephen Spielberg. 1993.

Schneider, Carl E. "What It Means to Be Sorry: The Power of Apology in Mediation." (2000) 17 *Mediation Quarterly* 265.

Scott, Colleen. "Amnesty and the South African Truth and Reconciliation Commission." <http://www.abc.nl/abc/general/guest/trc.html> (15 January 2002).

Sedgwick, Eve Kosofsky. *Epistemology of the Closet*. Berkeley: University of California Press, 1990.

Segal, Eliezer. "Jewish Perspectives on Restorative Justice." In *The Spiritual Roots of Restorative Justice*, edited by Michael L. Hadley, 181-97. Albany: State University of New York Press, 2001.

Sendor, Benjamin B. "Restorative Retributivism." *Journal of Contemporary Legal Issues* 5 (Spring 1994): 323-39.

Shakespeare, William. *Hamlet*. In *Shakespeare: The Complete Works*, edited by Peter Alexander, 1028-72. London: Collins, 1978.

–. *Merchant of Venice*. In *Shakespeare: The Complete Works*, edited by Peter Alexander, 223-53. London: Collins, 1978.

–. *Richard III*. In *Shakespeare: The Complete Works*, edited by Peter Alexander, 701-47. London: Collins, 1978.

Sharpe, Susan. *Restorative Justice: A Vision for Healing and Change*. Edmonton: Edmonton Victim-Offender Mediation Society, 1998.

Shearing, Clifford. "Transforming Security: A South African Experiment." In *Restorative Justice and Civil Society*, edited by John Braithwaite and Heather Strang, 14-34. Cambridge: Cambridge University Press, 2001.

Sherman, Lawrence W. "Two Protestant Ethics and the Spirit of Restoration." In *Restorative Justice and Civil Society*, edited by John Braithwaite and Heather Strang, 35-55. Cambridge: Cambridge University Press, 2001.

Sherman, Lawrence W., Heather Strang, and Daniel J. Woods. *Recidivism Patterns in the Canberra Reintegrative Shaming Experiments (RISE)*. Canberra: Centre for Restorative Justice, Research School of Social Sciences, Australian National University, 2000.

Shriver, Donald. "Where and When in Political Life Is Justice Served by Forgiveness?" In *Burying the Past: Making Peace and Doing Justice after Civil Conflict*, edited by Nigel Biggar, 23-39. Washington, DC: Georgetown University Press, 2001.

Shytov, Alexander Nikolaevich. *Conscience and Love in Making Judicial Decisions*. Dordrecht: Kluwer Academic Publishers, 2001.

Singer, Irving. *The Pursuit of Love*. Baltimore: Johns Hopkins University Press, 1994.

Singh, Avatar. *The Ethics of Sikhs*. Patiala, India: Punjabi University, 1970.

Singh, Pashaura. "Sikhism and Restorative Justice: Theory and Practice." In *The Spiritual Roots of Restorative Justice*, edited by Michael L. Hadley, 199-215. Albany: State University of New York Press, 2001.

Smith, Adam. *The Theory of Moral Sentiments*. Edited by C.C. Raphael and A.L. Macfie. Oxford: Clarendon Press, 1976.

Smith, Bruce. *The History of Little Orphan Annie*. New York: Ballantine Books, 1982.

Solomon, Robert C. *A Passion for Justice: Emotions and the Origins of the Social Contract*. Lanham, Maryland: Rowman and Littlefield, 1995.

Spelman, Elizabeth V. *Fruits of Sorrow*. Boston: Beacon Press, 1997.

Stowe, Harriet Beecher. *Uncle Tom's Cabin or Life among the Lowly*. New York: Penguin, 1986.

Strang, Heather. *Victim Participation in a Restorative Justice Process*. Oxford: Oxford University Press, 2001.

Strang, Heather, and John Braithwaite, eds. *Restorative Justice and Family Violence*. Cambridge: Cambridge University Press, 2002. <http://www.gu.edu.au/school/ccj/kdaly.html> (26 March 2003).

Tanner, Michael. "Sentimentality." In *Proceedings of the Aristotelean Society*, new series, 77 (1976-77): 127-47. Tisbury, UK: Compton Press, 1977.

Teays, Wanda, and Laura M. Purdy. *Bioethics, Justice and Healthcare*. Belmont, CA: Wadsworth, 2001.

Teitel, Ruti G. *Transitional Justice*. Oxford: Oxford University Press, 2000.

Truth and Reconciliation Commission of South Africa Report. Vols. 1-10. Capetown: CTP Book Printers, 1998.

"Truth, the Road to Reconciliation: Official Truth and Reconciliation Commission Website." <http://www.truth.org.za/index.htm> (6 June 2002).

Tutu, Archbishop Desmond. Interview with Danny Schechter. In *Globalization and Human Rights Interviews*. <http://www.globalvision.org/program/globalization/tutu.html> (6 June 2002).

Twain, Mark. *The Adventures of Huckleberry Finn*. 1885. New York: Dover, 1994.

Tweedie, Jill. *In the Name of Love*. London: Jonathan Cape, 1979.

Umbreit, Mark S. "Crime Victims Seeking Fairness Not Revenge: Toward Restorative Justice." *Federal Probation* 3 (1989): 53-7.

–. *Victim Meets Offender*. Monsey: Criminal Justice Press, 1994.

–. "Holding Juvenile Offenders Accountable: A Restorative Justice Perspective." *Juvenile and Family Court Journal* 46, 2 (Spring 1995): 31-42.

–. *Handbook of Victim Offender Mediation*. San Francisco: Jossey-Bass, 2001.

Umbreit, Mark S., and William Bradshaw. "Victim Experience of Meeting Adult vs. Juvenile Offenders: A Cross-National Comparison." *Federal Probation* 61, 4 (1997): 33-40.

Umbreit, Mark S., and Mark Carey. "Restorative Justice: Implications for Organizational Change." *Federal Probation* 59, 1 (March 1995): 47-54.

Umbreit, Mark S., and Robert B. Coates. "Multicultural Implications of Restorative Juvenile Justice." *Federal Probation* 63, 2 (December 1999): 44-51.

Umbreit, Mark S., and Howard Zehr. "Restorative Family Group Conferences: Differing Models and Guidelines for Practice." *Federal Probation* 60, 3 (September 1996): 24-9.

–. "A Reply to Andrew Ashworth." *Criminal Law Forum* 4, 2 (1993): 301-6.

Van Ness, Daniel W. "New Wine and Old Wineskins: Four Challenges of Restorative Justice." *Criminal Law Forum* 4, 2 (1993): 251-76.

Van Ness, Daniel W., and Karen Heetderks Strong. *Restoring Justice*. 1st ed. Cincinnati: Anderson Publishing, 1997.

Van Ness, Daniel W., and Karen Heetderks Strong. *Restoring Justice*. 2nd ed. Cincinnati: Anderson Publishing, 2002.

Van Ness, Daniel W., and Pat Nolan. "Legislating for Restorative Justice." *Regent University Law Review* 10 (1998) 53-110.

Voltaire. *Candide*. Boston: Bedford, 1999 [1759].

Wachtel, Ted, and Paul McCold. "Restorative Justice in Everyday Life." In *Restorative Justice and Civil Society*, edited by John Braithwaite and Heather Strang, 114-29. Cambridge: Cambridge University Press, 2001.

Walker, Lenore E. *The Battered Woman*. New York: Harper and Row, 1980.

Weiler, Joseph. "Federalism without Constitutionalism: Europe's Sonderweg" In *The Federal Vision: Legitimacy and Levels of Governance in the US and the European Union*, edited by Robert L. Howse and Kalypso Nicolaidis, 54-70. Oxford: Oxford University Press, 2001.

Weinrib, Earnest J. *The Idea of Private Law*. Cambridge: Harvard University Press, 1995.

–. "Legal Formalism." In *A Companion to the Philosophy of Law and Legal Theory*, edited by Dennis Patterson, 332-42. Oxford: Blackwell Publishers, 1999.

West, Robin. *Caring for Justice*. New York: New York University Press, 1997.

Whitney, Karen. "The Seriousness of the Offence: Proportionality in Sentencing Sexual Offenders in Western Australia." *Murdoch University Electronic Journal of Law* 3, 1 (May 1996). <http://www.murdoch.edu.au/elaw/indices/issue/v3n1.html> (17 March 2002).

Wilde, Oscar. *The Importance of Being Earnest*. London: Heinemann, 1967 [1899].

Williams, Patricia. *The Rooster's Egg: On the Persistence of Prejudice*. Cambridge, Harvard University Press, 1995.

Yazzie, Robert. "'Hozho Nahasdlii': We Are Now in Good Relations: Navajo Restorative Justice." *Saint Thomas Law Review* 9 (1996): 117-24.

Yeats, Mary Ann. "'Three Strikes' and Restorative Justice: Dealing with Young Repeat Burglars in Western Australia." *Criminal Law Forum* 8, 3 (1997): 369-85.

Young, Marlene A. "Restorative Community Justice in the United States: A New Paradigm." *International Review of Victimology* 6 (1999): 265-77.

Zehr, Howard. "Restoring Justice: Envisioning a Justice Process Focussed on Healing – Not Punishment." *The Other Side* 33, 5 (September/December 1997): 22.

–. *Changing Lenses: A New Focus for Crime and Justice*. Scottdale: Herald Press, 1990.

Index

Printed and bound in Canada by Friesens

Set in Stone by Brenda and Neil West, BN Typographics West

Copy editor: Robert Lewis

Proofreader: Arlene Prunkl